Controversies in Crime and Justice
series editor Victor E. Kappeler Eastern Kentucky University

Controversies *in* Criminal Justice Research

Richard Tewksbury
University of Louisville

Elizabeth Ehrhardt Mustaine
University of Central Florida

Controversies in Criminal Justice Research

Copyright © 2004
    Anderson Publishing Co., a member of the LexisNexis Group

    Phone 877-374-2919
Web Site www.lexisnexis.com/anderson/criminaljustice

LexisNexis and the Knowledge Burst logo are trademarks of Reed Elsevier Properties, Inc.
Anderson Publishing is a registered trademark of Anderson Publishing Co.

HV
6024.5
.C74
2004

Tewksbury, Richard
    Controversies in criminal justice research / Richard Tewksbury, Elizabeth Ehrhardt Mustaine.
    Includes index.
    ISBN 1-58360-547-9 (paperback)

Cover design by Tin Box Studio, Inc.

EDITOR Janice Eccleston
ACQUISITIONS EDITOR Michael C. Braswell

Dedication

To our friends, families, and colleagues:
thanks for supporting us in our careers.

Richard Tewksbury
Elizabeth Ehrhardt Mustaine

Acknowledgments

We are grateful to the anonymous reviewers who provided us with critiques regarding the content and organization of the book.

Richard Tewksbury
Elizabeth Ehrhardt Mustaine

Preface

Controversies in Criminal Justice Research presents students with challenging looks at some of the most basic, and sometimes most difficult, decisions faced by criminal justice researchers. Each chapter in this easy-to-read volume presents students with both an overview of a foundational question/issue in the conduct of criminal justice research, and discussions of the available options to resolve these controversies.

This volume introduces students to such basic questions as whether criminal justice research can and does affect social policy, whether a researcher should collect his/her own original data or draw on existing data sets, what types of approaches to use with interview subjects, and whether particular questions are best approached by quantitative or qualitative research methods. Where this volume stands out is that the authors never tell students what they "should" or "have to" do, but instead each selection lays out the merits of the various options, and challenges students to critically think through their own solutions to each controversy.

By emphasizing critical thinking and the application of concepts to the foundational issues faced by all criminal justice researchers, this volume provides a valuable complement or alternative to traditional "cookbook" approaches to treatments of research methods. Each selection is geared for the beginning researcher, and challenges students to look beyond surface level and cliché explanations for issues. Presented in a highly readable and concise manner, this volume promises to draw students into the real world of criminal justice research in a way that traditional textbooks typically avoid.

Table of Contents

Qualitative Methods

Introduction

Richard Tewksbury & Elizabeth Ehrhardt Mustaine

"Research methods? Why do I have to take research methods? I want to take classes that are relevant, or interesting, or at least easy! "

"I know, why do they make us take this stuff anyway? It's not like I'm ever going to use it! Why can't we take something that might be useful?"

"This sucks. There's no way I'm going to get anything useful out of this. And, I hear it's really hard, too."

Does the above exchange sound familiar? Of course it does! For many students reading this, you have probably had conversations very much like this. You probably feel this way right now. For instructors who teach research methods courses this exchange is something we have heard many times. We know students usually come to courses in research methods expecting to have to read dull material, to learn terms and ideas that they will never use again, and to have a difficult time earning a good grade. These feelings are especially common among undergraduate students, in all of the social sciences. Graduate students also feel similarly. During our own graduate school experiences we were faced with multiple required courses in research methods, and often felt that these classes were among the dullest, and the most challenging. As graduate students, though, we knew why we were taking these classes; the reasons were made crystal clear to us. "If you are going to be a scholar, you are going to do research. Remember, it's your research that will get you a job. It's your research that will determine whether or not you get raises, and whether or not you get tenure. Research is what the social scientist does!"

Yes, we learned that research is important, but we also learned that, despite all of the claims that social science is "science," there were an awful lot of grey areas and uncertainties about how to do research. The questions were not restricted to the finer points and decisions about how to measure particular variables, or how to draw an appropriate research sample, or how to most appropriately interpret our statistical results. The questions, many of which were large enough to be considered controversies, encompassed much larger issues. As graduate students, we quickly learned that there were two very distinct "camps" in the social science research world. First of all, there are the "quantoids" who believed that statistics were the answer to everything. If you could only come up with a good regression correlation or a strong path model, you could answer the mysteries of life, and solve the world's problems. Then, on the other side, you had your "soft" and "emotional" people who were dedicated to qualitative research methods. These were the researchers who always followed the quantitatively oriented researchers' explanations for social actions with questions like "that's fine, but how do those people feel?" or "but what does that mean in the real world, for real people?"

Our point here is that, although we like to think of ourselves as "scientists" with common standards, there are some basic controversial issues at the very heart of the activity that define us as scientists. Being able to recognize these controversies, and better yet being able to articulate what each side of each controversy advocates, is critical to being an informed practitioner, and consumer of research. For those of us who do research for a living, we know the controversies that are related to our areas/forms of research. We also know which side of the controversy is right (ours, of course!). Knowing and being able to explain the issues that comprise the controversies of research methods is perhaps even more important for consumers of research. This is because if, as a consumer of research, you do not understand the assumptions (and, honestly, the biases) that are behind the decisions that are made by researchers when planning, conducting, interpreting and writing research, you cannot know that there might be problems with research, or that a particular researcher might make some decision(s) for a political purpose.

Knowing what the questions (i.e., controversies) are in a specific field is one of the first major steps leading to being an informed, and critical, consumer of research. But, how can someone new to the world of social science research go about knowing what these controversies are? There are several ways this can be done. First, if you really pay close attention and read "between the lines" of many popular research methods textbooks, you can identify the "disagreements" or "decisions" that need to be made when planning, conducting, interpreting, and writing research. Or, you might be able to learn what these controversies are by embarking on a research project and asking advice from multiple other researchers. When you start to get different advice for how to handle a particular step in the research process, you can be pretty sure that you have stumbled onto a controversial issue. Or, to make learning what the controversial issues in social science research methods are, and what the major points of contention are in these controversies, you can go out and find a thorough, yet concise, book that outlines the controversies and explains the various views/sides of the controversy.

For you, this is definitely the path of least resistance. Why? Because you already hold this book in your hands!

Our goal in editing this book has been to draw together in one easily accessible place discussions of the major controversies that are found in the world of social science research methods. We are not saying that this book covers all of the controversial issues (because depending on who you ask to identify what the controversies are, you are likely to get different answers), nor do we claim that we have provided every piece of information about every view/side in each of the controversial issues that are addressed. However, what you will find in this book is a series of chapters that present concise, yet easily digested discussions of how some of the major questions facing research practitioners, and consumers, are to be understood.

In order to make sure that the discussions of research methods' controversial issues are explained in ways that today's students (whether undergraduate or graduate) can most effectively and efficiently understand the issues, we have carefully selected the individuals that were invited to write for this book. In some books where different scholars write different chapters, you will find that the editors have recruited "big name" scholars (i.e., researchers!) to write on their areas of expertise. This is not the strategy that we pursued in this putting together this book. Rather than go out and ask "famous" researchers to write about the controversies in social science research methods, we chose to invite scholars who, while all highly competent scholars with completed research to their credit, are all also excellent teachers; who endeavor to make their disciplines and areas of expertise accessible to students. Many of the scholars who have contributed to this book are only a few years removed from their own student years. However, even the "older" scholars among us are individuals who have made a commitment to be excellent teachers, and to provide students with interesting and easily understood materials. This book represents the collective efforts of this outstanding set of teachers-scholars.

So, while you may still not be convinced that a course in social science research methods really is relevant or interesting or something that can be enjoyable, we believe that this book will play a big part in (eventually) changing these views. Is gaining an understanding of how research is done important and relevant for your life? Of course it is, whether you are ready to believe it or not. Nearly everyday we read or hear about some new research findings. These findings may have an impact on the way we choose to live our lives. It is important to be able to assess the quality and validity of this new research as we become aware of it. Is studying research methods exciting? For some of us it is, and for some of us it will turn out to be a lot better than we may have expected when we first started out studying it. Is a research methods course one where you can earn a good grade? Perhaps, but that is really more dependent on the amount of effort that each student puts into the process. However, reading this book should help students to get a good grade. Let's be honest, it can't hurt your chances of getting a good grade. And, it definitely can help you to learn about social science research methods in more depth, and from a different set of perspectives. If reading this book actually does lead you to become a researcher, and eventually to want to share your love for research with others, then not only will we have fulfilled our goals, but we will have gone far above and beyond what we really hope to achieve. Helping you to become a more informed, and therefore "better" consumer of social science research is our real goal. We wish you luck as you progress toward that goal!

CHAPTER 1

Should (Does) Criminal Justice Research Influence Social Policy?

Elizabeth Ehrhardt Mustaine
University of Central Florida

Introduction

The relationship between criminal justice research and criminal justice policy is a controversial one. It could be one of give and take. Scholars such as Clear and Frost (2001) suggest that, theoretically, each informs the other. Questions about the type of policy to put into action, the timing of intervention or implementation, the target clientele/audience/recipients, and the effectiveness of any action taken or changes made necessitates the utilization of scientific research. Those interested in conducting social science and criminal justice research can develop this expertise and employ it to benefit the community and any social problems there, like crime. Ideally, then, the relationship between criminal justice researchers, practitioners, and policymakers should be an interrelated one.

Conversely, other scholars advocate that the policy arena is, at best, one of bias and ignorance and, at worst, one of agenda setting and corruption. These scholars argue that researchers would be better served, "taking up low paying posts in ivory towers, monasteries, and similar think tanks . . . (as this would be preferable to becoming) policy advisors in this repressive war on crime." (Cressey, 1978:189). Further, even when academic research addresses issues directly relating to social policy, often it is not used by policymakers and practitioners. To further complicate this controversial debate, several issues arise that have the impact of discouraging a harmonious relationship between science and public policy. This trend need not continue, however. With effort, consistency, high levels of communication between parties, willingness to work together, quality research, and thoughtful design and implementation of policy, criminal justice policy can become more effective.

What Is Public Policy?

Public policies are the actions that governments, other regulating bodies, and organizations take. Policy can also include the procedures, or guidelines, these groups use. Usually policy is used to outline acceptable procedures, guide present and future decisions, and/or regulate management
strategy. Criminal justice policy, then, refers to the acceptable procedures,
actions, decisions, strategies, and guidelines that regulate the criminal justice
system and the various organizations and programs with which it is associated. Policy can be as grand as the federal government requiring that all
police officers read suspects their Miranda rights before questioning them.
It can also be as minute as a local drug treatment center requiring an assessment be performed on each client to see which type of treatment would best
serve his/her needs.

Much of the time, policy is based on a philosophical orientation. When
policymakers implement strategies, frequently they utilize a guiding prin-
ciple, or way of thinking, to organize their strategies and plans of action. For
example, researchers and practitioners interested in preventing juvenile
delinquency typically formulate policy from one of three guiding main
beliefs: individual, education, and community. Each of these theoretical
views advocates certain types of intervention strategies to prevent illegal
youthful behavior (Lundman, 2001). To elaborate, those who believe that
juvenile delinquency is an individual-level issue, think that youth crime is the
product of personal problems, thus requires an individually oriented solu-
tion. Arguments include that youth violate the law because of individual-level
abnormalities (e.g., personality problems, improper parenting and supervision). As such, prevention strategies would need to include the identification
of youth who are headed for trouble and the implementation of treatment
to repair their flawed personalities. Such treatment might include regular visits to a counselor or adult mentor. Other scholars of juvenile delinquency
suggest that youthful misbehavior is the result of inadequate education
regarding the negative consequences of participation in delinquency. Hence,
these scholars believe that educational programming is the appropriate
and best-suited strategy for the prevention of delinquency. Programs such as
DARE (Drug Abuse Resistance Education), in which uniformed police officers teach junior high schoolers about the dangers associated with the use
of drugs, cigarettes, and alcohol, and how to resist such use, are examples
of this type of educational programming. Finally, supporters of community
strategies believe that juvenile delinquency is a community problem that
requires a community-level intervention. Theoretically, communities may
have other social problems present (e.g., low income, low rates of high
school completion) that contribute to a prevalence of youth crime in the
community. These advocates feel that delinquency is merely a symptom of
the other social problems present, therefore it makes little sense to treat misbehavior on an individual level, nor does the identification of associated dan-

gers. Effective prevention strategy should target the community. Examples of such interventions are midnight basketball, or the formation of community assistance organizations.

What Distinguishes Scientific Research?

Science is a way of producing knowledge. However, it is not the only way. Other forms of knowledge construction include mysticism, astrology, religion, and tradition. Today, science is the dominant method for the production of knowledge. Generally, science is said to have several components:

- Assumptions about the nature of the world and knowledge.

- An attitude or orientation toward knowledge.

- Special procedures, techniques, and instruments.

- An accumulation of knowledge.

- A social institution called the scientific community (Neuman, 1997)

Scientific research, then, is research that utilizes the above components and data as the evidence or information that allows researchers to make assessments about their guiding theories or ideas.

Criminologists and researchers in criminal justice generally use one of several methods when carrying out scientific research: surveys, interviews, observation, secondary data analysis, and the collection and organization of pre-existing data. As cases in point, Mustaine and Tewksbury (1998) conducted a survey of college students to find out about the prevalence, patterns, and sources of larceny theft victimizations they had experienced. Analyzing a data set that had already been collected by others, Jasinski (2001) examined risk factors for domestic violence that related to pregnancy. Such factors included whether or not the father wanted the child. As an example of interviewing, Feeney (1986) interviewed 113 male robbery offenders and examined the decision-making process they used when deciding whether or not to rob a particular target. Adler (1993), utilized participant observation (along with other methods) to examine a community of high-level drug dealers in Southern California. Finally, collecting and compiling data from the Federal Bureau of Investigation's *Supplementary Homicide Reports*, the NAACP Legal Defense and Educational Fund, Inc.'s *Death Row, USA*, the *Vanderbilt Television News Archive*, the *Annual Statistical Supplement to the Social Security Bulletin*, The *Statistical Abstract of the United States*, and *Current Population Reports*, Bailey and Peterson (1999) examined the impact of frequency of executions, number of women admitted to death row in penal institutions, and execution publicity, on female homicide rates (as measured monthly).

There are many reasons scientists engage in social research. As examples, academicians may use social research to test theories, and/or to produce knowledge about the patterns and sources of social phenomena. Marketing researchers may use social research to highlight spending patterns of various consumer groups. Political parties may use social research to identify the issues that voters feel are important and that reflect their views on these issues. Insurance companies use social research to identify claims patterns, patterns of injuries, and driving patterns among social groups. Newspapers use social research to inform the public about new knowledge that is produced. Regarding policy, practitioners, politicians, and researchers can use social research to assess the effectiveness of a particular philosophical orientation that guides specific policies, or the effectiveness of the specific policies themselves. Research can be used to advise policy implementers about which strategies will likely be the most effective. Science can be used to determine which clientele may be the most successfully treated in a particular program. Research can highlight any changes that occurred after a particular policy was implemented. Given the systematic nature of scientific inquiry, the findings from social research usually result in more informed, unbiased decisions than do the guessing, hunches, intuition, and personal experiences that people using the other forms of knowledge production employ.

Theoretical Implications for Criminological Policy

Many criminological theories have implications for social and correctional policy. While an in-depth exploration of all the theories that have policy relevance is beyond the scope of this chapter, a discussion of several theories as examples can be informative and highlight the need for the scientific evaluation of criminological theory.

Strain theory is an example of a criminological theory with policy implications. General Strain theory purports that when individuals are unable (usually due to negative/discriminatory treatment) to achieve positively valued goals they may commit crime in response (Merton, 1938). Several general policy implications that arise from this view on the causes of criminal behavior include minimizing the negative or discriminatory treatment of people and reducing the negative reaction of people who are treated in an unfair manner (Agnew, 1995). For juveniles, one example of a place where negative or discriminatory treatment can take place is the school. As such, programs that help to improve school performance might reduce the likelihood of future delinquency. Research has suggested that good preschool programs can both improve school achievement and decrease delinquency (Agnew, 1995). Other policy initiatives might include helping juveniles more effectively cope (using legal means) with negative or discriminatory treatment. An example of such an initiative includes programs that increase family functioning so that youth can turn to their parents for support when they are disappointed or frustrated with their circumstances. Functional family therapy tries to improve the expression and giving of emotional support among family members (Agnew, 1995).

Another example of policy initiatives that stem from criminological theory can be seen with Routine Activity Theory. Routine Activity Theory notes that criminal events take place when potential offenders, suitable targets, and absent/unwilling/incapable guardians come together at the same time in the same place (Cohen & Felson, 1979). Policy initiatives can be directed at individuals and communities as crime prevention strategies. Suggestions include guidance to residents of high-crime communities on measures of guardianship. Oftentimes, residents pay wrought iron companies to install iron bars on all windows and doors of a residence. Scientific research, however, has noted that most residential burglars gain access to homes via rear windows and doors (Felson & Clarke, 1995). Citizens can utilize this information and save money by installing bars only on possible rear entry points. Installing bars on front windows is probably a waste of money (Felson & Clarke, 1995). Further, research has suggested that persons who own dogs (among other indicators) are less likely to be victims of a significant theft (Mustaine & Tewksbury, 1998).

Using these two theories as examples, one can see that it is important not only for scientists to examine criminological theory for policy implications, to evaluate these policies for effectiveness, but also to share findings with citizens and policymakers so that useful crime prevention and treatment measures can be implemented. Indeed, perhaps it is part of the duty of academicians to share their findings (i.e., knowledge) and offer recommendations (Felson & Clarke, 1995).

Use of Scientific Research by Practitioners and Policymakers

Criminal justice policymakers and practitioners are two groups of individuals who could and should benefit from the knowledge gained by conducting scientific research. Policy based on the more informed, less biased findings of social research has the chance to be more useful, efficient, and cost effective than policy based on personal preference, gut feelings, and intuition.

As noted, many criminological theories have policy implications, however, many policymakers and practitioners often do not use the suggestions or findings that emerge from scientific research. This is unfortunate because in a time of heightened interest in criminological issues, growing correctional costs, and limited budgets, the need for an interrelated relationship between policy and criminal justice is crucial. Perhaps there has never been a time in our history when crime and crime policy were as important as they are today (Hancock & Sharp, 1997). Most national candidates have ideas for crime policy as part of their election campaigns. National political parties have crime policy as part of their political platforms. At the same time, federal granting agencies are calling for research that asks for community agencies and academicians to partner together, evaluate programming, produce knowledge that can be applied, and make suggestions about crime policy. Currently, research is available that addresses many of the issues that governmental legislative bodies are considering. This research could inform the policy initiatives governmental bodies, agencies, and community organizations are implementing. Often, however, it goes unused. For instance, plainly said, the criminal justice system is not effective at controlling or preventing crime. As an example, the United States has the highest incarceration rate among western industrialized countries in the world, and yet, we also have among the highest homicide rates (Hancock & Sharp, 1997). This implies that incarcerating a higher number of serious offenders does not reduce the amount of violent crime, like homicide, as two correctional goals imply (deterrence, incapacitation). Even so, policymakers and practitioners may wish to continue to use correctional strategies stemming from deterrence or incapacitation theory for several reasons. The nature of politics may be one reason. In this way, it may be that those types of policies are what their constituents want. Also possible is that some politicians are successfully lobbied by groups who support the greater use of incarceration. Politicians may not utilize criminal justice research for their policy suggestions because of agenda setting and the increasing politicalization of criminal justice policy.

Potentially, politicians, policymakers, and practitioners are unconvinced by or unaware of the scientific research that implies the use of these types of policies may be questionable. Clear and Frost (2001) indicate that it is because academic research is often not accessible to those who would use it. This may very well be the case. Most scholars who publish articles that are relevant to criminal justice policy publish them in academic journals that have a small and narrow target audience. Also, this body of research may not be characterized by consistent findings. For example, the research on the effectiveness of DARE is not completely consistent. Researchers evaluating DARE in Charleston County, South Carolina found that DARE participants were significantly more likely to hold strong attitudes against substance use than the non-DARE control group (Harmon, 1993). At the same time, the researchers evaluating a DARE project in Kokomo, Indiana found no significant differences between the DARE and non-DARE participants (Wysong & Wright, 1995). This body of research suggests, then, that while the success of DARE programming is questionable it is possible. This is certainly not a clear mandate to send to those interested in either utilizing DARE or devising alternatives to it. It may also be the case that the research is methodologically questionable. As an example, some research examining the effectiveness of Scared Straight policies (programs where juvenile delinquents spent the day in prison and were spoken to harshly by seasoned inmates in attempts to "scare them straight") is questionable because the researchers did not detail their methodological approach. Likewise, some of this research is suspect because of ethical issues (Lundman, 2001). Policymakers and practitioners may not wish to base initiatives on this research because they have doubts about it. For these reasons, scientists must carefully consider the methodological and ethical issues that arise with their research when undertaking projects that have policy implications, and utilize the methods of research that would be most appropriate.

Types of Research That Can Inform Policy and Relevant Issues

Differing philosophical views on research can impact the willingness of researchers to conduct scientific inquiry that has direct policy relevance as well as the willingness of policymakers and practitioners to find social research relevant. Because of their concern for "true science," generally it is scholars who recognize the importance of scientific methods. For example, most researchers acknowledge that the findings of a particular survey might have been different if questions were worded slightly differently. For example, a researcher could assess attitudes about the death penalty by using the question, "Do you support the use of the death penalty?" An alternative question is, "Do you support the use of the death penalty for persons convicted of violent crimes?" Undoubtedly, the number of respondents answering in the affirmative would vary depending on the question used. Also, findings from a particular study might vary depending on how researchers measure the concepts they utilize. For instance, in the debate about whether or not the death penalty acts as a deterrent, a researcher could measure the death penalty by looking at how frequently a given state actually executes someone. Anther measurement option would be to assess whether or not a particular state has the death penalty as a legal punishment (regardless of whether or not or how often it is used). Research findings may also vary depending on the sample used, as conclusions drawn from one sample may be different for another sample. Likewise, findings reached via survey research may be different than those findings that emerge from in-depth interviews, even if the topic of inquiry is the same. Methodological matters are often not the concerns of policymakers and practitioners, however, because they are not sensitive to issues of "true science." Because these people are focused on action and ideas leading to actions, they are concerned with the ideas that form the baseline of the research, the outcome of the research, and the cultural, political, and social implications raised rather than the methods used. For example, lawmakers are concerned with the interests of their constituents, their benefactors, and their networks of colleagues. They also may be interested in whether or not a certain policy under debate has been effective in the past. They are also likely to be concerned with the philosophy guiding any research they are reading. Given their agenda, and the necessity for action, it is unlikely that they will be able or willing to consider the type of method the research utilizes. Based on this, there appears to be mismatch between the interests of science and policy. These disparate elements of concern tend to widen the gap between scientific researchers and those who implement and develop policy.

Even so, several types of research are particularly well suited for aid in policy formulation, implementation, and evaluation. Research that is based on large random samples is well suited for making policy implications because of issues relating to generalizability. Generalizability refers to how representative a sample is to the larger population under study (or target population). In general terms, larger samples are more representative (that is, they are more likely to be small reproductions of their particular target populations). Because large samples and random samples usually have greater generalizability, findings from these samples produce a more informed "average" pattern or characteristic of the larger population upon which they are based. As such, policy stemming from these findings would be based more on typical situations rather than unique cases.

Nonetheless, research that utilizes smaller, nonrandom samples can be policy-relevant as well. First, however, it is important for subsequent research to validate the findings. Given the lessened, if absent, generalizability of findings from these types of samples, if several researchers consider similar issues on divergent nonrandom or small samples and find similar relationships, or if several researchers conduct similar projects and come to similar conclusions, we can be more confident in the conclusions than if they were based on just one research project. The idea here is that science can accumulate a *body of literature* that speaks to policy rather than just one research project that has policy implications.

Other research that is well suited for policy implications is research that has minimized methodological flaws and concerns. This is certainly a complex issue, however, because many theories of criminality have been criticized for being difficult to test. For example, Beccaria's (1819) principles of deterrence include *certainty*—the potential offender is certain that if he/she commits the crime, he/she will certainly be caught; *celerity*—the offender's punishment is carried out as soon as possible after his/her finding of guilt; and *severity*—the punishment given to any offender is just harsh enough to outweigh any pleasure or reward he/she got from committing the crime. In assessing or evaluating the policy worthiness of this theory, the concept of certainty can be measured in several ways. Researchers could survey individuals to see how effective they perceive the criminal justice system is at catching offenders. However, scholars could focus more on whether or not individuals actually think they will be caught (regardless of whether others are usually caught or not). Further, one could consider the Uniform Crime Report to assess the proportion of crime that is reported to the police vs. the amount of crime the police have classified as being cleared. Also problematic is the consideration of if we find that potential offenders are not certain they will be caught, does this mean that deterrence theory is inaccurate, or is it a flaw with the criminal justice system?

Amid these difficulties, it may happen that policy is formulated based on this theory (e.g., penalties for crimes and rhetoric by practitioners and politicians that represents the principles of deterrence theory) (Gilsinan, 1997). Now researchers and policymakers have a dilemma. They need to evaluate the impact and effectiveness of the policy, but this will be a difficult task, given that the theory upon which it is based is hard to test. This difficulty in testing may produce a variety of results that are hard to interpret. Research that does not find support for the effectiveness of a particular policy may infer the policy is not working. This research may erroneously purport that changes to the policy are necessary. To continue the example of Beccaria, his principles suggested a system of criminal justice based on deterrence. In order for deterrence to work, Beccaria suggested that persons must feel certain that they will get caught for committing the crimes they are considering. Research evaluating certainty would be hard-pressed to find would-be criminals who feel certain they will be caught. To make matters worse, official criminological data bear out this assessment: most people who commit crime do not get caught (U.S. Department of Justice, 1999, 2000). As such, science will have a difficult time testing whether or not the condition of certainty in the criminal justice system would prevent potential criminals. A finding of no relationship between certainty and prevention might suggest Beccaria was incorrect in identifying the combination of principles necessary to prevent crime. This research could also imply that the particular community under study did not have enough certainty to prevent crime, but if it were able to increase potential criminals' perceptions of certainty it would be able to prevent crime. It is also possible that certainty is not an element that influences would-be criminals' deliberations. Likewise, potentially, previous researchers have measured certainty inaccurately, producing invalid or unreliable results. In any of these events, the policy based on deterrence is hard to evaluate, thus making determinations about whether or not to continue the use of such a policy difficult at best.

Advantages of Developing Policy Based on Scientific Research

Amid the above-mentioned difficulties of testing policy effectiveness, there are advantages to designing, implementing, and evaluating policy based on scientific research. Research is more informative than other ways of acquiring knowledge, and when done correctly, research findings are generalizable. Policy should not be based on unlikely rare occurrences. If we base new policy on unlikely cases, then our criminal justice dollars and efforts are spent preventing or reacting to something that hardly ever happens. This takes money, time, and energy away from behaviors or circumstances that happen often and require attention. For example, the presence of illegal drugs in high schools is a far more prevalent problem than the likelihood of a mass shooting. When high schools spend money and policing efforts on metal detectors, searching students book bags, implementing and policing dress codes, and watching out for potentially troubled, mass-killing-spree-minded students, they may be neglecting or ignoring a far more prevalent problem: drug use among high-schoolers. When precious dollars are spent purchasing a metal detector on the off chance that one student has brought a weapon of mass destruction, these dollars cannot be spent implementing drug education programs, which might benefit many students.

Further, policy that is based on the typical situation or regularly happening phenomena has a greater chance of being successful/effective because we have a better, more complete understanding about the phenomena. Scientific research produces a higher level of understanding about regularly happening phenomena because of the frequency of occurrence and the greater number of cases from which to draw conclusions. The more completely we understand phenomena, the greater the ability we have to bring about effective policy.

Dangers of Basing Policy on Scientific Research

Not all research finds the same thing consistently. Sometimes research is hard to compare because it is characterized by the use of different samples (size, sample characteristic, etc.), different time periods, regional variation, or different variables to measure similar concepts.

Hancock and Sharp (1997) indicate that over the years, the United States has typically formulated crime policy based on one or more of the following goals: rehabilitation, restitution, retribution, deterrence, and incapacitation. Criminal justice scholars have long done research on the effectiveness of each goal. However, there tends to be a lack of consistency or issues of unresolved matters that preclude academics from forming a conclusive decision about the effectiveness of each goal. This may be one of the reasons that criminal justice policy can be characterized as having lack of congruity and short-sightedness. A policy may not be given enough time to assess whether it is working or not, or whether it could be effective if given more time or tinkered with in a particular way. This has typically ended up with a pattern of recycling of ideas evocative of the fashion industry, which often uses ideas from the styles of a generation or two earlier in current designs.

Political agenda setting exacerbates this pattern. As noted by Hancock and Sharp, "Agenda setting in criminal justice has often been based on reactive approaches to street-level crime while virtually ignoring white-collar, governmental, and organized crimes." (1997:2). This short-term, shortsighted reactive approach may result in seemingly haphazard ping ponging about which goal to utilize when formulating new policy.

Conclusion

Unfortunately, policymakers often do not utilize scientific criminological research when designing and formulating guidelines and procedures. There are many reasons for this neglect. It may be that the increasing politicalization of criminal justice policy causes agenda setting based on constituent, benefactor, or a network of colleagues preferences (which may be uninformed). Also, lack of complete understanding about the research process on the part of policymakers or practitioners may make it difficult for them to adequately assess scientific research. Additionally, the myriad issues surrounding the assessment of research, including the publication in academic journals, may make this important research inaccessible. Nevertheless, in the future, criminal justice researchers must make their highly relevant findings more accessible to policymakers, program planners, and other interested individuals. Scholars must minimize the methodological flaws of their research, as well as work to maximize the generalizability, quality, and consistency of their findings. When scholars produce quality academic research and present it in a concise and engaging way there is a greater chance for it to shape meaningful effective policy.

Recently, criminologists have taken significant steps to bridge the gap and open dialogues with policymakers and practitioners. A new journal, *Criminology and Public Policy* (CPP) was formed out of a National Institute of Justice initiative to create an avenue for the publication of sound, policy-relevant research findings (Clear & Frost, 2001). This journal is charged to strengthen the role of research in the formulation of criminal justice policy and put the most policy-relevant research into the hands of policymakers and practitioners. The editorial policy reflects this goal, "Authors are encouraged to submit papers that contribute to a more informed dialogue about policies and their empirical bases. Papers suitable for CPP not only present their findings but explore the policy-relevant implications of those finding." Additionally, this journal seeks to have academicians write up their findings in more practitioner friendly ways. For example, authors are encouraged to discuss the methodology for the study only briefly and refer only to that previous literature that is relevant for the study at hand. Graphs and tables should be clear and should be used only when necessary to make central points (Clear & Frost, 2001).

Similarly, the American Sociological Association has started a new journal called, *Contexts*. This forum for scholarly research "initiates an exciting effort to bring compelling social research to the attention of a wide, new audience." It is the goal of *Contexts* to present research with applied implications that addresses issues of critical public concern in a concise accessible way. In this way, teachers, journalists, civil servants, and policymakers can access important developments in social research in a forum that presents this information in a more user-friendly way, thus, increasing the likelihood that social research will be utilized in the development of public policy (Fisher, 2002). These new journals are important efforts for the ideal intermingling of policy and science.

With effort, consistency, high levels of communication between parties, willingness to work together, quality research, and thoughtful design and implementation of policy, criminal justice research can be more widely understood and used in the implementation and design of public policy. Subsequently, this policy can become more cost effective, useful, and successful.

Discussion Questions

1. What are the ways that criminal justice can have an impact on social policy?

2. What are the advantages of having criminal justice research and researchers address social policy issues?

3. What do you see as possible disadvantages or problems with criminal justice research and researchers trying to inform social policy?

4. What types of specific questions might be best suited for using criminal justice research in addressing social policy?

CHAPTER 2

The Value of Purely Theoretical Research vs. More "Practical" Research

Tracy L. Dietz
University of Central Florida

Merriam-Webster's Collegiate Dictionary, Eleventh Edition (2003) provides three definitions of research. These include, "careful or diligent search," "studious inquiry or examination; especially investigation or experimentation aimed at the discovery and interpretation of facts, revision of accepted theories or laws in the light of new facts, or practical application of such new or revised theories or laws," and "the collecting of information about a particular subject." While the focus of this book is reflected in the second definition above, it is clear that individuals actually conduct research informally every day. Research, in the broadest sense, is essential for human survival. We depend upon our logical interpretation of our environment to make sense of things and to make decisions about our lives. For example, research can be as simple as using unit pricing to determine which size and brand of a product to purchase to get the best deal.

Within the academy, however, intellectuals have come to accept that differences exist between scientific, academic research and those other ways of knowing that are typical of everyday human life—common sense and personal experience. Academic research relies upon a scientific approach to arrive at conclusions. This approach was first introduced by and to a small group of intellectuals between the late 1600s and the early 1800s. These philosophers believed that every aspect of human life could, and should, be critically examined. This time period is often referred to as the Enlightenment or the Age of Reason and is most often associated with French philosophy (Zeitlin, 1990). These philosophers were powerfully influenced by the intellectual pursuits of individuals such as Newton, Bacon, Hobbes, and Locke (Bierstadt, 1978). And, once guidelines were established for examining nature, examinations of human life and behavior using the same techniques soon followed. These same foundations continue to serve as a fundamental basis for examining human behavior today.

Types of Research

To begin our discussion, it is necessary to distinguish first between scientific and nonscientific inquiry. On the one hand, human beings, as well as nonhuman organisms, use inquiry to make sense of the world around them. However, in most cases, this inquiry falls within the realm of "common-sense" or nonscientific inquiry. Science, on the other hand, is a systematic process of inquiry . . . or "procedure for answering questions, solving problems, and developing more effective procedures for solving problems." (Ackoff, Gupta & Minas, 1962:1). Scientific inquiry relies upon the use of the scientific method. The scientific method, used by natural, social, and behavioral scientists in all disciplines requires that the scientist share his or her findings with the community, whether that be fellow scientists or the larger society of individuals who rely upon information to make decisions about programs, policies, or their everyday life.

Social research can have many purposes and can be classified based upon its purpose and its intended audience. The simplest distinction has existed for more than one century and is distinguished by classifying research as basic (or purely theoretical) research or as applied research (Neuman, 2000). This simplistic classification system, however, is not adequate for understanding the different types of research. Moreover, the two are not mutually exclusive. They share many characteristics and are difficult to discuss as entirely exclusive forms. For instance, social research, whether it is classified as basic or applied, can be exploratory, descriptive, explanatory, evaluative, or for validation, or even a combination of these, in nature. Nevertheless, the distinction between the two often receives a great deal of attention and has become a topic of heated debate among scientists. The difference that is typically acknowledged depends upon the intent of the research and the identity of the intended audience. However, even this distinction lacks clarity because two projects could be alike in all aspects except for the intentions of the researchers conducting the research (Ackoff, Gupta & Minas, 1962).

Purely Theoretical Research

The purpose of purely theoretical, or basic, research is the advancement of knowledge about the social world. Purely theoretical research is conducted to examine theories more closely using empirical data. The primary goal of this research is typically to refute or support one or more theories that purport to explain social patterns. Basic research, often conducted by scientists in academic settings, may result in new ways of thinking and understanding the world and the way it works. For example, a basic researcher might want to examine more closely the degree to which a person's educational attainment affects his or her likelihood of committing a crime. Likewise, scientists frequently utilize basic research to develop the methodologies that are used in all types of research, both basic and applied. In the example of the examination of the relationship between educational attainment and criminal delinquency, the researcher may develop a new way to measure likelihood of committing a crime. To examine a more detailed example of basic research in criminal justice, the reader is directed to the Program of Research on the Causes and Correlates of Delinquency (www.ojjdp.ncjrs.org), which is comprised of three coordinated longitudinal projects. The causes and correlates projects were initiated in 1986 by the Office of Juvenile Justice and Delinquency Prevention to improve the understanding of serious delinquency, drug use, and violence by examining the ways that youth develop within the context of their social environments.

Although many nonscientists do not fully understand the utility of purely theoretical research, purely theoretical, or basic, research is generally the core of new scientific ideas. The outcomes of these activities often lack concrete practical applicability at the time. Yet, future developments and understanding hinge upon the merit of such endeavors. Basic research provides the important foundations upon which applied research relies and the results of purely theoretical research are generalizable to "real-world" problems, issues, and policies (Neuman, 2000). In addition, basic research may be presented and discussed in terms of its policy implications. Thus, in the example discussed above, if basic research results in knowledge that suggests that higher levels of education lower the likelihood of at-risk people becoming involved in criminal activities, programs can be developed and expanded to support the educational attainment of at-risk individuals. Conversely, if science demonstrates that such an argument is not supported, new ideas about intervention efforts can be addressed.

Applied or "Practical" Research

While researchers conducting basic research are generally more interested in developing theories, methodologies, and an understanding of phenomena that will last over time, practical, or applied, research is generally conducted to obtain an immediate answer to a question or to solve an urgent problem (Neuman, 2000) in an organizational, clinical, or community environment (Sinnott, Harris, Block, Collesano & Jacobson, 1983). Ultimately, the goal of such research is to help practitioners and policymakers conduct their jobs in an informed and effective manner (Neuman, 2000).

Thus, it is often referred to as "practical" research. Many government agencies connected with the criminal justice system are oriented toward applied types of research. For example, the mission of the National Institute of Justice is to research crime control and justice so as to meet the challenges of crime and justice at the state and local levels.

Theoretical explanation is not as central to applied research (Neuman, 2000). Nevertheless, theories play an important role in determining the methodologies used to conduct the research appropriately and to understand the results and implications of those results (Sjoberg & Nett, 1997; Gelfand, 1975). For instance, Sherman and Berk (1984) combined theory testing and application, examining deterrence and labeling theories in their study of mandatory arrests on domestic violence recidivism. Applied research may be conducted by individuals and teams from a variety of settings. The researchers may be scientists who are conducting the research on their own or they may be sponsored by an individual or agency interested in the outcomes of the research. Similarly, the researcher may be affiliated with or employed by an organization interested in the outcomes (Neuman, 2000).

While basic research is often made public, either through publications or professional presentation, the results of applied research is less likely to become public information. The results may become known only to a small group of individuals, who may be different from the actual individuals who conducted the research. The researcher, in this case, has the responsibility of translating the scientific findings into the language that the consumers of the knowledge can understand and use. These practitioners and policy-makers may decide how to use the information and whether or not to share the results with others, including the general public (Neuman, 2000). Not surprisingly, some researchers may have concern over the pressures that may be placed upon them by the consumers of the knowledge who may be funding the research project to produce specific results. Likewise, they may be concerned with how the results of the research will be used. For instance, Neuman (2000) notes that while basic researchers are more likely to maintain high standards with the methodologies used to conduct their research, applied researchers "may compromise scientific rigor to get quick, usable results" (2000:24). The results of the research, regardless of the rigor of the methodologies employed, may be used to make important decisions or to justify decisions about policies and programs. Neuman further notes that applied research may produce conflict because of its immediate impact, and often controversial, nature. Officials may simply use applied research on programs and policies as a means of delaying decisions that might become divisive, for example (Merton, 1973).

Although not always, applied research is frequently descriptive in nature and may be classified into many different types, depending upon the function of the research. Applied research may be used to develop or evaluate policies, processes, or programs. Regardless of the function, however, the strength of the different types of applied research is its immediate practical use (Neuman, 2000).

Action Research

In 1949, Max Weber called for sociologists (and implicitly other researchers) to be "value-free." As such, he argued that researchers should not use their positions as researchers to support a particular perspective but rather to report the "truth" as seen in the data gathered from reasonable scientific methodologies. Action research, which is sometimes referred to as policy research, is research that is conducted for the purpose of developing a knowledge base on a social problem. This information is typically used to create practical, action-oriented recommendations to assuage social problems that are then targeted toward policymakers (Majchrzak, 1984). For instance, the NAACP Legal Defense Fund maintains and disseminates statistical records on a quarterly basis pertaining to the relationship between the death penalty and race. The organization hopes to demonstrate the potential racist manner in which the death penalty is used and to urge Americans to pressure policymakers to abolish the death penalty (please refer to: http://www.deathpenaltyinfo.org/dpicrace.html for a detailed discussion of these data). Action research violates the standard of "value-free" research, using knowledge as power to motivate social and political action. Ultimately, the goal of action research is to increase public awareness of an issue and to encourage the public to help in efforts to produce social change. This type of research is often associated with a critical science approach that is considered to be in opposition to the position promulgated by Weber (Neuman, 2000). Arising and growing in popularity in the 1970s as a method for providing policymakers with relevant information (Majchrzak, 1984), feminists and Marxists often conduct this type of research. It is often utilized by various human and animal rights groups as well as organizations that are interested in expanding and supporting their agenda (Neuman, 2000).

Social Impact Assessment

Social impact assessments are another form of applied research. These projects are conducted with the purpose of predicting the consequences of a proposed change (Neuman, 2000). Policymakers, program planners and directors, and citizen groups have become increasingly concerned with the potential social and economic effects of proposed policies, programs, and projects (Leistritz & Ekstrom, 1986). Policy changes may result in either positive or negative changes (and often both) (Neuman, 2000). Predicting these effects is often referred to as social impact assessment or socioeconomic impact assessment (Leistritz & Ekstrom, 1986). For instance, Young (1998) conducted an analysis of residents' resistance to prisons being built in their community to determine the potential negative effects on the community. He discovered that the residents did not adhere to the "not-in-my-backyard mentality" and were not afraid of increased crime rates or negative economic effects.

In some cases, socioeconomic impact assessment has been used to mean an analysis of all but the social effects while "sociocultural impact assessment has been used to denote evaluations of the effects on social organization and structure, social institutions, social perceptions and attitudes, and processes of interaction" (Leistritz & Ekstrom, 1986:xiii). Social impact assessments, conducted in a rigorous, systematic, scientific manner can become useful in understanding the potential impact of policy changes and developments. Unfortunately, these useful research projects are often neglected (Neuman, 2000), occasionally resulting in devastating unintended consequences that could have been avoided if a well-designed impact assessment had been conducted.

Evaluation Research

Evaluation research is a broad category that is used to describe research projects that examine the effectiveness of a policy, program, process, or procedure (Neuman, 2000). According to Rossi, Freeman, and Lipsey (1999), evaluation research can trace its roots back to the 1600s. However, research used to systematically evaluate programs is a relatively new methodology, its expansion coinciding with recent political, demographic, and ideological changes that have resulted in an expansion of the welfare state and formal social service provision, the enhanced reputation of the social and behavioral sciences and the type of research produced by these scientists, and a move toward fiscal conservatism (Rossi, Freeman & Lipsey, 1999).

Evaluation research can take two forms, both of which are important to developing a clear picture of effectiveness. Formative evaluation provides continuous observation while summative evaluations examine the final outcomes (Neuman, 2000). Program evaluations generally focus on program design and planning, monitoring, outcome evaluations, or economic efficiency, or a combination of these (Sullivan, 1992). Needs analysis is a type of research that is related to evaluation research and plays an important role in planning and managing programs. While evaluation research examines the outcomes of the program, needs analysis is instrumental in addressing current and potential problems of the future and how to best address these problems by identifying needs and assessing the importance and relevance of the problems and possible solutions (McKillip, 1987). Program evaluations are useful in determining whether a program works or identifying areas where the program has failed to achieve its goals and should be modified or abandoned (Sullivan, 1992). For example, numerous evaluations of DARE have been conducted over the past decade or so. Ironically, while the goal of program evaluation may be to determine the effectiveness of programs and identify potential changes that need to be addressed, while the evaluations of DARE typically find it be unsuccessful in achieving its goals, the program continues to be funded (Zagumny & Thompson, 1997; Wysong, Aniskiewicz & Wright, 1994; Clayton, Cattarello & Walden, 1991).

The Tense Relationship between
Applied and Basic Research

However, while the relationship between applied research and policy has had a long history in the United States, that history has been an arduous one.

While basic and applied research have common historical roots and are intricately intertwined with one another, a tense relationship between the two designations developed in the twentieth century. Basic researchers may argue that their efforts are of a higher order because they are seeking knowledge for knowledge's sake. Conversely, applied researchers may contend that basic research is irrelevant for the "real world." At the same time, however, the interdependence of the two is undeniable. Moreover, basic researchers would often like to see their research endeavors become important contributions to the world around them.

The distinction between "basic" and "applied" science is one that has commanded the attention of scientists in disciplines for some time (Olsen, 1981; Blumer, 1992); yet, the distinction between purely theoretical and applied research is almost impossible to draw. The types of research outlined above are interdependent upon one another. Indeed, as noted by Ackoff, Gupta, and Minas (1962), "the distinction is based not on a difference in the kind of research conducted, but on a property of the researcher" (1962:8). Olsen (1981) argues, for example, that "the basic scientist views himself or herself as a scientist dedicated to the pursuit of knowledge for its own sake, while the applied (scientist) identifies himself or herself as a practitioner who contributes to solving or eliminating social problems" (1981:565). In the study of crime and criminals, for instance, criminology is largely a theoretical discipline while criminal justice is more often an applied discipline. In sum, the distinction between the two may be summarized as science is a means to an end for applied researchers while science is the end for basic researchers (Berk, 1981). However, research described as pure at one point in time and by one individual may eventually be applied to practical problems later. Likewise, applied research projects may eventually produce pure research projects (Ackoff, Gupta & Mina, 1962) and problems identified in applied research projects have led to the development of research tools that have contributed to social and behavioral science on the whole (Rossi, 1986). The distinction has become even more muddled as universities, the traditional centers of basic research, have been drawn into the applied research arena by the growth of research centers on campuses (Lazersfeld & Reitz, 1975) and as researchers are increasingly required to draw the obligatory conclusions regarding the utility of their research in their proposals to funding agencies.

In spite of the controversy that has developed over the distinction in the twentieth century, Blumer (1992) contends that social and behavioral scientists in many disciplines expected, even hoped, that the research that they conducted would contribute to society in a meaningful way. Moreover, while many people first think of the stereotypical academic when they think about research, early American social scientists gathered together in Boston in 1865 at the Massachusetts State House to discuss their concerns with the economic and social conditions that developed just after the end of the Civil War. This group of social reformers, the founders of the modern-day American Social Science Association, considered their interests to be scientific in nature (Smith, 1994). In the early 1900s, applied research first became common in education and public health (Rossi, Freeman & Lipsey, 1999). The applied role of social science was expanded in the 1930s and 1940s as part of Roosevelt's New Deal policies and with the increasing United States involvement in World War II and Roosevelt's interest in the opinions of the American voters (Lazersfeld & Reitz, 1975; Flynn, 2000). At that same time, the German psychologist Kurt Lewin began to advocate for a systematic relationship between academic research and action, coining the term "action research" (Lazersfeld & Reitz, 1975) and the social sciences began to move toward specialization. The role of research in public policy again expanded through Johnson's Great Society programs of the 1960s (Flynn, 2000). During that time the War on Poverty and the War on Crime led to the Law Enforcement Assistance Administration and the allocation of larger research budgets for criminal justice research, for example.

Utilization of Academic Research

As previously mentioned, many types of people may be involved in conducting research. While the academic researcher is perhaps the most recognized, teachers, students, practitioners, politicians, program directors, nonprofit organizations, researchers employed by businesses and organizations, attorneys, and even individuals with an avid interest in a topic may conduct research. For obvious reasons, basic research is most often used by other researchers, educators, and students. The utility of basic research to others may not be as obvious. However, basic research is essential to the development of well-designed applied research projects as well. A thorough understanding of research methodologies and theoretical explanations is crucial to applied researchers whose mission is to solve problems. Moreover, although they are not representative of the typical consumer of basic research, decisionmakers and the general public might find the results of basic research valuable to them in their everyday social lives.

Applied research is conducted and used by a heterogeneous group of people and organizations. While the largest proportion of the members of the American Evaluation Association's members are employed in colleges or universities, the members represent many different types of organizations and disciplines and a minority of them list evaluation as their major professional responsibility. (Rossi, Freeman & Lipsey, 1999). The profile of those who do, could, and should use research is just as indistinct. While the concept of research-informed decisionmaking is not new, scientific research, has played a limited role in social service programs and in the various levels of governments (Chelimsky, 1991), as well as in education and in the criminal justice system. However, the opportunities for researchers to play an important role in decisionmaking in our society are limitless. Indeed, scientists are often called upon to conduct assessments of needs and program evaluations for social service programs. Likewise, scientists may find themselves reporting to government officials on everything from public opinion to cost-benefit analysis and the potential impact of new program changes. Similarly, educators occasionally rely upon social and behavioral scientists to conduct research on the needs of their students and the outcomes of program implementation. Scientists working in the area of criminal justice, criminology, or related fields may also become expert witnesses in court proceedings or assist attorneys in jury selection. Or, a researcher might evaluate whether or not a law or legal change has produced the intended effect or if it has produced a non-intended effect. These are, of course, just a few of the areas in which scientists have played important roles in the past. Whether or not scientists are able to expand their influence in the public arena in the future depends largely upon scientists' decisions about the path that we want to take and how we choose to get there.

Although researchers working in the area of criminal justice and crime, as well as other disciplines, have had a history of influencing decisionmakers and contributing to progress, the role of applied research in decisionmaking has grown over time. From beginnings related solely to education and health, by the 1950s such research was common in such areas a delinquency prevention (Rossi, Freeman & Lipsey, 1999). Yet, in 1975, Lazersfeld and Reitz reported that it was actually rare that policymakers rely upon research when they make decisions. And, while there has been dramatic growth in applied research over the past 60 years or so, such research has changed from an endeavor of scientists to one shaped largely by decisionmakers, service providers, and interested citizens (Rossi, Freeman & Lipsey, 1999). The influence of applied research appears to be greatest among government agencies. However, in recent years of fiscal conservatism, the responsibility for conducting or sponsoring applied research has been shifted to state and local agencies who are ill-equipped to complete the task. At the same time, though, concerns about the appropriate use of funds for programs will likely require intense scrutiny of existing program in the near future (Rossi, Freeman & Lipsey, 1999). And, even though scientists have not made as many advances in marketing their expertise to private business and industry as they have to government agencies, many corporate managers are becoming increasingly more conscious of the social causes and effects of the issues confronting them in the workplace (Olsen, 1981). Although researchers working in criminal justice and other disciplines have not been as influential in government agencies and the corporate environment as they might be, science has much to offer these various types of organizations. To be sure, while the limited influence of research in the non-academic world can be explained by a variety of factors, scientists themselves must accept a great deal of the blame for not making their research relevant and useful to decisionmakers in government agencies, corporations, and the like.

Making Research Available

Scientists (Blumer, 1992) are generally interested in contributing to the improvement of the world around them. However, most are not successful in their efforts to introduce research to the public and to policymakers and program directors. Far too often, they isolate themselves into a world in which they interact with other scientists and their research is generally presented to other scientists in a way that that community can understand (Olsen, 1981). Thus, while their research may have important relevance to improving the human condition, the message is often not heard by those who make decisions about policies.

Few of the decisionmakers share the scientists' perspective. For example, many of the individuals who make decisions about programs and policy aim at understanding social life from a more individual perspective, whereas the researchers often espouse a more statistical and generalizable approach (Lazersfeld & Reitz, 1975). Moreover, Chelimsky (1991) notes that decisionmakers often are not sure when researchers can be of help to them and often are reluctant to admit that they need assistance because doing so would suggest that they are uncertain about their decisions and it might result in relinquishing some control over the process. However, they may be very likely to embrace at least some of the message if research is presented in a way that emphasizes the relevance of the research to decisionmakers. Accordingly, scientists can assume a variety of roles that can advance their research and make it accessible to the policymakers, program planners, and ultimately the general public. Moreover, it becomes imperative for the scientists to carefully communicate their research findings to those who do not share their perspective. This requires developing a more sophisticated understanding of the perspectives of policymakers, organizational leaders, activists and others who might benefit from our message. It also demands that the message be communicated with clarity and humility (Prosavac & Carey, 1997; Olsen, 1981).

Techniques for Communicating to Nonscientists

As previously mentioned, scientists often isolate themselves, interacting only with other scientists. But, if we are to make our research useful to others, we must be proactive in making it accessible and appealing to them. The methods involved with making our research accessible to the public are varied and dependent upon the initial goal of the researcher. Making basic research accessible to the public may require different techniques from making applied research accessible. Because applied research is more likely to result in detailed discussions of how the results affect real-world programs and decisions and basic research focuses more on the methodological and theoretical discussions pertaining to the subject, the relevance of research findings obtained in an applied project may be more obvious than those of basic research. Thus, it is important for scientists to make the relevance of results of basic research, as well as applied research, clear. Researchers may need to adjust their writing style to make the relevance clear.

One way to accomplish the goal of making research accessible to policymakers, program directors, and the public is to rewrite technical findings for a more general audience after a technical research report is developed for the discipline. Writing reports for magazine or newspaper articles or books requires a different writing style than the professional writing style to which most academic researchers are accustomed. Nevertheless, it is imperative that researchers develop these skills if the information that we have is to become useful to the public. Similarly, researchers can carefully choose to become important resources for journalists who report on issues relating to their area of research interest. For instance, criminologists might become part of the list of resources for journalists compiled by the university for which they work and agree to be interviewed by reporters working on stories related to crime in their area. In either case, it is essential for scientists to avoid jargon that is too technical for the public and to be clear and concise in communicating their message (Olsen, 1981; Vaughan & Buss, 1998). Researchers can further improve the chances that their research will influence decisionmakers by identifying those who make decisions and communicating the results directly to them. Once appropriate individuals are identified, findings and resultant recommendations should be communicated to them in a concrete and specific manner (Rylko-Bauer, van Willigen & McElroy, 1989). Contrary to the experiences of the researcher within his or her academic field, the presentation of findings may be more effective if it is communicated orally rather than in writing (Posavac & Carey, 1997). Similarly, the use of multi-media presentations may increase the attention that decisionmakers give to the presentation (Marjchrzak, 1984; Andranovich & Riposa, 1993). Marjchrzak (1984) outlines several suggestions for improving the effectiveness of presentations. She suggests that presenters be concrete and use examples for clarity, establish objectives for the presentation, present conclusions first, explain the relationship of the study to policy questions, avoid jargon, discuss all options rather than a single option, state study limitations, and reduce the presentation to its essentials. These recommendations apply to written reports as well. Additionally, Andranovich and Riposa (1993) recommend using visual aids whenever possible in written reports to agencies and decisionmakers. Graphs and charts may be particularly helpful in presenting information to non-academics (Posavac & Carey, 1997). Furthermore, it is important that researchers avoid becoming involved with politics. Vaughan and Buss (1998) suggest, for instance, that researchers should analyze policy but not politics and that they explain, identifying the positives and negative of specific options, but not be too quick to advocate a particular course of action. Likewise, they emphasize the importance of understanding the limits of science. Researchers, in their eagerness to encourage the use of their research in the public, may have been guilty of exaggerating the value of research. This, coupled with the demand for immediate results, may have led policymakers in the past to conclude that researchers in the United States cannot deliver on their promises (Street & Weinstein, 1981; Wilensky, 1997).

Researchers working in the area of criminology and criminal justice, as well as in other disciplines and areas, can also become active members of task forces, citizen groups, agency boards and other committees that are relevant to their research interests. For instance, scientists who conduct research in the area of domestic violence might become actively involved with domestic violence task forces in their area or serve on the board of directors for the local shelter. Criminologists might become actively involved with the neighborhood crime watch program in their community in an effort to help educate the citizens about crime statistics in their area and the like. Although the time commitment involved with these activities can be high, they provide a remarkable opportunity to educate policymakers about research and how it can be used to inform decisions. Similarly, attending policy conferences outside academe that relate to the scientists' research interests allows them to introduce policymakers to research and perspectives with which they may not have been previously familiar (Olsen, 1981).

Strategies to Improve Utilization of Applied Research

Researchers whose research projects are of a more applied nature might incorporate strategies that allow the intended primary audience to become part of the research process, either by direct involvement or by the researcher being more cognizant of the needs and problems of the audience. First, perhaps the most important factor in increasing the utilization of research is the involvement of the potential consumer of the research in the research process. The involvement of the client increases the likelihood that the research will be used because it demystifies the research process (Rylko-Bauer, van Willigen & McElroy, 1989; Majchrzak, 1984). Involvement also allows the researcher to better understand the situation of the client and makes the project more relevant to them. Likewise, it allows the users to better understand the ways that the research can be used and increases the stake that they have in the project and its successes (Chelimsky, 1991;

Rylko-Bauer, van Willigen & McElroy, 1989). Frequent communication between the researcher and the potential consumer can also be beneficial to the researcher's understanding of the constraints and realities of the decisionmakers' environment and about changes in the policy arena that might affect the study (Marjchrzak, 1984). Open dialogue between the two parties may also help the potential consumer develop a clearer understanding of the constraints and realities of the researcher.

Applied social researchers should also understand the organizational culture of the agency or organization to which the research applies as well as the community and political factors that may contribute to the utilization of the research in the public arena. Indeed, good quality research may never be used to implement change if the findings of the research are perceived as potentially threatening to other agencies or groups in the community. And, of course, factors relating to the research process itself can be vital to utilization. The research methodologies that are employed must be considered credible by the decisionmakers. Decisionmakers will be more likely to use research that appears to be timely, of high quality and applicable to the problem or issue at hand (Rylko-Bauer, van Willigen & McElroy, 1989). The researcher can also increase the utilization potential of his or her research if he or she communicates with other agencies and organizations with an interest in the research (Marjchrzak, 1984). In fact, Hallinan (1996) suggests that scientists might improve the utilization of their research if they were to develop a mechanism for translating research into policy recommendations for nonresearchers.

Finally, a discussion of the problems with accessibility to and utilization of research would be replete without at least mention of the controversy over the production and utilization of applied scientific research among researchers. Applied research has long been considered by basic researchers to be inferior to basic research with those who conduct such research considered to be "little more than technicians" and "real social scientists," respectively (Whyte, 1998:16). Applied research has been harshly criticized by researchers themselves. Applied researchers are accused of being more likely to compromise sound methodology just to get quick results (Neuman, 2000). Furthermore, Street and Weinstein (1981) argue that applied research may be too closely tied to the clients' definition of problems thereby decreasing the researcher's control over the project, which in turn may lead to less rigorous research. They also argue that the applied researcher may be pressured to, or inadvertently become too committed to, the status quo and fail to see reality. Conversely, they also suggest that in some instances the applied research project may become so politicized that the researcher is discredited and unable to provide useful insight. Regardless of the validity of these criticisms and regardless of the degree to which basic research may be criticized, controversy among scientists themselves does little to promote the use of research by non-academics. Thus, it is imperative that the separation and status differentiation between basic and applied research be reduced if the use of research in policymaking and program development is to be realized (Whyte, 1998).

The social and behavioral sciences, such as criminology and criminal justice, have not been held in as high regard as physical sciences (Ackoff, Gupta & Minas, 1962). Nevertheless, research, both basic and applied, has played an integral, although admittedly sometimes hidden and sometimes less significant than it could have, role in society for quite some time. Science has been used to educate the public and it has been used to justify and support perspectives of decisionmakers. The role that it will have in the future will depend upon the decisions of researchers themselves as well as upon the path that society takes as a whole. If our research is to be used in decisionmaking in the future, we must take it upon ourselves to be vigilant in our efforts to make research available and relevant to the world around us (Olsen, 1981). Making the research available and relevant requires that researchers make concerted efforts to do so. First, because basic and applied researchers often are addressing the same issues from different perspectives and each could benefit from the insight of the other, we also must resolve the status differential between basic and applied research (Whyte, 1998). The division and hierarchy that has developed between basic and applied research has resulted in a lack of communication between basic and applied researchers. And ultimately, the progression of science as a discipline can be slowed or halted altogether by such discord. Moreover, researchers who do not provide policy implications of their work run the risk of someone else attempting to do so and making errors in that attempt (Vaughan & Buss, 1998). Second, researchers must learn better methods of communicating to interested parties outside the academy and research institutions. At the same time, of course, policymakers and other consumers of research must make an effort to become more aware of what research has to offer and how they can best inform research ideas and planning. This is particularly important because both researchers and practitioners are realizing reduced budgets at a time when demand for well-constructed and implemented programs is high (Vaughan & Buss, 1998). Researchers who may find it more difficult to secure financial support for basic research and consumers decisionmakers and service providers may find it increasingly more difficult to conduct adequate assessments of community needs and programs with dwindling budgets on their own can rely upon one another in hard economic times. Finally, social and behavioral science research will have the most profound influence in societies that are dedicated "to humane and rational planning and that are 'governable'." (Street & Weinstein, 1981:xxii). Scientists can participate in supporting the development and maintenance of such societies as well. Thus, while the potential is great, the part that science and scientists will play in the future is not guaranteed.

Discussion Questions

1. What is the difference between purely theoretical and "practical" criminal justice research?

2. Why would researchers choose to do purely theoretical research?

3. How do purely theoretical and practical forms of criminal justice research inform one another?

4. How do researchers differ in their approaches to conducting theoretical and practical research?

CHAPTER 3

How to Know if a Piece of Research Is Good/Valuable

Jeffrey L. Helms
Kennesaw State University

Jeanne J. Johnson
Alliant International University

As a student in the social sciences, reviewing and evaluating research consumes a large portion of time. Of course, this is something professors forget to tell you. But that is another story. Learning how to determine if research is good and/or valuable to the selected topic of interest is something of an art form and is best learned through practice which consists of reading many, many articles, books, and reports. There are many different ways of determining if a piece of research is useful to you in your quest for material for your purpose. However, there are some useful hints that will help in deciphering what is good research.

This chapter will assist the student by providing some helpful hints on how to determine the positive as well as the negative aspects of many different types of research. Every piece of research has some type of flaw that will inevitably raise questions in the mind of the experienced researcher. Some of these flaws may be less of an offense than others. However, even the best research is not perfect, especially when one chooses to dissect it. As a result of this inevitable fact regarding research, this chapter will be discussing the quality of research based on a continuum rather than a dichotomy of good vs. bad research.

What Is Research Evaluation?

Research evaluation is a method of asking pertinent questions of a piece of research in order to understand better what the author has done and what gap in our current knowledge base the research is filling or solidifying. Evaluation of research needs to be meticulous in the questions that one asks in order to determine if the research has been done properly and whether or not it is applicable to the world outside of the setting in which it was conducted.

There are certain problems with evaluating social science research. The first, and probably most evident, is that much research that is done is inaccessible to those who do not have training in how to evaluate research. As a result of this, oftentimes research is intimidating to those who are interested but may not understand how to effectively evaluate and review research (Locke, Silverman & Spirduso, 1998). Research alone can be difficult to understand without having to translate the technical jargon that is often used by researchers. Because of the belief that one needs specialized training to understand research, many feel that they lack the intellectual demand that reading and understanding an article or source may require. Because of the lack of self-confidence (and sometimes the lack of direction by the instructor/professor) the novice often does not attempt to read research.

When one does read research, many times they are faced with the realization that research findings may conflict with one another, or the findings are so complex that it is extremely difficult to understand them. When this occurs, how does one possibly make sense of what is being reported? How does one evaluate information he or she does not understand? How does one evaluate research by someone who obviously has more experience in the field? There is also research that has been done that at least on the surface has no "usefulness" to anyone in the real world. Therefore, how does one determine what is good research and what is trivial given their particular needs, or what is generalizable to those who live in other settings, cultures, etc.? When this happens, as it does to the best researchers, frustration is certainly the next consequence in the research evaluation process.

When one begins to review research, it is essential to keep in mind that every reviewer brings to the research a different perspective. There is a particular knowledge base that every reader possesses before they pick up the research. One must also understand that the author is trying to convey a particular point, test a specific hypothesis, or answer a certain research question (Katzer, Cook & Crouch, 1978). With these many different viewpoints and understandings, it may at times be difficult to differentiate fact from opinion. This is why knowing how to evaluate research is essential to the conscientious reader and student.

Being able to distinguish "good" from "bad" research as well as understanding what it is that the author is trying to convey to the reader is an essential part of any professional's understanding of his/her field. It is important to be able to evaluate research and conduct a thorough review in a manner that allows a better understanding of what is being discussed, in any form of research. Although at times it may not be the most glamorous portion of one's career or studies, it is certainly one of the most important.

Getting Started: The Basics of Evaluation

In order to evaluate research, one must have a general understanding of some of the purposes of research, types of sources, and formats where research is found. This section will start by discussing the purposes of research. Within this discussion will be a review of the types of research likely to be encountered (applied and theoretical). Following from this will be a discussion of the types of sources that can be accessed (primary and secondary) as well as the benefits and drawbacks to the use of each. Ending this section will be a discussion of the various formats where research can be found (journal articles, books, and reports).

The Purposes of Research

Research has two general purposes. The first is to increase knowledge within a specific discipline, and the second is to increase one's knowledge as a consumer of research in order to understand new developments within one's discipline (Morgan, Gliner & Harmon, 1999a). Within these two purposes, there are also two general types of research; these are theoretical and applied research. Most research is conducted with the purpose of finding some way to apply the outcome to real-world situations. This is considered to be applied research, whereas theoretical research is, although necessary, generally not as easily applicable to real-world situations.

Theoretical research is defined as being conducted to investigate issues relevant to the confirmation or disconfirmation of theoretical or empirical positions. The goal of theoretical research is to acquire general information about a hypothesis or more generally a research question, with little emphasis placed on applications to real-world examples of these questions (Bordens & Abbott, 1996). There are many different ways to evaluate this type of research. Because there is little emphasis placed upon the application of the research question that is being researched, the evaluation is strictly from a standpoint of obtaining knowledge rather than learning a new skill that can be used (i.e., Does it add to your knowledge and how?).

Applied research on the other hand has a different focus. The goal here is to investigate a problem based in the real world. Although a theory may still be the origin of the research question/hypothesis, the goal is to generate information that can be applied directly to a real-world problem (Bordens & Abbott, 1996). When reviewing this type of research there is a different focus and purpose in mind. Here not only is knowledge absorbed, but there is also a necessary understanding of the research outcome as it may affect one's practices or understanding of a frequently used theory. Applied research may have a direct impact upon the way one targets problems within an individual, group, organization, or institution. Applied research has more readily usable purposes than theoretical research. There is however, a certain amount of overlap between theoretical and applied research. As mentioned previously, much applied research springs out of theory.

Primary vs. Secondary Sources

There are two types of research sources that one must consider before conducting a thorough evaluation of the research. These two types of research are primary and secondary sources. Primary sources contain the full research report, including all details necessary to duplicate the study. A primary source includes descriptions of the rationale of the study, its subjects/participants, apparatus (special instruments used), procedure/methodology, results and references.

A secondary source is one that summarizes information from primary sources. These include literature review papers and theoretical articles that briefly describe studies and results, as well as descriptions found in textbooks, magazines, etc. Another type of secondary source is a meta-analysis, where a researcher statistically combines the results from research in a particular area in order to determine which of the variables studied are important contributions to the phenomenon under review (Bordens & Abbott, 1996).

It is essential to know what type of source is being evaluated and reviewed because primary sources are considered more reliable than secondary sources. This is because the author of a secondary source may be misinterpreting what the author of the primary source is trying to convey. Complicating the matter further is the fact that there are different formats where these primary and secondary sources are found. However, with some helpful hints to follow, the review of primary and secondary sources will be made easier.

Publication Formats

There are three main publication formats where research is found. These are books, reports, and journal articles. There are particular things which one should be aware of with each type of publication. There are also different parts of each as well as different ways in which one should review these types of manuscripts. We will begin this portion looking at the positives and negatives to each type of publication, as well as discussing how to properly go about evaluating these types of research publications. We will also discuss some important questions to ask while one reads through each type of manuscript. These questions will help to determine where the research stands on the continuum from good to poor, its usefulness, and also whether one should consider the research a reputable and reliable source of information.

Books—Many believe that books may be too outdated as reference material. However, much research that is held in books can be considered a good (although primarily secondary) source. It is important to note that this section will discuss topical books (e.g., textbooks and edited collections on a particular topic). Other books that can be rich resource material (e.g., monographs, extensive/lengthy studies published in book format) are better evaluated utilizing the information found in the section covering journal articles.

The research found in books is heavily screened on the basis of importance and quality by various sources (e.g., publishers, editors, authors, research assistants, and manuscript reviewers). By the time the research has been incorporated into a book, it has also been integrated with other research to form a consistent body of knowledge. This is helpful because the author of the book has done much of the research for the reader already. It is considered an important piece of research that is relevant to other research and incorporated in a way such that it is integrated in a large body of information (Martin, 1996).

Often a good place to start one's research is with a book. If the author has done a good job of integrating the relevant information, there will be a good summation of all the most important research on a particular topic. One possible problem with this approach is that every author is biased toward a particular orientation or theoretical approach and may select research that supports his/her opinion. Therefore a good way to get around this is to consult more than one book for a general summation of information in a particular area. This is specifically the reason that professors do not want students to rely completely (or heavily) on secondary resources.

Another important issue regarding this secondary source is that of delays in publications. By the time the book reaches the shelves and is ready for the reader, a year or more may have passed since the last review of the literature for the book. If a book is utilized it will be necessary to investigate not only the primary sources upon which the book is based but also any new research that may have come out since the writing of the book. A good rule of thumb for this is reviewing the available literature on the relevant topic beginning at least one year prior to the copyright date listed and moving forward in the search to the present. As a result and as mentioned earlier, books may be an excellent place to start but they are not the end of the road for the student.

Journal Articles—It would be a disservice to any piece of writing to only consult books, as one cannot be assured of the quality or the breadth of any book. Also and as mentioned earlier, some information in a book may be outdated or there may be newer, conflicting data on a particular subject. The best way to obtain more current research that is from a primary source is from journals. Although the time from completion of the study to the appearance in a journal can still be quite long, journals generally still provide more current publications of research than books. Now with the accessibility of computer databases, one can obtain research that was published as recently as a month ago in a minimal amount of time and sometimes without even having to go to the library or having to search through the actual journal.

When considering journals, one must also keep in mind the reputation of the journal within the social science community. Also, some journals are refereed journals, which means that the articles included are usually reviewed by two (or more) reviewers prior to acceptance by the journal for publication. Furthermore, most refereed journals have blind reviews in order to limit the bias in the review process. In contrast, a nonrefereed journal does not have such a review process; therefore, the articles may be published in the order in which they are received or according to a fee that the author pays (Bordens & Abbott, 1996; Browne & Keeley, 2001). The review process for journal articles is intended to ensure that high-quality articles appear in the journal. While the type of review process is usually found at some place in the journal (oftentimes at the beginning or in a section titled something like "information for potential contributors"), when there is doubt, simply asking the reference librarian for assistance can aid in the determination. In summary, while it is oftentimes difficult to assess a journal's reputation, the following general guidelines can be helpful:

- Is it abstracted in one of the well-known databases (e.g., Criminal Justice Periodical Index, ProQuest, MedLine, PsycInfo)?

- What is its circulation? How many individuals, institutions, and libraries subscribe to the journal?

- What is the number of articles submitted for publication relative to the acceptance rate? (This information can be found in the journal's annual report or from the editor. Usually a lower acceptance rate equals a higher level of respect in the field.)

- Does the journal have a blind, peer review process?

- Have your peers and professors heard of the journal? Do they believe it has a good reputation?

Journal articles (as well as any other piece of research) should be read with a critical eye and with many questions in mind that should be answered. Reading journal articles involves taking a skeptical point of view, which includes dissecting each section of the article carefully and evaluating adequacy and accuracy of what the author has to say (Bordens & Abbott, 1996).

Although primarily utilized by psychological journals, many journals in the social sciences have adopted the guidelines set forth in the fifth edition of the *Publication Manual of the American Psychological Association*

(2001). It is important to note that this is often considered the "holy text" of all social science writing and an essential part of any social scientist's library.

As a result of the wide acceptance of the *Publication Manual*, most articles will have very similar formatting of the various parts/sections of the article. Typical parts/sections are: the title page, abstract, introduction, method section, results section, discussion/conclusions and references. Although these are traditionally used, some journals may organize the information differently or use somewhat different headings. With a minimal amount of additional time, these can be easily understood and translated although the specific terms may be different. There are very specific items that must be included in each section. This allows for easier review as well as location of specific information that may be of particular interest. Also within each section there should be specific things that one looks for when evaluating the research.

Before diving into the journal article, one should ask specific questions that are to be answered by the journal article. The following checklist will help to determine if a particular piece of research is a valuable contribution to the field and your purposes. The checklist as found in the fifth edition of the *Publication Manual* (APA, 2001) is as follows:

- Is the research question significant, and is the work original and important?

- Have the instruments [data collection procedures] been demonstrated to have satisfactory reliability and validity?

- Are the outcome measures clearly related to the variables with which the investigation is concerned?

- Does the research design fully and unambiguously test the hypothesis?

- Are the participants representative of the population to which generalizations are made?

- Did the researcher observe ethical standards in the treatment of participants—for example, if deception was used for humans?

- Is the research at an advanced enough stage to make the publication of results meaningful? (2001:6, bracketed material added)

This list is just a beginning point of things to consider before combing through the research article. There are specific questions that need to be asked of each section of a journal article. These will be discussed next.

The specific parts of a manuscript, as mentioned above, need to contain very specific information. The first two parts of a journal article that one will encounter is the abstract and introduction. The abstract is a brief paragraph that summarizes the article. This can be used as a starting point for the reader to determine if a more precise and careful reading is necessary or if the article is not useful for the current purpose. The abstract should be self-contained, concise, and specific, as well as coherent and readable. The introduction should introduce the problem, develop the historical background of the problem, and state the purpose and rationale for conducting the research. The purpose of the research is also an important factor to determine. This lets one know exactly what the researchers intended to accomplish and why the research was originally conducted (Girden, 1996).

While the goal of the abstract is to concisely summarize the research, the goal of the introduction is to assist the reader in understanding why the research was conducted. One must first consider the importance of the question that is being asked by the researcher. Is it significant? And if so, how would it change our thinking about the particular area of study? One way to assess its significance is to consider how it relates to previous research. Is the summary of previous research complete and accurate? Does the research add or change current perceptions of theoretical understandings? Does the research add to current knowledge and will it lead to future research done in this area? After thoroughly reading the introduction, what predictions would other researchers make? Are there other predictions or possible explanations for the findings (Bordens & Abbott, 1996; Browne & Keeley, 2001; Oleson & Arkin, 1996)?

The method section should identify the participants in the research, describe the materials or apparatus used if appropriate, and detail the procedures used for collecting the data (APA, 2001). Research consumers need to consider what ideas the author is trying to study and what steps need to be present to adequately measure those ideas/phenomenon (Oleson & Arkin, 1996). Readers of research should look for the methods section to clearly convey the key elements of the design of the study, such as the sources of the data, when the data was collected, a discussion of instruments or other data collection methods used, as well as the basis for judging effects of the independent variable if it is an experimental design (Fischer, 2000).

The method section should be viewed as a set of directions for conducting the study. When reading the method section of an article, evaluate who the participants were, taking into consideration their race, sex, age, or ethnicity. Could these limit the degree to which the results apply beyond the research situation? Does the design of the study allow adequate testing of the hypotheses as stated in the introduction? Are there any flaws in the materials or procedures used that might affect the validity of the study (Bordens & Abbott, 1996; Browne & Keeley, 2001; Girden, 1996)? For some studies, it will be important for the reader to look critically not only at how the variable under study is defined in measurable terms but also the number of ways the variable was measured. In general, are there other ways of measuring the variable(s) under investigation and if so, why were those not utilized? While there are certainly limitations regarding resource expenditure for research, a multi-method investigation (i.e., an investigation that measures the variable in numerous ways) has a tendency to be superior to a uni-method investigation.

Although many of the aforementioned questions should be asked of all research studies and their respective methodologies, additional consideration will need to be given to qualitative research, research that does not try to quantify (i.e., use numbers and statistics) the area of study. The following are some of the supplementary questions that the reader will want to ask:

- How was the collection of data structured?

- Were there converging operations/triangulation? In other words, was there diversity in settings and methods used to collect data (e.g., different environments, group and individual interviews)?

- What was the protocol used to collect the data? Structured interview? Observational?

- If it is observational research, how much interaction was present between the researcher and those observed? Was this an appropriate level of contact?

- How was the data collection limited (because everything cannot be studied in every possible situation)? Were these limitations justified or arbitrary? How were they explained?

There are two major types of validity that need to be considered when evaluating quantitative research studies. These are internal validity and external validity, both of which can compromise the findings of any research study. Internal validity depends on the strength or soundness of the design (Morgan et al., 1999b). When assessing internal validity there are two important factors that need to be considered. Were the participants randomly assigned to conditions and were there proper control or comparison groups that did not receive the experimental variables? If the research has external validity, the findings may be generalized to populations and settings outside of the experiment (Morgan et al., 1999b; Oleson & Arkin, 1996).

For qualitative research, there are two broad types of threats to validity, bias and reactivity (Maxwell, 1996). Bias can be seen when a researcher selects data simply because it fits her/his pre-existing notions of the area being studied. In doing this, the researcher may ignore conflicting data that may be present or likely would have been present, given a different or additional research method. Maxwell (1996) defines reactivity as "the influence of the researcher on the setting or individuals studied" (1996:91). While both bias and reactivity can/do have significant influence on the data collected, they are somewhat inescapable. As a result, the reader of the published studied should review these possibilities with the following questions in mind: How would the data collection and the subsequent results have been affected if a different researcher had conducted the study? A different setting had been used? A different collection procedure utilized? Did the researcher acknowledge any biases or reactivity in the study? Did the researcher attempt any strategy to limit these threats (e.g., independent observers or raters/coders)?

The purpose of the results section of the journal article is to present the findings of the study. The results section of a journal article should include any tables and graphs that are needed to report the data. They should be clearly presented. The statistical tests, if any, that were performed on the data should also be reported in the results section. This should be a thorough report of all statistical information needed to clearly understand the statistical procedures performed. The statistical significance should also be reported here as well as the strength of the relationship between the variables used in the study (APA, 2001). Of course, some studies do not require such information like some qualitative research (e.g., some forms of naturalistic observation and participant-observer research). If the inclusion of statistical operations is not necessary for the particular study, obviously it is not a weakness. For qualitative research, the procedure utilized to develop categories or organize the data needs to be explained. In qualitative research, sometimes tables are utilized to illustrate typical data gathered.

When evaluating the results section of a quantitative research article, one should look for which effects are statistically significant, generally whether the differences are too large or small (Bordens & Abbott, 1996). Assessing the statistical validity from which conclusions are drawn is a very important part of properly evaluating a research article. Mistakes may be made, or improper statistics may be used that confuse the findings. This is often considered the most difficult part of a research article to understand, especially for a beginning consumer of research (Oleson & Arkin, 1996).

The next to last section of a journal article is that of the discussion/conclusion/implications section. In the discussion section the author is expected to interpret the findings of the research study, especially with respect to the original hypothesis or research question. The author is expected to examine and interpret the results as well as draw inferences from them. In this section, similarities and differences between the current findings and findings of other research should be clarified. The author also is expected to state any flaws of the research without dwelling on every possible shortcoming (APA, 2001).

In particular, what needs to be evaluated are whether or not the authors found "significant" results and whether or not they are stating them fairly (Fischer, 2000; Oleson & Arkin, 1996). It is additionally important to evaluate whether the authors were too broad or too narrow in their conclusions. Were there alternative ways to look at the data? Could different conclusions have been drawn? This is the section in which the authors will reach some conclusions regarding the outcomes of their study. Readers will be asked to consider whether threats to validity could have been reduced or eliminated. Also, if the results are intended to be generalized to the other populations, one may be asked to assess threats to external validity, which may render the conclusions less reliable (Girden, 1996).

There are some helpful questions that need to be kept in mind when reading the discussion section as this section determines if the study was successful and, if so, what conclusions one can draw from the research. Do the author's conclusions follow from the results that were reported? Does the author offer speculations about what the results may mean? How well do the findings of the study mesh with previous research and existing theories? Are the results consistent with previous results or are they uncommon? Does the author make suggestions for future research? If the study evaluated a program (e.g., an anger management program) and found significant problems, does the author offer recommendations on how to improve the program? Do they point out other variables that should be taken into account for future research (Bordens & Abbott, 1996)? Generally speaking, the more thoroughly these questions are addressed and/or answered by the author, the better and more useful the study.

The final section is that of the references. This should be considered a valuable resource for finding other literature on the same or similar topic. The section includes all the references cited in the body of the paper. Because of the very nature of references, they include all information necessary to obtain them should the reader wish to access them.

Before moving to the next section, one last but important mention needs to be made. It is important when reviewing the article for your particular purpose that a true critique is made of the article. To do a "true" critique, the reviewer must evaluate whether or not the author achieved his or her goal. Too many times, a critique ends up evaluating the study on aspects that were not the aim of the study in the first place. Criticism should stem from what the author says will be done in the study. Did the authors do what they said they were going to do? Was the undertaking worthwhile to the respective area/discipline? Criticism can always be launched regarding potential expansions or additional inclusions in the project (e.g., study of additional populations). When these types of criticisms are given they are not "true" criticisms but rather additional areas of study that can be done.

Reports—The last type of publication to find research in is reports, which are often ignored. Often reports may be published by government agencies, private companies, or businesses. One of the main problems that many people have with reports is the technical jargon associated with them. Here, the problem is no longer simply comprehension of the material, but translating the report into language that can be understood by the novice or student reader (Locke et al., 1998).

Reports are similar to journal articles but are usually more in-depth about the procedure and materials used to conduct the study. Some reports may even list the actual data collected. As a result of these similarities, reports can be evaluated in much the same way as journal articles. Most reports that are published are not reported in journals, and most libraries do not routinely order them because they quickly fill shelves and are difficult to organize. Many consider technical reports to be a waste of time for particular areas of research; yet for research that is truly comprehensive, they can be an excellent source of information (Martin, 1996).

Unfortunately technical reports are sometimes difficult to obtain, especially if a nongovernmental agency publishes them. When it is a governmental report, oftentimes the document number is needed. Now many reports are available through the Internet Web site of the particular agency publishing the report (e.g., The Office of Juvenile Justice and Delinquency Prevention, www.ojjdp.ncjrs.org; National Criminal Justice Reference Service, www.ncjrs.org) and can be read entirely on the Internet.

How Do Different Audiences Evaluate Research?

When searching for research the student must ask what he or she is trying to get out of the research found. Different people will look for different types of research, depending on what their purpose is in finding the research. There are two main distinctions of focus here, the academic audience and the practitioner audience.

Professionals who work in academics, or academicians, generally look for the theoretical implications that the research has; they are looking to see if the information can be easily translated into possible future research. Oftentimes more important to the academician is whether or not the research is sound in its methodology and resulting implications. The academician wants to know if there is enough information in the research article to replicate the study with ease. When searching for research and in trying to determine if the research is of use to them, the academician generally looks at the following research aspects quite closely: the methodology, analytic method, and theoretical implications.

On the other hand, the practitioner is typically looking for something much different in research. The practitioner wants to learn of alternate ways of intervening with their clients and recipients of their services (e.g., improving security within a correctional facility). They want to improve the services provided to their clients. The practitioner wants to be able to walk away from an article or book having learned a new skill that can be implemented easily and readily. When a practitioner looks at a journal article, for example, oftentimes they will read the abstract first to determine if the research is pertinent, and if so they often move on to the discussion section. Here there is less emphasis placed upon the methodology and data obtained; the data analysis procedure is less important to most practitioners than it would be to an academician. However, somewhat different from the academician, there is more emphasis placed on the ramifications which are usually found in the discussion section.

Practitioners also are concerned with the implications the research has in noncontrolled environments, that is, the generalizability of the findings. The practitioner wants to know if the conclusions will work in the real world, not just the laboratory or study setting. The practitioner is less concerned with the stringent guidelines that were used in the research and is apt to place more weight on case studies that have been shown to be effective. In essence, what the practitioner is looking for is what works and what does not work. They want straight-to-the-point information; they want to know how they can improve what they are currently doing. They want something practical.

No Research Is Perfect

By this point, you may be thinking that no piece of research will withstand the rigors set forth in this chapter. Although we have reviewed how to properly and thoroughly review and evaluate research, what has not been discussed is the fact that no research is perfect. Knowing this, how does one determine what is good research and what is poor research? This is where critical thinking skills come into play. Developing a mental checklist of the points described in the chapter can assist you in evaluating for yourself the strengths and weaknesses of a particular piece of research or study. While not simply a tally that can be quantified easily, carefully considering the strengths and the weaknesses of a particular study and its relation to other studies in the area can help assist in weighing its worth along the continuum of good to poor research. Furthermore, it is important to keep in mind that even poor research offers the reader an opportunity to learn about the field in question. Also, just because the research may not be valuable to your current efforts does not translate into it having "no value." Instead, it may be valuable to another researcher with a different agenda or even to you at a different point in time.

Conclusion

At this juncture, you are probably telling yourself that there is no way you will be able to determine what is good research and what is poor research. Keep in mind that as time goes by and the more research you read the easier this distinction will become. Practice is the key to being a good consumer of research. Although it may not be straightforward in terms of what to do and when to do it, over the course of time the skills described in this chapter can be acquired, learned, and honed.

The greater the amount of material that you read in your area of interest, the better able you will be to evaluate the quality of the research. Not only will your knowledge base expand, but also your research skills will improve. Not all research is equal in terms of implications for that particular subject area, however all research falls onto a continuum from good to poor. For your purposes you will find out where on that continuum your research falls with practice.

Discussion Questions

1. What does the statement mean, "a piece of research is good/valuable"?

2. What are the three most important things to consider when assessing the quality and value of a piece of criminal justice research?

3. Why is it important to evaluate the quality and value of research products?

4. What is the value of research that has 'flaws' or is not "perfect"?

CHAPTER 4

Methodological Yin and Yang: Qualitative and Quantitative Research in Social Science

Angela D. West
University of Louisville

Lanette P. Dalley
Minot State University

Introduction

Although all scientific inquiry into human phenomena is conducted to gain a better understanding of human nature in a systematic way, the goals of various approaches and methodologies are often quite different (Parse, 2001). Historically there has always been a great deal of debate concerning the application and value of quantitative versus qualitative methodologies, particularly in the social sciences (see Sil, 2000, for an excellent summary of this heated debate). Quantitative strategies generally have been given more respect in the social science fields as well as by the general public (Denzin & Lincoln, 1998; Berg, 1989), most probably because it is easier to justify a conclusion based on numerical analysis as opposed to "feelings" or "perceptions." Thus, social scientists have a propensity to rely solely on numeric descriptions of phenomena under study rather than on data generated from ethnographic and field research.

This chapter, however, argues that, while both quantitative and qualitative methods each can provide robust data, such data can be substantially enriched when the two methods are used in conjunction with one another (see also Maxfield & Babbie, 2001; Tarrow, 1995, Murphy & O'Leary,

1994). For example, it is possible to judge your friends based on how often they call you, how many times they ask you how you are doing, or how often they realize something is bothering you, but the odds are that you choose your friends not based on a pure numerical analysis, but on more substantive frames of analysis: Do we get along? Do we have things in common? Do we like each other? In sum, most of the important decisions in life are decided not just on "the numbers" but on less quantifiable analysis. Quantity *and* quality matter, not only in life, but in research. In fact, both methods complement one another. Unfortunately, many researchers become familiar with one or the other methodology, become comfortable with design, implementation, data collection, analysis, interpretation, and application in this methodology, and avoid the method with which they are less familiar and comfortable. This has resulted in fewer studies that attempt to answer research questions through the use of an integrated or "triangulated" design (Tarrow, 1995; Sil, 2000; Hagan, 2000; Murphy & O'Leary, 1994).

According to Campbell and Fiske (1959), triangulation is the use of multiple methods to study the same phenomenon. Although this chapter describes and delineates quantitative and qualitative methods as separate strategies, each having distinct advantages and disadvantages, and each having particular problems and situations to which they are best suited, we argue that triangulated methods, using both quantitative and qualitative strategies are necessary to more clearly, accurately, and precisely describe phenomenon under study.

The Quantitative Question

Measurement is the goal of research. Just exactly how that measurement is taken depends largely on the questions being addressed. Often, research projects involve asking questions about the quantity of whatever it is under study. Researchers often ask how many, how often, how big, how small, how fast, how tall, and how long. These are all questions that beg a quantitative answer. They all will be answered with numbers that express anything from feet, inches, years and dollar amounts, to frequencies, proportions, percentages, rates, and ratios.

Numbers can provide description and help answer questions about the nature of relationships among variables. Description involves describing topics of interest in terms of basic characteristics. Demographic information, for example, is often used to describe individuals or groups of individuals. Suppose, for example, I asked you to describe the class for which you are using this text. Your first instinct would probably be to tell me about the demographics of the people sitting in the classroom. You might tell me that the class has 50 students, with 25 men and 25 women. You might also tell me that there were 28 white persons, 15 black persons, four Hispanic persons, and three Asian persons in the class. You might also determine that five persons had a cumulative grade point average (GPA) of 4.0, 18 persons had GPAs of between 3.0 and 3.99, 23 persons had GPAs of between 2.0 and 2.99, and four persons had GPAs of below 2.0. This information is represented below in Table 1.

Table 1
Class Demographics

	CLASS #1		CLASS #2	
	#	%	#	%
Sex				
Male	25	50%	75	60%
Female	25	50%	50	40%
Race				
White	28	56%	98	78%
Black	15	30%	10	8%
Hispanic	4	8%	10	8%
Asian	3	6%	7	6%
GPA				
0 – 1.99	5	10%	32	26%
2 – 2.99	18	36%	55	44%
3 – 3.99	23	46%	23	18%
4	4	8%	15	12%

What good is this information? If you are only interested in describing your class in terms of these characteristics, then it might be useful. Kritzer (1996) calls this type of information "brute data" because it does not require interpretation. Description, however, is rarely used alone. It is most often used as a basis for comparison among similar groups. For example, what if you wanted to compare your class (as described above) to Class #2 as presented in Table 1? Class #2 has 125 members, whereas your class has only 50. Can you make comparisons between these two classes just by looking at the raw numbers? Obviously not. Consider sex, for example. Just comparing frequencies gives the impression that Class #2 has more women than Class #1. While Class #2 obviously has more women in pure numbers, it is only because Class #2 has more members overall than Class #1. Once you compare the percentage of women in each class, it is apparent that women are *underrepresented* in Class #2 as compared to Class #1.

When you translate raw numbers or frequencies into percentages, you are able to compare among groups of differing sizes. That is the beauty of percentages; size does not matter because percentages standardize groups using 100 as a base. As you examine Table 1 more closely, you will be able to see the value of translating raw numbers into percentages.

But what if you were interested not only in comparing the groups, but also in making inferences about the relationships among the variables? That is, from the information on this table, I can describe Classes #1 and 2 in terms of their sex, their race, and their GPAs. I also can compare the two classes on these characteristics and say that one class has more or less than the other class in a particular area (e.g., Class #2 has more male members than Class #1, or Class #2 has more members in the highest GPA than Class #1). This is useful, but limited, information.

What if I wanted to know *why* Class #2 has more members with higher GPAs? Can this table answer that question? Descriptive statistics, as presented in Table 1, only describe things. Inferential analysis can help answer questions related to the relationships between and among variables, to determine how well any particular sample represents the population from which it came, and whether observed differences between and among groups in a sample reflect actual differences between and among groups in the population (the purpose of statistics). It is these areas in which quantitative data become necessary.

Quantitative Design, Data, and Analysis

Quantitative data is quantifiable information collected from a particular source. That is, it is information that is measurable through the assignment of numerical values. These assignments often are arbitrary. Sometimes these values imply a quantity of some characteristic (e.g., GPAs imply a quantity of knowledge, academic achievement, or education), but often these values are used only to keep track of distinct categories (e.g., there are four racial categories in Table 1 that could be numbered from 1-4). In the latter case, the numerical assignments have no real meaning—they do not indicate the level of any particular characteristic.

Quantitative analysis is the process of examining quantitative data in order to make conclusions about the problem under study. It involves gathering the data, "cleaning" the data, and manipulating the data for ease of handling. More specifically, it involves the use of statistical procedures to determine whether and to what extent particular concepts (such as "fear of crime" or "stress") are present or absent, to determine whether and to what extent particular variables are related ("fear of crime" is related to "stress"), and to test hypotheses that variables are related in a theorized way (individuals with more "fear of crime" have higher levels of "stress"). These statistical procedures often involve complex mathematical equations that provide a researcher with a number or set of numbers to interpret.

Quantitative design involves constructing a research project based on research questions involving concepts that can be defined and measured numerically. This is not to say that *only* quantitative designs can address these questions, but that the variables involved lend themselves to numerical measurement. The concept of "stress," for example, can be defined in such a way that a researcher can develop a numerical measurement to determine whether an individual has "stress," and to what extent. In this manner, levels of stress among different individuals in different situations can be compared. Qualitative methods, such as interviews, also could determine the presence or absence of stress, but it would be more difficult to make comparisons among individuals in different circumstances based on a contextual examination of interview data. In addition, quantitative research "generates more precise predictions" about such relationships by providing numerical ranges or values within which one can predict individuals or samples of individuals are likely to fall (Caporaso, 1995:459).

The most important consideration is the research design itself. Researchers should construct designs with the purpose of the study, the questions to be addressed, and how the findings will be used in the forefront of their minds. As King, Keohane, and Verba (1994) emphasize, no amount of clever data analysis can salvage a weak design.

One primary difference between qualitative and quantitative designs is in the number of data sources and the scope of information collected. Quantitative designs often involve larger numbers of data sources with a more narrow scope of inquiry. In contrast, qualitative designs often involve fewer data sources with a broader scope of inquiry. That is, quantitative designs often involve more breadth but less depth, and qualitative designs often involve less breadth but more depth.

In what situations would a researcher prefer breadth at the expense of depth or depth at the expense of breadth? Quantitative techniques generally are used when one desires breadth more than depth. With quantitative methods, it is easier to obtain large amounts of summary statistics about a particular problem among a particular group. Nearly every type of agency, for example, keeps statistical information about the populations that they serve. State departments of transportation keep records on all licensed drivers. State departments of health keep records on all individuals who utilize their services. Law enforcement agencies, courts, correctional facilities, and offices of probation and parole keep information on cases and persons processed through their agencies. Quantitative data abound, and often more data are collected than anyone could ever use.

Studies on public opinion, for example, are obviously more concerned with breadth rather than depth. Researchers often measure public opinion on a wide variety of topics because public opinion often is extremely important to many different groups, agencies, and organizations. In fact, certain research organizations exist only to measure public opinion and to maintain databases of trends and patterns in those opinions over time (e.g., Gallup, the National Opinion Research Center).

Gauging public opinion is crucial because these groups, agencies, and organizations rely upon public opinion for their very existence. Lawmakers, for example, keep a watchful eye on public opinion to help them determine trends in social philosophies that might eventually result in required policy changes. To illustrate, public opinion on the death penalty has traditionally tilted toward support for capital punishment. Lately, however, public opinion has shifted away from a preference for death toward a preference for life imprisonment without parole (see, for example, Vito, Keil & Andreescu, 1999).

Representative and Generalizable

When researchers study a particular problem, it is rare that they are able to access the entire population affected by that problem. As an alternative, scientists collect information from selected members of that population. Theoretically and ideally, this sample is randomly selected and representative of the entire population because each and every member of that population had the same chance of being selected for the sample. Given that this sample represents the population, we can use whatever we find within the sample to represent the population, with a known and specified chance of error. (A complete discussion of probability theory is beyond the scope of this chapter.) A significant task of quantitative data analysis, therefore, is to assist researchers in making the determination of whether one sample represents a population well enough to make valid inferences (generalizations) about that population.

One cannot accomplish this task with qualitative analysis. Qualitative methods usually do not rely on random selection and are not, in general, as concerned with making broad generalizations about the populations from which the data sources were drawn. The point of qualitative studies is to make conclusions about the data sources from which the information originated, not only in using the data source to make generalized conclusions about some larger group. Often, qualitative researchers are interested in observing and describing some phenomenon that does not lend itself to numerical description and correlational analysis.

If the research goal is to describe a problem or to describe relationships among variables within large populations that may be difficult to identify and to reach, it is best to use quantitative design. For example, Tjaden and Thoennes (2000) examined 1,785 domestic violence reports compiled by the Colorado Springs Police Department over a five-month period. Their goal was to make conclusions about the relationship between stalking allegations and other case characteristics such as arrest of the offender or the charge issued.

They found that cases in which stalking was alleged differed in several ways from cases in which stalking was not mentioned. For example, stalking victims were significantly more likely to have a restraining order on the offender. Most importantly, however, law enforcement behavior seemed to significantly differ between the two types of cases. In cases that alleged stalking, officers were significantly less likely to make an arrest. When they did arrest, they were reluctant to charge the offender with domestic violence stalking, and instead charged them with the less serious charge of harassment or violating a restraining order.

This type of quantitative research provided crucial empirical data on the prevalence of stalking in domestic violence cases, risk factors associated with stalking, and police response. This is valuable in that it reveals potentially serious problems with the justice process, like the differential application and enforcement of the laws, that may impact many lives. This information can be used to develop more focused inquiries into this phenomenon and to effect policy and procedure changes within law enforcement and within the court systems, if necessary.

The relationships that Tjaden and Thoennes measured through quantitative design would likely have been missed with a qualitative design. Qualitative design is better suited to situations in which the research goal is to describe a problem within smaller, more easily identified and more accessible populations. This is especially true if you are dealing with "deviant" behaviors that involve small groups of participants, such as "bath house" behavior (Tewksbury, 2002), "exotic" dancing (Sweet & Tewksbury, 2000), and female impersonation (Tewksbury, 1993). In the former, researchers are more concerned with the breadth of information, and not as concerned with the depth. In the latter, researchers have little interest in being representative or in generalizing to a larger population. In many cases, it is possible to obtain information from an entire population, so generalizing is unnecessary. The main concern in this case is to comprehensively describe a problem as it exists among data sources.

Context and Interpretation

Along with depth of information goes the idea of context. With quantitative analysis, one often is unaware of the context surrounding information. Data is usually gathered with little regard for time, space, and circumstance. An event, belief, perception or other response is reduced to a number or to a check mark beside a category. In most cases, information is missing about why or under what circumstances that response is given. Perhaps more importantly, the researcher might not ever know why those responses might change given different sets of circumstances. This is the context that is usually absent from quantitative studies. As Babbie (2001) points out, most quantitative research (with the exception of longitudinal studies) provides only a "snapshot" of reality as it exists at a particular point in time. This may be detrimental if you are concerned with developing a deeper understanding of a particular problem or behavior.

To illustrate, Seiter and West (in progress) surveyed probation and parole officers to determine the type of supervision style that the officers used in dealing with clients. Part of this survey asked the officers to report how much time per week they spent working with clients on various tasks, such as office visits, home visits, conducting urine tests, etc. This is quantitative information that will allow the researchers to measure and compare time spent on each type of activity by the officers. This is useful if we are interested only in reporting the distribution of time spent on various tasks during an average week.

However, this information would be much more valuable and useful if we could understand how officers responding to these surveys interpreted these particular questions, and if we could ask the officers to describe the context surrounding these events. For example, one activity on which officers were asked to estimate their time expenditure was "home visits." One officer's interpretation of "home visits" might be very different from another officer's interpretation of "home visits." A home visit might mean that an officer visited a parolee's home to discuss progress in finding employment or in obtaining social services. On the other hand, a home visit might mean that an officer went by an offender's home late at night to determine if curfew requirements were being followed. Clearly, these two types of "home visits" are different and the context is crucial. In fact, qualitative data in the form of officer interviews helped Seiter and West recognize this limitation within their survey data.

While respondents to quantitative questions often must interpret what they are being asked, quantitative analysts also must interpret the resulting data. Researchers typically have discussed interpretation as critical to qualitative studies given that qualitative data are primarily textual or observational and therefore more subjective, or dependent upon interpretation to derive meaning. Although the importance of interpretation to qualitative studies is fairly obvious, Kritzer (1996) argues that "rather than being more divorced from the human process of interpretation, quantitative social science probably involves more levels of interpretation than does qualitative social science" (1996:3).

To illustrate, Kritzer (1996) describes three levels at which interpretation operates to assess the meaning and adequacy of quantitative results. First-order interpretation relies upon the definition of the statistical measures. One must recognize the definition of any statistical procedure in order to interpret results from the completion of that procedure.

Second-order interpretation identifies "problems" in the data and the analyses by examining statistical results. In this type of interpretation, the researcher moves beyond merely focusing on the simple meaning of statistical results to understanding patterns that might be less than obvious. Kritzer (1996) provides the example of large regression coefficients that imply a relationship among variables, but that happen to be in the "wrong" direction. He questions whether this means that the variables are unrelated, whether the theory involved (from which the regression equation was derived) was "wrong," or whether some of the variables have strong collinear relationships (that is, as one changes, so does the other one) with one another. The recognition and addressing of these types of problems require a deeper understanding of statistical procedures, a familiarity with theoretical models, and a willingness to look beyond the obvious.

Third-order interpretation, according to Kritzer (1996), is the "most complex and the least understood," and involves "connecting the statistical results to broader theoretical patterns" (1996:9). At this level, a researcher attaches probabilities to a variety of potential explanatory models. For example, a scientist studying the criminal behavior of burglary is aware that there are several known theoretical explanations for this behavior such as "strain theory," "differential opportunity theory," and "rational choice theory." It also is highly likely that there are other, unknown explanations that have yet to be recognized or adequately articulated into theoretical models. As Kritzer explains, the scientist operates under the basic assumption, expressed in a probability, that "THE" model is true, with the unexpressed assumption that some "OTHER" model is not true. This makes the questionable assumption that "SOME" model is "true." According to Kritzer, "the process of linking data (and data analyses) to the substantive theory is one of revising the probabilities associated with the substantive models" (1996:9).

The use of data to assess and develop theoretical propositions is "closely tied to contextual elements such as substantive theory, data collection/generation, and side information available to the analyst" (Kritzer, 1996:10). With this statement, Kritzer is arguing that even quantitative data need to be contextually considered in order to be properly interpreted and useful in making inferential conclusions.

Kritzer goes beyond the rather obvious recommendation that quantitative data be interpreted within context, to the slightly less obvious suggestion that context also involves the theoretical issues that motivated the collection and analysis of the data. These contexts also beg interpretation. For example, one often hears essay exams called "subjective" tests, while multiple-choice exams are termed "objective" tests. The rationale behind this terminology assumes that the grading of essay exams requires interpretation by the reader/grader, making the meaning and grade "subject" to that reader/grader's interpretation. In contrast, multiple-choice exams call for no such interpretation on the part of the reader/grader, and therefore are more "objective." What often is overlooked in this argument is that even "objective" exams have some measure of subjectivism. The person who constructed the exam obviously had a reason for asking the questions that were asked in the way that they were asked. The provision of potential answers also called for subjective choice by the person making the exam. The construction of quantitative data collection instruments follows the same reasoning.

Kritzer (1996) also argues that researchers make decisions between qualitative and quantitative methods not only by determining which method best addresses the questions under consideration, but also based on "what they like doing" (1996:25). He says that "data are fun" because "they sometime confirm what we know; they occasionally tell us things we did not know; [and] they often confuse and confound us (i.e., relationships we "know" must exist do not appear to be present in the data)" (1996:26). He contrasts the benefit that qualitative researchers derive from the fieldwork experience with the enjoyment quantitative researchers find in "the data themselves (or the interaction of data and theory)" (1996:26).

The Qualitative Question

Qualitative research is a generic term for investigative methodologies described as ethnographic, naturalistic, and anthropological (Jacob, 1987; 1988). The backbone to qualitative research is *grounded theory* that focuses on the research process (Babbie, 2001; Glaser & Strauss, 1967). "Essentially, grounded theory is the attempt to derive theories from an analysis of the patterns, themes and common categories discovered in observational data" (Babbie, 2001:284). Thus, a theory evolves during the research process whereby observations are summarized into conceptual categories which are eventually refined and linked together (Shutt, 2001; Glaser & Strauss, 1967). Special attention is given to the research procedures, particularly to systematic observations and coding (Strauss & Corbin, 1990; Berg, 1989).

Unlike quantitative research, qualitative research provides a wide range of methodologies to collect data, but by definition, none of the methods relies solely on numerical measurements (King, Keohane & Verba 1994), although a quantitative numerical analysis can be employed (such as ranking a professor's teaching abilities on a scale of 1 to 10). Researchers interested in conducting qualitative studies can use in-depth interviews, case studies, focus group interviews, field research, and participant observations. The choice of one or more of these methods largely depends on the research questions (or hypotheses) and population under study. Deciding which method to employ is discussed next.

Qualitative Design, Data, and Analysis

It is useful to determine whether qualitative methods are appropriate within the larger context of research decisions in general. These questions largely revolve around the advantages and disadvantages of qualitative methods. As Patton (1987) points out, the choice of the research process and data collection strategies depend on the answers to several questions:

1.   What is the focus or goal of the study?

2.   What are the primary research questions?

3.   How large will the sample be?

4.   Is the sample easily accessible?

5. When are the data needed?

6. What types of resources are available to conduct the research?

7. Does the researcher have the necessary skills to conduct qualitative studies?

One of the primary strengths of qualitative research methods is how qualitative research provides a thorough perspective of the population that is being studied; unlike experimental or survey research qualitative research allows the population to be studied in its own environment (Babbie, 2001). By observing the actual phenomenon as it occurs and observing it as completely as possible, researchers can obtain a more complete understanding of it.

Qualitative methodology is particularly suitable for studies where the purpose is to examine the nuances of motivations, attitudes, and beliefs. "As such, this mode of [methodology] is especially, though not exclusively, appropriate to research topics and social studies that appear to defy simple quantification" (Babbie, 2001:275). For example, if the researcher desires to gain an understanding of human behavior and interaction as it is related to addiction, mental or physical illnesses, or criminality, qualitative studies are an appropriate methodology. Researchers who developed well-known qualitative studies (such as Howard Becker's, *Outsiders: Studies in the Sociology of Deviance*) use field observations and interviews. More importantly, such studies demonstrated that qualitative studies can have significant scientific and social value if conducted with the necessary skills and insight (Babbie, 2001; Patton, 1990). In fact, Becker's study is still regarded today as a major contribution to social sciences because of his ability to describe the population holistically.

Typically qualitative studies involve smaller samples than quantitative studies, primarily due to the time necessary to obtain all of the relevant data. For example, a prison researcher may spend a few days reviewing files to determine the ages, gender, and type of crime that relates to each inmate. The result may be three charts worth of aggregate data that numerically describe the inmates' criminal histories and demographics. A qualitative researcher, on the other hand, may spend weeks delving into the family histories of each inmate for the purpose of finding factors that might be related to criminal behavior.

If the researcher expects that the sample will be large (i.e., more than 100 participants) and the researcher has few, if any resources (i.e., help in interviewing participants, transcribing tapes, and analyzing data), he or she may want to consider using a quantitative method instead. In essense qualitative studies are known for their time-intensive labor usually taking several months or perhaps as long as several years to collect data. Clearly, researchers need to first consider the relevant time needed to complete the research task, particularly if they have few, if any, resources.

Another concern relating to qualitative research is the issue of whether a qualitative study based on a small sample size can be appropriately used to generalize findings to the general population. Small sample sizes often associated with qualitative methods is perhaps the most common area of criticism. However, most qualitative researchers are not interested in generalizing to the entire population but rather are more interested in gaining a thorough understanding of the sample population, as it exists in its own environment. In addition, Stake (1995) points out that while qualitative studies are not intended to make "grand generalizations" it is possible to make "petite generalizations" with valid modifications (1995:8).

The last issue associated with the sample is that qualitative methods typically involve some form of nonprobability sampling procedure. Unlike quantitative samples, there often is no official list of the population from which to randomly select respondents. For instance, there is no official list of all gang members, prostitutes, or gamblers in order to conduct a stratified random sample. Thus, researchers are often faced with finding a participant who is willing to be interviewed and who also refers other possible participants to the researcher. This process of locating individuals to make up the sample is known as a snowball sampling technique. The most difficult aspect of this type of sampling procedure is acquiring access to certain groups of people who are often quite suspicious of outsiders in general. Another concern inherent in a snowball sampling technique is the lack of randomization and selection bias. Thus, in nonprobability samples everyone in the sample population may not have an equal chance of participating because of the lack of systematic selection of participants (Babbie, 2001).

The last area that researchers need to be concerned with when considering qualitative research methods is regarding whether they feel comfortable with actually interviewing the respondents. A researcher who desires to conduct qualitative research should actually enjoy interacting with people. This is critical in the sense that individuals usually cannot "fake" genuinely liking people and the respondents may pick up on this, thereby negatively impacting the quality and quantity of data collected. If the researcher is not comfortable with interviewing, another option is to arrange for someone else to conduct the interviews and the principal researcher later analyzing the data separately. As can be seen from this discussion, there are a variety of ethical issues associated with qualitative research, some of which can be complex and difficult to address. Nonetheless, the researcher is responsible not only for identifying the ethical issues but, more importantly, for taking responsibility for the consequences of his or her involvement (Shutt, 2001). This is discussed next.

Ethical Considerations

By their very nature, qualitative methodologies have more potential ethical problems than quantitative methodologies. Abuses of research participants have been well documented. For instance, Laud Humphrey's study *Tearoom Trade* (1970) involved the subsequent nonconsensual interviewing of men who frequented public restrooms to engage in same-sex sexual activities. This study caused a great deal of controversy involving a whole host of what many researchers considered ethical violations: lack of informed consent, invasion of privacy, and deceit.

Another study conducted by Haney, Banks, and Zimbardo (1973), often referred to as the *Simulated Prison Study*, involved college students participating as either prisoners or prison guards in a simulated "prison" at Stanford University (see http://www.prisonexp.org). Aside from the physical ordeals that several of the participants endured, this study also generated controversy due to psychological trauma inflicted upon the participants. The major bone of contention was that the participants were not fully aware of what consequences they might face before they volunteered for the study. Thus, they were not fully informed, and could not provide informed consent. As a result of these types of abuses, Institutional Review Boards (IRBs) were established at universities, hospitals, and in some correctional systems for the purpose of preventing any harm to research participants (Babbie, 2001; Raymond, 1993; Rosnow, Rotheram-Borus, Ceci, Blanck & Koocher, 1993).

The ethical issues outlined below describe the general research concerns as established by the Department of Health and Human Services (DHHS) when human subjects are involved in studies. DHHS is the federal agency that oversees, approves, and manages the ethical operation of federally funded research (DHHS, 2001). Researchers and IRBs often use the DHHS guidelines as a model to develop their own policies and procedures when conducting research with human subjects (see also, DHHS & The Office for Protection from Research Risks, 2002). It is important to note however, that because each study is unique, some studies may have more complex ethical issues that are beyond the scope of this chapter.

Informed Consent

This concept is one of the most essential ethical issues. Participants are informed in writing of the details of the research process, especially the potential risks (emotional or physical) and benefits. After being informed of these details, the participant (and/or the participant's parent or guardian, if necessary) must indicate their consent by their signature. This is called "active" consent. In addition, participants are informed that they can withdraw from the study at any time or refuse to answer any questions without any potential negative consequences. Participants who are given compensation but who terminate their participation before completing the study still are compensated on a prorated basis, according to the term of their participation.

In some studies, particularly studies involving minimal risk and larger numbers of respondents (and most likely quantitative data), written consent is not necessary. This type of consent is called "passive" consent and often involves studies with large samples (and most likely quantitative data). Informing the potential research participant of passive consent is specifically explained in a cover letter or as an introduction to the study instrument (i.e., "by completing this survey you are consenting to participate in this study").

Regardless of whether the study is appropriate for active or passive consent, the researcher should always "debrief" the participant after participation by describing the study, the purpose of the research, the potential risks and benefits to the subject, who the researcher is representing, and how the data will be used. If the researcher fails to provide this information, the participant is, for all intents and purposes, uninformed and cannot technically provide informed consent. Researchers also should always address confidentiality and anonymity in the description of the study.

Anonymity/Confidentiality

The collection of data often involves the ability to identify the person from whom that data was obtained. Personal identifiers, such as name, social security number or other identification number, date of birth, race, sex, age, ethnicity, and education are common pieces of data that are collected in much research. In corrections research, for example, inmates usually are associated with an "inmate number" that is assigned them when they enter the correctional system. This number provides access to the inmate's file within which his or her entire social, psychological, and criminal history is maintained.

One cornerstone of ethical research is the attempt to shield research participants from unnecessary and invasive use of their personal information and to protect their identity from persons who might be interested in the study findings. This involves the confidentiality of research. Researchers are obligated to protect, to the best of their abilities, the confidentiality of a person's participation in a research project. This implies that, while data may be collected from individuals, this data will not be traceable back to those individuals but will instead be analyzed and reported on an aggregate level.

Confidentiality is a bit easier to promise than is anonymity. According to Babbie (2001), "a research project guarantees anonymity when the researcher—not just the people who read about the research—cannot identify a given response with a given respondent" (2001:472). Anonymity often is achieved by using numerical codes on surveys, using fictitious names, and deleting any possible identifiers in final reports (Shutt, 2001). This type of protection is difficult in quantitative research, but becomes even moreso in qualitative studies. Interviews, for example, usually require that the researcher know the name of the person that is being interviewed.

Although the rule of thumb is for researchers to take precautionary measures to the best of their abilities in order to protect the identity of research participants, there are some exceptions. For example, research with inmates may require violating confidentiality assurances if, during the course of the study, the inmate indicates intentions to harm themselves or others. Under such conditions, it is good practice to inform respondents that certain situations, behaviors, and statements may necessitate an exception to their general confidentiality protections. Understandably, most prisons require that researchers do this prior to conducting the research, and inmates usually are well aware of this policy. Thus, when establishing research guidelines and exceptions to confidentiality, researchers must understand and clearly communicate these conditions to the potential participants.

Another potential ethical issue involves the ownership of data. When information is collected within an agency or about an agency, to whom does that data legally belong? Researchers and agencies must clearly establish data ownership, preferably at the beginning of any research project, and preferably in writing. Ownership of data may have certain political, practical, and legal implications. For example, a publicly funded agency such as a police department, may be forced to provide raw data to the local newspaper under the Freedom of Information Act (FOIA) (USC 552, 1966). If, however, the researcher owns the data, provisions under the FOIA do not apply. This issue may be particularly crucial when the research involves data of a sensitive nature. Data ownership may be especially important as it pertains to qualitative data. Taped interviews, photographs, or life history narratives would make it very easy to identify a particular person as the source of the data, thereby violating anonymity and confidentiality protections.

It is also important to point out that, unlike relationships and communications between the medical, counseling, and legal professions and their patients or clients, the researcher-subject relationship generally does not qualify in most states as a relationship within which communication is privileged or protected. Most states limit such protected communications to specific relationships, such as between a husband and wife, doctor and patient, priest and parishioner, and attorney and client. Thus, the information provided to researchers by study participants usually has no "automatic" legal basis for creating a privilege. Researchers nonetheless attempt to protect participants by contractual agreements contained either in the signed informed consents or by other written agreements between the researchers and participants. Although such contractual provisions do not provide the same level of protection afforded by the more traditional privileged relationships, such provisions nonetheless provide participants with a guarantee of a certain level of privacy and confidentiality that can be enforced through the law. Conversely, such contractual provisions place on the researcher the legal responsibility to maintain the privacy of the subjects as delineated in the written document. A researcher who fails to comply with this agreement can be sued for breach of contract and, potentially, for invasion of privacy. Thus, although the law does not automatically guarantee confidentiality, certain protections are provided to participants through the research process itself.

Protected Populations

Voluntary participation and informed consent are the two most frequently cited ethical concerns when dealing with children, prisoners, mentally ill, mentally handicapped, students, the elderly, and minorities. Unfortunately, researchers have in the past exploited these populations. As such, these categories of individuals have been deemed protected populations "because of their lack of political, social, and financial power, these disadvantaged groups are more accessible to researchers due to their lack of power" (Berg, 1989:135).

Understandably some of these populations may be very difficult to study simply because of the vast issues involving informed consent. For example, if a researcher wanted to study juvenile delinquents who have been diagnosed with depression, the first question should concern whether a minor can give informed consent, particularly if he or she is depressed. Clearly, the researcher needs the juvenile's parents' informed consent. However, juvenile delinquents often have more than one guardian or agency who have a legal interest in the child (e.g., guardians ad litem). Thus, the researcher in this case is obligated to track down all those individuals who have (or represent) a legal interest in the juvenile and obtain informed written consents from each of those individuals and entities. This is perhaps one of the biggest reasons why children are not often the focus of studies.

In correctional settings, the issue is not guardianship or ability to give consent, but one of a coercive environment. Inmates are under the control of the state. As a result, it is argued convincingly that a request for an inmate to do something while incarcerated is tantamount to an order. Convincing an IRB that an inmate can refuse to participate in a study or can freely withdraw his or her participation at any time is a Herculean task.

Researcher Qualifications

The researcher must have training or experience in using qualitative methodologies, particularly where interviewing respondents is part of the research process. Sufficient experience can be gained through professional experience in the field or by role-playing in the classroom with the underlying idea that they have studied various interviewing styles. Perhaps the most important interviewing skill that a researcher can foster is the ability to develop rapport with the participants (Tewksbury & Gagné, 1996; see also Berg, 1989). In addition, in some studies it is important that the researcher have experience working with the population, as well as with the type of data collection method that will be used. A great deal has been written regarding the impact (both positive and negative) that researchers have in the interviewing process (see Kvale, 1996; Jacob, 1987; Whyte, 1982; Burgess, 1991). Sufficient training and experience in the art of interviewing and the science of data collection can go a long way in preventing potential harm to the respondents.

Participant Observation

One of the more contradictory ethical dilemmas associated with qualitative research concerns the researcher's degree of participation in the phenomenon under study. Obviously, some groups prefer not to be studied, such as drug dealers, terrorists, or hate groups such as the Ku Klux Klan (KKK). Researchers have been known to study such groups "undercover," without the knowledge of the individuals being studied. Clearly such research entails deceiving members of the groups or participants in the behavior of interest. In conducting such nonconsensual research, researchers not only may violate the potential legal rights of the participants, but also may place themselves at risk of physical harm. The use of deception as part of the research process is a debatable topic among researchers primarily because of the lack of informed consent (Stainback & Stainback, 1988).

Currently, no rule forbids participant observation or the use of deception simply because in some studies the benefits of deception (or that which will be gained through deception) outweigh the costs (the ethical violations). Clearly, without the use of deception it would be very difficult (if not impossible) to study some groups, their members, and their members' behaviors. If the researcher identified himself or herself the group might not allow access or might change their behaviors in response to the researcher's presence (Patton, 1987). Essentially, in order for most IRBs to allow participant observation or any form of deceit to occur in a study, the researcher must be able to justify that such conduct is necessary and to show that the benefits outweigh the costs. Yet even if the researcher can clearly demonstrate the value of such an approach, an IRB may refuse the study because of the inherent risks to the researcher, to the participant, or to the institution in the form of lawsuits (Babbie, 2001; Berg, 1989).

As one can imagine, more complicated problems may arise with respect to confidentiality concerns. Researchers need to carefully consider any potential conflicts that may arise within the context of the population under study and decide before conducting the research how he or she will handle these situations.

Qualitative vs. Quantitative

While some argue that there are clear guidelines for determining when to use which design, others claim that the choice between qualitative and quantitative designs is more a matter of personal choice. Obviously, some research problems are better suited to one design or the other. In fact, some methodologists insist that choice of method is determined by the problem under consideration. Studying steroid use among college or professional athletes, for example, would be very difficult to accomplish with field research. One could conduct interviews, but the likelihood of getting very many people to volunteer to be interviewed is pretty slim. Survey research, on the other hand, yields quantitative data and may be more likely to generate participants given that respondents may feel more anonymous responding to a survey than being interviewed.

Aside from personal choice and the nature of the questions being addressed, choice of method also is affected by the type of information being collected and by what one plans to do with that information. As previously argued, quantitative designs are best suited for breadth of information over depth, and when one is attempting to make generalizations from a sample to a larger population.

Choice of method also should be made after careful consideration of theoretical implications. In designing any research project, theory should guide the inquiry and can help the researcher decide which method is best suited for the research process.

Other important considerations are time and expense. The collection of quantitative data can become expensive if large samples, special collection techniques, or extensive follow-ups are used. For example, telephone interviews can be very expensive, but so can copying and mailing several hundred surveys and conducting mailed follow-ups. The collection of qualitative data involves fewer individuals and little or no paper and mailing costs, but other expenses can quickly add up. The costs of hiring and training teams of interviewers can quickly accumulate. In addition, interviews must be recorded and transcribed into text, which can quickly decimate a research budget. In general, the process of collecting and analyzing qualitative data is more time-consuming (and therefore more expensive) than the process of collecting and analyzing quantitative data.

Along these lines, qualitative research, especially interviewing, often requires skills developed through training and/or experience. An interviewer seeks to capture the richness of people's life experiences in their own words. As a result, the validity and reliability of qualitative data in these types of situations largely depend on the methodological skill, sensitivity, and training of the researcher (Patton, 1987). Systematic and rigorous observation involves far more than just being present and looking around. Observations must be documented systematically within a short time period of when the observation occurred. Careful note-taking is essential.

Skillful interviewing involves much more than simply asking the right questions. It involves using sophisticated social skills, providing appropriate verbal and nonverbal cues, and being able to read the respondent's non-verbal body language (Denzin & Lincoln, 1998). Analyzing this type of data requires considerably more than just reading the transcript of an interview. Whereas most people understand that the collection, analysis, and inter-pretation of quantitative data requires training in statistics, some may have the misperception that qualitative methods are "easier" because they do not involve any sort of mathematical interpretations. This may be far from the truth. As Patton (1987) notes, "generating useful and credible qualitative data through observation, interviewing, and analysis requires discipline, knowl-edge, training, practice and hard work" (1987:8).

One might be tempted to argue that qualitative and quantitative method-ologies are so distinct as to be unrelated and impossible to reconcile. On the contrary, despite their superficial differences, they share a common goal—to aid researchers in the search for understanding by assisting in the col-lection, analysis, and interpretation of information. In fact, Kritzer (1996:27) claims that:

> moving from the data and the statistical results to an understand-ing of the significance of the findings involves working at a variety of levels and using a variety of skills that transcend particular methods. These skills of interpretation, when used well, serve to bind together social scientists working with either quantitative (statistical) or qualitative (textual) data because, regardless of the type of "text," interpretation relies upon similar processes.

In fact, while some have argued the merit of one method over the other (see discussion in Sil, 2000), the current movement is toward a unifi-cation of methods (King, Keohane & Verba, 1994). Unification suggests that the interpretation and comparison of qualitative data follow the same quasi-experimental logic used in quantitative research and subject to the same rules for drawing causal inferences, and that all quantitative data be deposited in some sort of central data bank so that future researchers could replicate and therefore validate studies.

While this may be an interesting suggestion, Sil (2000) argues that it is unnecessary. Sil's contention is that, like Durkheim's proposal of a unified organic solidarity in a division of labor in society (1984/1933), qualitative and quantitative methods can be used together in a "scholarly division of labor" to understand the "quite distinct, yet interdependent, roles played by different research products and methodological approaches" (1984/1933:500). Tarrow (1995) concurs and claims "a single-minded adherence to either quantitative or qualitative approaches straightjackets scientific progress" (1995: 474).

Quantitative and qualitative methodologies not only complement one another but also can provide a more holistic view of the population under study. Dalley's (2002) study on inmate mothers provides a simple but illustrative example of how both methods can be employed together. This study involved interviewing 44 inmate mothers about their relationships with their children. Dalley used a questionnaire followed by focus group interviews. The questionnaire was valuable in that it provided numerical descriptions of the children's problems, and simultaneously "stimulated" the women into thinking more about their children's problems. This had the desirable side effect of enhancing thoughtful participation in the focus group interviews. Similarly, data from the focus group interviews enriched the questionnaire data by providing in-depth information and personal illustrations or experiences necessary to fully understand the children's problems. Below is an example of the type of data generated from the questionnaire and focus group interviews. The first question and marked response is from the questionnaire:

In your opinion, what types of problems does this child experience? (check all that apply)

_____ learning/school
__X__ behavioral
_____ health
_____ drug addicted newborn
_____ mental health
__X__ fetal alcohol syndrome
_____ teen pregnancy
_____ alcohol/drug
_____ developmental delays
_____ none
_____ don't know
_____ other_____

Compare the questionnaire response to the response the same inmate mother gave during the interview process. When asked how her "drugging and drinking" affected her behavior and her relationship with her nine-year-old son, the mother said:

> My older son, he was my little man. I'd have him hide it [booze] so his dad wouldn't see it. . . . I'd tell him to get me a drink. So he would bring out my bottle. I don't know where the kid hid it because I went looking for it once and I couldn't find it. So I asked him and he'd said, 'Wait!' So I sat down on the chair and he'd take off. And he'd come back with my pint. As long as we lived in that house I never did find his hiding place because he has a little temper too. So if I as much as got out of that chair, he'd scream because I wouldn't do what he wanted me to do. It's like you're the kid, you sit still and I'm the big person.

This statement not only describes the behavioral problems that the inmate mother reported in the questionnaire, but more importantly, it clearly describes the role-reversal that was occurring in the mother-child relationship. Child development experts agree that role-reversal or "parentification" can seriously impact a child's ability to perform necessary child development tasks in order to become emotionally healthy adults (Chase, 1999). However, it is very doubtful that this information could have been obtained from the questionnaire alone. Thus, without the qualitative focus group data, Dalley (2002) argues that she would not have been able to portray a holistic or completely accurate view of the population's needs or problems.

Other examples of researchers using a combination of qualitative and quantitative methods involve police officer perceptions of date rape (Campbell, 1995), attitudes toward needle sharing among injection drug users (Carlson, Siegal, Wang & Falck, 1996), and spouse abuse (Murphy & O'Leary, 1994). The Project on Human Development in Chicago Neighborhoods triangulated strategies by using a community survey, an observational survey, a survey of neighborhood experts, police, public health, and social service records, and census data to gather information regarding factors that may be related to neighborhood crime (Earls & Visher, 1997).

Conclusion

As demonstrated in this chapter, the purposes and functions of qualitative and quantitative data are indeed different, but complementary. As Malterud (2001) suggests "although procedures for textual interpretation differ from those of statistical analysis because of the different type of data used and questions answered, the underlying principles are much the same" (2001:483). Indeed, as Kritzer (1996) emphasizes, "the process of data analysis, regardless of whether the data are qualitative or quantitative, involves an interaction between the analyst and the data" (1996:474).

The earlier example of the inmate mother describing her child's problems clearly illustrates how both quantitative and qualitative methods can measure the same variable in two different ways. Designs that use both methods may also have increased validity in that they are attempting to measure a particular concept or phenomenon in a variety of ways. If multiple measures of a concept yield consistently similar results, validity is enhanced.

Both methods provide valuable but different data and, when combined, provide a more complete and accurate picture of the phenomenon under study. Quantitative data allow researchers to create precise, numerically based summaries, comparisons, and generalizations. Qualitative data provide context, explanation, and clarification. This is a process Tarrow (1995) creatively calls "putting qualitative flesh on quantitative bones" (1995:473).

The current trend in research is for researchers to think of qualitative and quantitative methodologies as compatible, complementary methodologies that can be used in concert to create a more useful research design. As Tarrow (1995) urges, "whenever possible, we should use qualitative data to interpret quantitative findings . . ." and to "use different kinds of evidence together and look for ways of triangulating different measures on the same research problem" (1995:474). So, "the good news is that we don't need to choose" because both methods are "useful and legitimate" (Maxfield & Babbie, 2001:24).

Researchers and students, however, should remember that reality may present constraints on the choice of research design. While it may be desirable to employ both qualitative and quantitative strategies, the problem under study may involve situations or circumstances that necessitate the choice of one method or the other. Good research does not automatically evolve from a particular method. Instead, good research is the result of thorough contemplation of a problem and good judgment on the part of the researcher to develop the most practical, ethical, and effective measurement of that problem, no matter the method chosen.

Discussion Questions

1. Which type of research is "better": quantitative or qualitative research methods?

2. How do the types of research questions examined with quantitative and qualitative methods differ?

3. What are the major differences between quantitative and qualitative approaches to research?

4. How do quantitative and qualitative research methods work together?

CHAPTER 5

Original vs. Secondary Data Collection: The New Dilemma for Research

Jana L. Jasinski*
University of Central Florida

Original vs. Secondary Data Collection

For a new researcher, the process of developing a new empirical study can be, at the same time, both exciting and overwhelming. Among the many decisions that need to be made are the type and source of data to be collected. At this stage one of the most basic choices researchers are faced with is whether to collect original data or to use secondary data. Throughout this chapter the pros and cons of each of these types of data are discussed.

What Is Secondary Data Analysis?

Research using data that were created for some purpose other than that of the current research project is called secondary data analysis. The data can take generally two formats, pre-existing data sets (data files that are ready to be analyzed by the researcher, e.g., General Social Survey [Davis & Smith, 1996]) or existing statistics (available information that needs to be organized into a format that can be analyzed by the researcher, e.g., burglary rates for the 100 largest cities in the United States).

Sociology, criminology, and criminal justice as disciplines have a long history of conducting secondary data analysis. Sociologist Emile Durkheim ([1897] 1951), for example used existing data including suicide rates, reli-

*The author would like to thank Kim Daniels for her assistance with the content analysis of journal articles.

gious affiliation, and marriage and divorce rates to examine fluctuations in suicide. Durkheim's goal was to examine the relationship between indicators of social solidarity and integration, and the deviant act of suicide. To examine the geographic distribution of juvenile delinquency Shaw and McKay (1942) used official data on delinquents brought before the juvenile court, committed to correctional institutions, and dealt with by probation officers. In addition to research on crime and delinquency, available statistics have been used to investigate a variety of issues. Karl Marx, for example, used economic statistics to test his theory of class struggle ([1867] 1967) and Max Weber used church documents to investigate the relationship between religion and sociopolitical behavior ([1904] 1977).

In addition to these early empirical studies, researchers are increasingly utilizing secondary data analysis in order to conduct their research. An examination of the leading journals in criminology, criminal justice, and sociology showed that, in 1990, 27.6 percent of the articles appearing in *Justice Quarterly*, 26.7 percent of those in *American Sociological Review*, and 28 percent of the articles in *Criminology* used secondary data sets. By the year 2000, 45 percent of the articles appearing in *Criminology* used secondary data sets. Among the most commonly used data sets in the journal *Criminology* were the Uniform Crime Reports (FBI), the Supplemental Homicide Reports, and the United States Census. Other data sets used included the National Youth Survey, the MacArthur Foundation's Violence Risk Assessment Study, and the 1993 Canadian General Social Survey. Almost 40 percent of the articles published in *American Sociological Review* in the year 2000 used secondary data. Census data were used most often. However, researchers also used the General Social Survey, the Panel Study of Income Dynamics, and the Current Population Survey. Almost one-third of the articles published in *Justice Quarterly*, the leading journal in the field of criminal justice, in the year 2000 used pre-existing data sets. Among the data sets used were the Supplemental Homicide Reports, the National Youth Survey, and the Youth in Transition Survey. Although researchers' use of pre-existing data sets has certainly increased over the 10-year period between 1990 and 2000, it has not replaced the collection of original data. Instead, it has become part of the research design process involving an increasing number of decisions for the researcher to make. One of the steps in this process is to decide whether or not to use secondary data.

Why Would You Want to Use Pre-Existing Data Sets?

There are a number of reasons for using secondary data, particularly in the form of pre-existing data sets. These include, availability, cost, flexibility, time, and issues related to sample size and representativeness. Each of these will be discussed in more detail below.

Availability and Access

Pre-existing data sets (sometimes also referred to as canned data, or sec-ondary data) can be extremely useful for researchers. Existing data sets cover a wide variety of areas including public attitudes, corrections, courts, the criminal justice system, crime and delinquency, victimization, police, drugs, alcohol, and crime (See Appendix for the list of the most popular data sets archived at the National Archive of Criminal Justice Data). Perhaps one of the most obvious benefits of using a pre-existing data set is the availabil-ity. Today there exist a range of locations at which data sets dealing with issues related to criminology and criminal justice can be found. For example, the National Archive of Criminal Justice Data (NACJD) (part of the Inter-uni-versity Consortium for Political and Social Research (ICPSR)) is located in the Institute for Social Research at the University of Michigan. NACJD archives data from a number of government agencies including the Bureau of Justice Statistics (BJS), the National Institute of Justice (NIJ), the Office of Juvenile Justice and Delinquency Prevention (OJJDP), and the Federal Bureau of Investigation (FBI). In addition, NACJD also receives data from individual researchers in the criminal justice field, and other U.S. governmental agen-cies, as well as international sources. The diverse types of data archived at the NACJD make it possible for researchers to find a data set for just about any crime-related topic.

In addition to the wide range of crime-related data sets, archives like the NACJD often make acquiring the data relatively simple as well. For the majority of researchers wishing to use archived data, the World Wide Web site provides the simplest method of acquisition (www.icpsr.umich.edu/NACJD/index.html). Most computers today have a large enough hard drive and a relatively fast Internet connection and therefore should not have any difficulty with the downloading process. If the Internet is not an option for acquisition of the data, some of the data collections are available on CD-ROM. If the researcher's organizational affiliation is a member of ICPSR, he or she has downloadable access to more than 500 data collections relating to criminal justice, free of charge. Data archived through ICPSR have gone through a process by which they are assigned a unique study number, the documentation and data have been checked to make sure they match, con-fidential information has been removed or recoded to protect the original respondents, an abstract summarizing the project is prepared, and the orig-inal data file is duplicated and stored off site.

Another place for researchers to locate crime-related data is the Nation-al Criminal Justice Reference Service (NCJRS). The NCJRS is a federally sponsored information clearinghouse for people around the country and the world involved with research, policy, and practice related to criminal and juvenile justice and drug control. In addition to abstracts of more than 160,000 criminal justice publications, NCJRS also maintains links to other Internet sites providing information on available data for researchers and instructions on how to use them. In fact, there are many locations at which researchers can find information on pre-existing data sets (see Appendix for a list of other sites to acquire data)

Price

Another benefit of pre-existing data sets is their price, or rather their lack of. Many data sets are free of charge to the individual researcher if he or she acquires them via the Internet. In other words, if a researcher is using data archived through ICPSR, as long as the institution where the researcher is located is a member of ICPSR, the individual researcher can download data and all relevant codebooks for free. This means that the researcher does not have to invest in the cost of actually doing the survey. Although for small scale projects (both quantitative and qualitative) the costs are not high, for national or multi-site studies, the cost of actually doing the research can be prohibitive for any one individual researcher. For example the National Crime Victimization Survey (N=50,000) costs approximately $14 million a year to collect and process the data (Personal Communication Mike Rand (BJS) 8/28/01), and the General Social Survey, comprised of a national sample of approximately 3,000 individuals, costs more than $2 million (Personal Communication, Tom Smith (NORC) 12/6/01). The 1975 National Family Violence Survey (N=2,500), originally fielded at a cost of $140,000 would cost approximately $500,000 in year 2000 dollars (Personal Communication, Murray Straus [Family Research Lab], 12/9/01). Although the average researcher will not conduct national surveys with samples as large as these, even smaller non-probability samples can be expensive. For instance, a colleague and myself recently completed administering 2,000 surveys to a convenience sample of students. The cost for photocopying alone was approximately $1,000.

Flexibility

In addition to the low cost of using pre-existing data sets, institutions that archive data, such as ICPSR, tend to store data covering a wide range of topics. For example, within the NACJD, topics range from victimization, public opinion, and sentencing practices to arrest patterns, and police practices. Moreover, the NACJD is only one part of ICPSR. The holdings of ICPSR include Census enumerations, community and urban studies, education, geography and environment, organizational behavior and social indicators, to name just a few. In fact, ICPSR maintains the world's largest archive of computer readable social science data.

Greater flexibility for the researcher is also possible because data storage facilities like ICPSR often combine data files so that researchers can easily investigate trends without having to go through the time-consuming process of combining data files. For example, both the National Crime Victimization Survey (NCVS) and Supplemental Homicide Reports (SHR) are available as multi-year files. Accessing these files of the SHR would make it possible to examine trends in homicide victimization over time, including patterns of victim-offender relationship, geographical location, age, gender, and race/ethnicity. The NCVS files contain even more information, allowing the researcher to analyze patterns over time in risk factors for a variety of personal and property victimization types.

Time

Perhaps one of the greatest benefits of using pre-existing data sets is the possibility of saving time. Original research using information from human subjects must complete the process of human subjects review to ensure that the research will not harm the participants and that it is conducted in an ethical manner. Researchers using public use data sets, on the other hand, do not have to go through this process as the original author already took care of it. This saves the researcher valuable time waiting for approval from his or her individual institution. The wide scope of pre-existing data sets may also save time. For example, by using data from sources such as the United Nations World Crime Surveys, researchers are able to make global comparisons relatively easily and in much less time than if they were to collect data from different countries themselves. Pre-existing data sets are also useful for the purposes of triangulation (using more than one method to study the same topic) and replication (repeating research in order to develop more confidence in the findings). For example, a researcher could use the National Violence Against Women Study (Tjaden & Thoennes, 1998) to examine whether or not victims of physical assault report their victimization to the police and for those who did not contact the police, reasons why they chose not to report their victimization. Although this would be a very interesting study, it might be even more informative if the results from the secondary analysis of this survey were combined with focus groups comprised of victims of physical assault. The survey data would allow the researcher to conduct inferential statistics and make generalizations about the population; however, the focus groups would provide richer detail and greater context for the decision of whether or not to call the police. In this instance, using triangulation might provide more useful information for developing policies to encourage reporting victimization to the police.

Issues of Sample Size and Representativeness

Many data sets that are available for researchers to use are from large national samples, such as the National Crime Victimization Survey, the Violence Against Women Survey, and the National Youth Survey. Large sample sizes make complex analyses possible. Moreover, many of these studies used sophisticated sampling techniques, thus making it possible to generalize reliably or make statistical inferences about the population. In addition to large national samples, however, much of the data available to researchers represents the complete enumeration of the population (e.g., the Census). Researchers can obtain definitive results with complete population data.

How Do You Go About Finding the Appropriate Data Set for Your Project?

There are literally thousands of data sets from which a researcher may choose, and the task of finding a data set that will be the most reliable and valid for the particular research project may, at times, appear daunting. In fact, there is no simple method for locating the perfect pre-existing data set with which to conduct a particular research project. The process could be considered analogous to locating articles for a literature review in that it involves looking in multiple places, using different keywords, and reading more about the different data sources than you will actually use in the end project.

Some archives offer assistance to individual researchers looking for data; ICPSR is one of them and is a good place to begin the search for data. This is not the only place to look for data, however, and the savvy researcher interested in using pre-existing data sets should always keep an eye out for new sources of data. In addition, to ICPSR, the American Statistical Association (ASA) and the Bureau of Justice Statistics have sponsored a Web site maintained by the Center for Criminology and Criminal Justice Research at the University of Texas at Austin with information on crime and criminal justice data. The purpose of this site is to provide information on the many BJS data sets on crime and criminal justice in the United States, in order to encourage researchers to learn about and use these data in their research.

Another data archive designed to provide a central location for data on issues related to violence is the National Consortium on Violence Research (NCOVR) located at Carnegie Mellon University. Outlined in its mission statement, the purpose of NCOVR's Data Center is to facilitate the accumulation and exchange of scientific knowledge, reduce the overhead costs of doing research and remove the barriers to accumulating and replicating study results. The data center has two levels of accessibility to their data collection. The general public can access public domain data sets, while NCOVR members can access all public domain data sets, and their own private research data sets that have not yet been made public. What sets this center apart from some others is that some data have already been linked with Census data, thus saving steps for the researcher and creating more detailed data files.

The few archives discussed in this chapter are in no way meant to represent all of the possible data sources available to researchers. Instead, they can be used as a jumping-off point from which the process of trial and error begins. Many government web sites that publish crime and criminal justice data also provide links to other resources on related topics that may represent potential data sources. Keeping in mind that using secondary data means that it is much less likely that a researcher will find the perfect pre-existing data set, it is imperative that the goals of the research project be well formulated before beginning any search for data. This will make the process of evaluating potential data sources that much quicker and the end product that much stronger.

Benefits of Using Data One Has Collected

Control Over Research Method

Although using pre-existing data sets has many advantages, there are certainly many reasons for original data collection. First and foremost is the degree of control that the individual researcher has when collecting original data. When a researcher designs a project that will involve original data collection, he or she can determine exactly what questions to ask, how to ask them, and in what format they will be asked (e.g., phone survey, self-administered questionnaire, qualitative interview). Using a pre-existing data set, however, means that this part of the research design process has already taken place without any input from anyone other than the original researcher or research team. Moreover, original data collection guarantees that the research instrument is designed specifically for what the researcher wants to accomplish, thus avoiding the frustration often experienced when using a pre-existing data set that may not cover exactly what he or she had in mind for the project. For example, although the National Survey of Families and Households includes several questions on intimate partner violence, the questions are not based on any established measure of violence. This means that it is impossible to make comparisons between research using this data set and prior work using more widely used measures of violence. Additionally, because the purpose of the survey was to generate general information about family life and family interactions, it lacks key variables that researchers generally would include in a survey specifically designed to measure intimate partner violence.

Control Over Sampling

Another advantage of developing an original data set is that the researcher has control over the sampling process. He or she can determine what type of sample (probability or nonprobability) and the specific characteristics of individuals who should be in the sample in order to best answer the research question. This may be particularly important if the researcher is involved in applied research, where there is a specific client interested in analyzing the effects of a particular program. In this case, pre-existing data would not be very useful. On the other hand, original data collection would allow the researcher, together with the client, to address issues relevant to the program being evaluated and to conduct the research with a sample of individuals affected by the program. Researchers who use pre-existing data sets do not have the option of working through this process because the sampling has already been completed.

Qualitative Analysis

Existing data sets also tend to be quantitative in nature. For example, some of the most widely used data sets (e.g., The National Crime Victimization Survey, The National Household Survey on Drug Abuse) contain quantitative data from surveys. Although these data sets may provide useful information, at the same time, they are not necessarily the best source of information for a particular research topic. Moreover, it would be a mistake to assume that just because these data sets are available, they are the only way with which to examine a topic. If the focus of a research project is an in-depth analysis of context and meaning, these data sets would be inappropriate.

Problems with Original Data Collection and Design

Relying on pre-existing data also means that any mistakes in or problems with the original data collection are passed on to any other researchers who use the data. Although data archives conduct extensive consistency checks before making the data available, this occurs after the data have already been collected by the original researcher, and does not address the issues of reliability and validity that are important aspects of all research designs. By using these data, researchers run the risk of perpetuating these problems. Although original data collection also may not be free of mistakes, researchers are more likely to be aware of the limitations of their own data and how they might affect their analyses.

Researchers who design their own projects and collect their own data also have the advantage of being able to expand the body of literature on a topic by looking at research issues with their own innovative and creative fashion, rather than relying on someone else's vision. This helps to create new knowledge and direction for research and keeps the field moving forward. Rather than relying on existing data, original data collection makes it possible for the researcher to examine issues differently and in more detail than if he or she only relied on what was already available.

Greater Flexibility

Original data collection is also of vital importance for exploratory research. By its very nature, exploratory research breaks into new, previously unexplored areas of inquiry, and requires original thought and creativity. This type of research is only possible with original data collection. It is also an extremely important part of the development of any discipline because, without it, knowledge would become stagnant and the field of study would cease to advance.

When the researcher creates and implements his or her own empirical study, he or she maintains complete creative control of the entire project, something that does not occur when pre-existing data sets are used. This allows the researcher to have more knowledge about the reliability and validity of the entire process, to design a data collection instrument that is specifically targeted toward one research topic, to select the most appropriate sample, and to expand the knowledge base of the discipline into new directions.

Disadvantages of Each Source of Data

The increasing availability of secondary or pre-existing data sets is making it possible for a greater number of researchers to conduct more research using secondary data sets. Although there are many benefits to this type of research, it would be a mistake to assume that using pre-existing data sets should replace the collection of original data. For example, although there is a diverse selection of public-use data sets available, they were most likely created for a purpose different from what the researcher who is using them might want. For example, the National Violence Against Women Survey, a national data set available through ICPSR, surveyed 16,000 men and women about their victimization experiences and is a unique source of information for studies of sexual assault, physical violence, and stalking victimization. Unfortunately, this data set does not contain any questions about perpetration, thus limiting the type of research that can be conducted with it. The National Crime Victimization Survey (NCVS), another commonly used data source, is also limited by the nature of its sampling design. As part of the design of the NCVS, all individuals in a household age 12 and older are interviewed every six months for a three-year period. New households are rotated into the sample on an ongoing basis. The available data files, however, do not provide information with which to determine if the individuals living in the household for the first survey administration are the same individuals for future survey administrations. This makes it virtually impossible to conduct individual-level analysis over time. In other words, the sample available to the researcher, in the form of a pre-existing data set, may not be the appropriate sample for the project the researcher wishes to conduct. Moreover, the variables included in the original project may not be the necessary variables with which to test hypotheses that were not part of the original study design and development. Even if the needed variables are included in the data set, the response choices, and therefore the options for analyses, may not work for the project a researcher wishes to conduct.

Many existing data sets, particularly those for large national samples, are very complex. Data collections archived at ICPSR, for example, are comprised of data files and documentation files, typically including a data file, an abstract file, a codebook file, and SAS and SPSS data definition statement files. Researchers downloading data from this site will need to understand the process of combining the data definition statements with the data to create a system file to be read by SPSS or SAS. ICPSR, however, does a lot of behind the scenes work to make the acquisition of data as easy as possible for the researcher. Before any data set is available for public use, ICPSR goes through a process of checking for wild codes (i.e., data-entry mistakes), recoding and/or calculating derived variables, standardizing missing data codes, performing consistency checks on variables with skip patterns, converting hard-copy documentation to computer-readable documentation, reformatting of computer-readable documentation, creating computer-readable codebooks, and generating SAS data definition statements and/or SPSS data definition statements. The result is that data archived on this site follow a consistent format, and can be easily understood, therefore reducing the amount of time the researcher needs to spend learning about the data before actually using it.

Even with a process like that employed by ICPSR, however, researchers using this type of data will need to invest both the time and energy to read the available codebooks and methodology reports describing how the original research was conducted, how the data file was created, and the appropriate way to use it. Occasionally additional information must be acquired from other sources in addition to the institution at which the data are housed. For example ICPSR has archived the Violence Against Women Survey, however, the actual survey and methodology report are not on ICPSR website. Researchers may also want to read any and all technical reports that have been published, as well as any published articles in which the particular data set was used so as to acquire background information on the data set, how to use it, and how it has been used.

Additionally, it is necessary to learn about the sampling methodology used in order to decide what, if any weighting procedures should be used. In some cases, the original authors may have already created specific weights and may have specified when to use them, however, they are not always easy to locate and may be buried deep within a codebook. It is a mistake to assume that secondary analysis is the easy way to conduct research and that the complexity of data sets will be understood immediately. In fact, in some cases, it may take a great deal of time, and several contacts with either the original investigators or the archiving agency in order to confirm that the data are being used properly. In contrast, researchers who design and carry out their own research projects are already intimately familiar with every nuance of the project and do not need to go through this process.

Although time was discussed previously as a benefit to using secondary data sets, it can also be a disadvantage. Many public use data sets are not available immediately after the original project is completed. Data from government agencies like the National Institute of Justice become available relatively quickly after the original researcher files the final grant report. However, not all data that will eventually be available to the public is accessible in a timely fashion. Often, by the time a particular data set becomes accessible to the public it may already be five to six years old or older. Data age is a relevant issue to consider, particularly if the topic of a given study is directly related to policy changes. For example, police policies and practice with regard to response to domestic violence have changed dramatically since the publication of Sherman and Berk's (1984) seminal study. It would be difficult to make relevant generalizations about today's police practices using data that were collected prior to the 1980s.

So, when are data too old? The answer is not simple, and really depends on the purpose for which the data were intended. For example, researchers are still using data from the 1975 National Family Violence Survey. Although the data are more than 25 years old, they are useful for a number of purposes, primarily analyses of trends over time. For example, in 1997 Straus and colleagues published an analysis of changes in cultural norms approving marital violence. In their analyses, Straus et al. (1997) used data from 1968, 1985, 1992 and 1994 to assess changes over time. Other researchers have used data sets such as the Supplemental Homicide Reports, which are available from 1976 to 1999, to conduct longitudinal research (e.g., Chew, McCleary, Lew & Wang, 1999; Puzone, Saltzman, Kresnow, Thompson & Mercy, 2000).

When Is Each Type of Data Appropriate to Use?

When planning an empirical study, one of the first steps, after developing a research question and potential hypotheses to test, is to identify the method of data collection. More and more frequently today, this involves the decision of whether to collect original data or to use a pre-existing data set. Secondary data are extremely useful for getting information from a large sample that otherwise would be out of reach for the individual researcher. Using pre-existing data also allows for the analyses of trends without waiting as long. For example homicide data are available for more than 20 years. By using secondary data sets of large national samples researchers are better able to generalize to the entire United States population. On the other hand, researchers should not limit themselves to secondary data only, and certainly should not assume that the existence of a secondary data set on their topic means that it is the best option for them. As is often the case, the pre-existing data sets that are available are not always sufficient to address a particular research question, and researchers should not try to force the data to fit the question, or alter the question to fit the available data. Exploratory research, for example, is often better served by the collection of original data. Once the research question is fully developed, however, the decision of what type of data to use may become much clearer.

Conclusions

Beginning a new research project is, at the same time, both exhilarating and frustrating. Part of the challenge is developing a research question that can be answered with empirical data. Once that issue has been addressed, one of the next choices involves whether to collect original data or use data that some other researcher has collected for his/her research project. There is no right or wrong choice, however, researchers should begin this process with eyes open to both the advantages and disadvantages of each source of information. Although the use of secondary data is becoming more common, it will not, and should not, replace collecting original data. Instead, by using pre-existing data sets, researchers may have more opportunities to conduct studies that were previously out of their reach due to time and funding constraints.

Appendix

Locations at which to begin search for secondary data sets:

Inter-university Consortium for Political and Social Research (ICPSR)
http://www.icpsr.umich.edu/index.html

National Archive of Criminal Justice Data (NACJD)
http://www.icpsr.umich.edu/NACJD/index.html

NCJRS–National Criminal Justice Reference Service
http://www.ncjrs.org/index.html

Justice Research and Statistics Association
http://www.jrsainfo.org/

Federal Statistics
http://www.fedstats.com

National Consortium on Violence Research
http://www.ncovr.org

The following list represents the most requested data sets from the National Archive of Criminal Justice Data for the months January – Aug 2001. During this time period, 802 studies were requested by 24,148 users.

1. Uniform Crime Reporting Program Data

2. National Crime Victimization Survey

3. National Household Survey on Drug Abuse

4. Capital Punishment in the United States

5. Survey of Inmates in State and Federal Correctional Facilities

6. Monitoring the Future: A Continuing Study of American Youth

7. National Youth Survey

8. Census of State and Federal Adult Correctional Facilities

9. Law Enforcement Management and Administrative Statistics (LEMAS): Sample Survey of Law Enforcement Agencies

10. United Nations World Surveys on Crime Trends and Criminal Justice Systems, 1970-1994

11. Directory of Law Enforcement Agencies

12. National Opinion Survey of Crime and Justice

13. Federal Court Cases: Integrated Data Base

14. Homicides in Chicago

15. Violence and Threats of Violence Against Women and Men in the United States

16. Survey of Inmates of Local Jails

17. National Incident-Based Reporting System

18. United States Supreme Court Judicial Database

Discussion Questions

1. What types of research questions can be answered using original and secondary data?

2. What are the advantages and disadvantages of collecting original data for a research project?

3. What are the advantages and disadvantages of using secondary data for a research project?

4. How does the choice to use original or secondary data affect the social policy implications of a research project?

CHAPTER 6

Does Theory Really Guide Survey Research? Why Is Theory Important in Surveys?

Tracy L. Dietz
University of Central Florida

Jana L. Jasinski
University of Central Florida

Most social scientists today agree that an important symbiotic relationship exists between theory and research. A clear understanding of theory is essential to the development of a sound research project that adds to the state of knowledge. Ultimately, too, the application of a well-developed theory can enable researchers to explain the results of their research project. Similarly, data collection and analysis enable researchers to evaluate and test theories and to further expand upon them. The purpose of this chapter is to discuss the linkage between theory and survey-based research; however, a better understanding of and attention to the role of theory will strengthen other types of research as well.

What Is Theory?

To understand how theory informs social research in general and survey research specifically, it is important to distinguish what does and does not constitute "theory." Moreover, theories must be differentiated from theoretical paradigms. A theory is "an account of the world that goes beyond what we can see and measure . . . that organizes our concepts of and understanding of the empirical world in a systematic way." (Marshall, 1994:532).

The term paradigm, which was first introduced into the realm of science by Thomas Kuhn, represents the preferred theoretical perspective and manner of conducting scientific inquiry at any given point in time. Kuhn referred to this as "normal science" (Kuhn, 1962). It can be argued that theories flesh out specific paradigms and make them testable.

In addition to these basic definitions, it is important to understand that there are different levels of theories. Most people, at least in the United States, tend to think primarily in terms of micro-level of reality (Neuman, 1997). Micro-level theories focus upon small group or individual action, interaction, and the construction of meaning (Marshall, 1994). Examples of micro-level theories in criminology include the various types of social learning theories such as Sutherland's Differential Association Theory (1947), Differential Identification Theory (Glaser, 1956), and Travis Hirschi's (1969) Social Bond Theory. Conversely, macro-level theory deals with larger social structures, such as institutions or entire societies (Neuman, 1997). Anomie or Strain Theory that Merton (1938) developed based upon Durkheim's (1952[1897]) application to suicide is an example of a macro-level theory. Other examples include Thomas and Znaniecki's (1927) Social Disorganization Theory and Shaw and McKay's (1942) Social Ecology Theory. Meso-level theories are relatively rare and are an attempt to link micro-level theories to macro-level theories in a logical way (Neuman, 1997). Delbert Elliott's (Elliott, Ageton & Canter, 1979) Integrative Theory that combines strain, social learning, and social control theories into a more comprehensive theory is an example of a meso-level, or middle-range theory. The concept of "middle-range theories" was first introduced by Robert Merton (1968) to bridge the gap between the empiricists and abstract theoreticians in social science. These theories seek "to integrate observed empirical regularities and specific hypotheses within a relatively limited problem-area." (Bullock & Stallybrass, 1977:390).

The Relationship Between Theory and Data

Humans and other organisms understand the world around them using a variety of theories and data collection strategies every day. Indeed, it is through the process of theorizing, hypothesizing, data collection through observations, and drawing conclusions that the world is understood. Early philosophers recognized that careful systematic observation could be used to explain and predict the physical world. Soon, philosophers adopted these same techniques or ideas to understand the social world. Scientific inquiry differs from the techniques that are used to understand the world by humans on a daily basis in that science relies upon a carefully designed systematic plan. Moreover, theory is more or less often applied to these observations in a precise manner to explain and predict.

Most social scientists agree that theory and research should be linked to and dependent upon one another. The degree to which the relationship is delineated by the researcher, however, depends upon the purpose of the research and researcher's own beliefs (Sjoberg & Nett, 1997). Indeed, a debate regarding the relationship between theory and data can be traced over time with some researchers advocating an emphasis upon data and others an emphasis upon theory.

Theoreticians and Empiricists

Early philosophers debated the issue of the relative importance of theory versus data and observation in understanding. Kant, for instance, gave priority to concepts and theory, while Locke and Hume emphasized data. These same proclivities can be identified in the writing of more contemporary social scientists as well (Sjoberg & Nett, 1997). This division between social and behavioral scientists who emphasize "theory over those who emphasize observation (or data) reflects to some degree the cleavage between scholars who are committed to a logico-deductive approach in science and those who are oriented toward discovery." (Sjoberg & Nett, 1997:35). Robert King Merton, whose focus upon Structural Strain Theory and its relationship to deviance (1938), was instrumental in the late twentieth century in building a bridge between theoreticians and empiricists, arguing that theory and data interact with one another and cannot be disentangled from one another. Arguably, most social scientists agree that there is an important relationship between the two. And, while a number of social scientists have given lip service to the notion of the relationship between theory and research, there seems to be a disjunction between what they argue should be and what they actually do when they conduct research (Sjoberg & Nett, 1997). Consequently, while Sjoberg and Nett (1997) argue that the issue of the role of theory in actual research demands more clarification, the significant relationship between the two is evident in the major theoretical paradigms and criminological theories that are recognized and used by researchers today.

Ways in Which Theory and Data Complement One Another

As previously mentioned, theory and data are interdependent upon one another. Theory may be used as the foundation for the development of a research project in which data are used to test a theory, or data may become the foundation upon which a theory is constructed. The testing of hypotheses derived from a theory is referred to as deductive reasoning. Theory is important to deductive research projects in several important ways. It molds the ways in which the research approaches and understands the research topic. Moreover, theory defines the concepts and basic assumptions as well as providing a foundation for the questions and hypotheses to be examined and tested. Likewise, it provides a base for interpreting the results of the project. It also enables the researcher to make a connection between single studies and a larger knowledge base. Furthermore, it helps the researcher to better understand the significance of the data and findings to the larger body of literature (Neuman, 1997).

In contrast to the deductive model discussed above, the inductive research model begins with data. These generalizations are then used to build theory. Typically, the researcher formulates a general hypothesis from the observation of initial cases and then examines subsequent cases to determine the degree to which those cases support the hypothesis, revising as needed (Marshall, 1994). While the degree to which theory informs inductive reasoning may be less obvious, it is important to realize that theory is nevertheless important in the initial development stages of this type of research.

In a word, the deductive model uses theories to formulate testable hypotheses that are used to test the theories themselves and the inductive model focuses primarily upon the development and reformulation of theories through data.

Major Theoretical Approaches in Criminology

The classical approach in criminology represents the first approach to extend beyond traditional notions of magic and the supernatural as explanations of crime and deviance. This approach was the first to take into account ideas of free will and rationality on the part of the deviant (e.g., Beccaria & Bentham). The neoclassical approach extended this early approach by allowing for other mitigating circumstances, such as environmental and psychological factors (e.g., Ferri, Garofalo, Cornish & Clarke). Not long after the initial development of the neoclassical approach, which witnessed a resurgence in the latter half of the twentieth century, the ecological school of criminological theory, which focuses upon the relationship of the actor (criminal) with their environment, arose (e.g., Guerry & Quetelet). Similarly, in the mid to late 1800s, economic theory, based upon the philosophies of Marx and Hegel, developed and was applied to the study of crime with the primary explanation for crime being centered in the social inequalities that led to social problems (e.g., Bonger). Also, during the early to mid 1800s, the positivist theory, which emphasizes an empirical rather than a philosophical orientation to understanding crime, developed (e.g., Lombroso & Sheldon). Included under the heading of positivist theory are the more contemporary psychological and sociological theoretical approaches to explaining crime (Hagan, 2002).

As stated previously, theory and research are inextricably connected. According to Akers (2000) part of the criteria for evaluating theories is first the degree to which they are testable, and second whether or not there exists empirical evidence to support the propositions of the theory. Research methodology represents the attempt to obtain the empirical evidence with which to evaluate the utility of theory for the purposes of application and a more complete understanding of the behavior in question. Although there are a variety of research methodologies, they can generally be grouped into two main styles, qualitative and quantitative. Within each style exists a variety of different research techniques. For the purpose of this chapter, the focus will be on survey research, a technique most commonly associated with the quantitative style of research (Neuman, 1997).

What Is Survey Research?

Although one of the characteristics of the scientific method in general is systematic observation, survey research—as a scientific enterprise—uses a particular type of instrument, the questionnaire, or interview schedule, to collect data. In quantitative research, this tends to be a standardized instrument that a large number of respondents complete.

What Is the Purpose of Survey Research?

Survey research, as with many other types of scientific inquiry, generally has four objectives: Description, Exploration, Explanation, and Evaluation (Neuman, 1997). Descriptive surveys are designed to depict the characteristics of a given population or sample. For example, research describing the characteristics of those individuals who smoke marijuana would be considered descriptive in nature. Exploratory surveys are used when researchers know very little about the population of interest and may provide information with which to generate hypotheses (inductive reasoning). A study investigating Internet crime would be illustrative of research with an exploratory objective. Surveys with the objective of explanation would be focused on identifying the cause and effects of the phenomenon of interest. Studies that attempt to identify why individuals age out of crime would be examples of this type of research. Finally, evaluative surveys attempt to systematically review the effectiveness of a given program or policy. An example of an evaluative survey might be evaluating the effectiveness of a drug education program such as DARE (Drug Abuse Resistance Education).

Survey Methodology

Survey Design

Once the researcher has identified the objectives of the research, one of the next steps involves selecting the specific design. In many cases the respondents are asked to complete the questionnaire themselves. These self-administered surveys may be conducted through the mail, in person either individually or in group settings, or through electronic means. Survey research may also be conducted through interviews where the researcher asks the questions orally and records the respondent's answers. Interviewer-administered surveys may be completed either face-to-face or by telephone.

Which survey design is appropriate? Each type of survey design has a number of advantages and disadvantages. Although there are exceptions, (e.g., large-scale national surveys), self-administered surveys, tend to be more efficient in terms of both time and cost than face-to-face interviews. Group administered surveys, for instance, allow the researcher to acquire large samples relatively quickly, particularly if student samples are used. Self-administered surveys have an additional benefit that may be particularly useful regarding research on crime, delinquency, and deviance. Individuals may feel more comfortable reporting controversial or deviant attitudes or behaviors anonymously on a questionnaire than directly admitting to those same attitudes or behaviors to another person. Not all self-administered surveys share the same advantages, however. Mail surveys in particular suffer from a high nonresponse rate (Neuman, 1997). Additionally, there is no control over who actually completes a mail survey, or even if it is completed by only one person.

Interview surveys also have a number of strengths. Response rates tend to be higher than for self-administered surveys; this is particularly true for face-to-face interviews (Neuman, 1997). In addition, the surveys conducted as interviews tend to be more complete (a result of using probing questions) and have fewer skipped questions and questions where no meaningful response is indicated. Interviews are also more effective for gathering information about complicated issues that require more detailed explanations than could be given with a self-administered format. For example, collecting a life history of an individual who engages in criminal activity. The advantages of interviews over self-administered surveys are most pronounced in face-to-face interviews. In-person interviews offer an additional advantage. The interviewer can supplement the survey data with information from direct observation. For example, researchers investigating domestic violence using the face-to-face data collection would be able to note the presence of a spouse or partner and the reaction of the respondent to him or her. With the exception of this final advantage, telephone interviews have similar advantages over self-administered surveys. However, those benefits are not as pronounced as in the case of in-person interviews (Babbie, 2001).

The choice of which survey design to use, self- or interviewer-administered, may depend on the topic of the survey, purpose of the research, available resources, time limitations, and respondent abilities (e.g., literacy). For example, surveys administered over the phone are generally less expensive than face-to-face surveys (Babbie, 2001). They may also take less time to administer, particularly if a Computer Assisted Telephone Interviewing (CATI) system is used. Phone surveys may also be more appropriate for sensitive topics such as criminality because the respondent does not have to report law-breaking behavior in person. However, at the same time, the length of surveys administered over the telephone is more restricted than if the survey was administered either in a face-to-face format or a self-administered format. Similarly, mail surveys require an address list and, in order to be cost effective, bulk mailing rates may need to be used. However, even telephone and mail surveys may still be more expensive than group administered surveys. Self-administered surveys, on the other hand, are valuable because of the greater level of privacy.

In addition to the administrative issues surrounding the choice of survey design, theory also guides this decision. Researchers following a deductive approach (theory followed by research [Popper, 1968]) would choose a research design to test the theory or model they have developed. The design therefore, would need to translate the propositions dictated by the theory into measurable concepts. In contrast, researchers approaching the study from an inductive perspective (research followed by theory) might not be faced with the same restrictions in choosing a design because the theoretical framework is derived from the actual data collection rather than applied to it.

Development of the Survey Instrument

Central to survey research is the development of the instrument, called either a questionnaire or interview schedule depending on the type of research being conducted (self- or interviewer-administered). This process is guided by a clear understanding of the objectives of the research. According to Schutt (1996), the researcher should also consider the substantive variables to be measured (as they are related to the study objectives). This understanding, combined with the theoretical framework for the study aids the researcher in the development of the survey instrument.

What Questions Should Be Included in a Survey?

One of the first decisions researchers must make in the process of developing the survey instrument is which questions to include and in what format the questions will be asked. It is at this stage of the research process that the connection between the theoretical and the empirical is made. The development of survey questions translates the ideas (concepts) into a format that can be observed (measured) (Frankfort-Nachmias & Nachmias, 1992). This is completed through the processes of conceptualization and operationalization. Conceptualization is the process of defining the abstract concepts. Operationalization is the process by which the procedures for measuring the concepts are specified (Neuman, 1997).

Building upon the work of Merton, Cohen, and Cloward and Ohlin, for example, Agnew (1985) revised strain theory to examine delinquency. The revision added the idea that in addition to goal-seeking behavior, sometimes pain-avoidance behavior is also blocked. Furthermore Agnew (1985) suggested that adolescents who reside in these aversive environments, places where they are forced to remain, would be more likely to engage in deviant and criminal behavior. Additionally, he argued the possibility of an indirect relationship between aversive environments and delinquency through anger. The concepts of aversive environment, anger and delinquent/criminal behavior were operationalized using the Youth in Transition Survey. To assess environmental aversiveness, respondents were asked questions regarding perceptions of parental punitiveness, and mean teachers. Anger was measured with questions asking about feelings of verbal and physical aggression against parents and teachers and irritation over small things. Finally, delinquent/criminal behavior was measured with questions assessing the extent of the respondent's behaviors, such as theft, arson, and serious fighting, over a three-year period as well as questions about their involvement in interpersonal aggression. Agnew's revision of Strain Theory provides an excellent example of the process of moving from conceptual ideas to empirical assessments. Neuman (1997) suggests that this process, forging a link between ideas and reality, in a deductive sense, is central to the quantitative process. In contrast, analytical induction, developing concepts from the data, is much more common in qualitative research (Marshall, 1994).

Theory also plays an important role in the question development and design stage of the research process. Although substantive theories might suggest to the researcher the relationship between concepts (for example deviant peer associations and deviant behavior), auxiliary theories suggest the relationship between concepts and the indicators of these concepts (Carmines & Zeller, 1979). For example, Hirschi's Social Bond Theory (1969) suggests that deviant behavior occurs when social bonds are weak. Furthermore, these social bonds are comprised of four different dimensions, attachment, commitment, involvement, and belief. Researchers interested in investigating the utility of this theoretical framework to explain a particular type of deviant or criminal behavior would need to include in their survey indicators representing each of these four different dimensions.

What Is the Role of Theory in the Analysis and Interpretation of the Data?

The discussion so far has focused on the role of theory in the design stages of a research project. However, it is also important in the analysis and interpretation of research results as well. Once the research project has been carried out and the data have been collected, the researcher is faced with many data analysis choices. These decisions are often informed by theory. If the study involves the testing of a particular theory, for instance, the choice of analytical models will be guided by the propositions of the theoretical framework. Agnew's (1985) study discussed previously, for example, empirically tested a theoretical model built around Strain Theory. This revised Strain Theory specified the particular model to be tested with the survey data. Theory also provides the framework with which to interpret and understand the results of the data analyses. In other words, it helps the researcher make some sense out of the findings and couch the results in a larger body of knowledge. Additionally, use of theory assists the researcher in making practical application of the results to address some real-world problem. In other words, theory plays an important role in both basic and applied research.

The Role of Theory in Basic vs. Applied Research

Basic and applied research differ from one another primarily in the purpose of the research. Chapter 2 of this book provides a more detailed discussion of these two types of research, but generally basic research is concerned with identifying phenomena and explaining them, while applied research is conducted in an attempt to provide practical solutions to problems and/or evaluate or examine phenomena in an applied setting. Generally speaking, criminology is more closely associated with basic research (explanation of criminal behavior) while criminal justice is more closely associated with applied research (evaluation of policies and/or programs to prevent, reduce, or eliminate crime). Theory is an important component in both types of research.

Basic research in criminology seeks to utilize theory to understand criminal behavior. For example, although many studies have found that delinquent teens are more likely to have delinquent friends, the causal ordering of this relationship is not well understood. Differential Association Theory (Sutherland, 1947) suggests that people learn to be deviant from deviant peers with whom they are close and have frequent and ongoing contact. These deviant peers are more accepting of delinquent behaviors and attitudes. More recent theoretical development first introduced by Terence

Thornberry (1987), suggests that there is a reciprocal relationship between delinquent peers and delinquency. This is often referred to as Interactional Theory. Research such as that conducted by Matsueda and Anderson (1998) where interactional theory was supported with data from the National Youth Survey, could be characterized as basic in nature.

Conversely, Sherman and Berk (1984) utilized Deterrence Theory as the framework for developing their hypothesis that the belief that one would be arrested if they committed violent acts against their partner would deter people from repeat domestic violence offenses. As part of the well-known Minneapolis Domestic Violence Experiment, they collected data to test whether the response of the police officer (arrest, separating the couple, etc.) was associated with repeat offending. The results of this study became a foundation for discussions of, and changes in, policing policies in many communities. Thus, this illustrates how theory can inform applied research projects in studies of crime.

Other Types of Theory That Relate to Survey Research

While this chapter has focused primarily upon the role of theory in developing research projects and explaining results, it is appropriate to mention that there are additional types of theory that guide survey, as well as other types, of research. In particular, good research is only possible through the appropriate consideration and implementation of theories that are specific to research methodology rather than to substantive topics. For example, sampling theory informs research projects by helping the researcher to determine what type of sampling technique is best for a given project and in particular, how that sample will be drawn and what size it should be. In addition, measurement theory is also important in the development of a research project in that it helps the researcher to determine what level of measurement is needed to complete the project, how those measures should be constructed, and what types of statistical tools to use. A more detailed discussion of the ways in which these types of theories influence survey research is beyond the scope of this chapter. However, readers are directed to Carmines and Zeller (1979) for a discussion of measurement and Kalton (1983) for a discussion of survey sampling for more information.

Conclusion and Discussion

As Neuman (1997) notes, it is the naïve researcher who is not aware of the intricate relationship between theory and research. Nevertheless, the degree to which theory actually does inform and is informed by survey research is likely less than what would be hoped. Indeed, while in a utopian research world, theory and research would always inform one another and research projects would be developed in a way that would make their results generalizable and useful to the world. However, numerous factors impose upon this "ideal" way of conducting science. As in the study of norms of other forms of social behavior, there are ideal and actual or real norms that relate to scientific endeavors, both in terms of the practical way in which science is conducted and in terms of the way in which theory informs research.

According to Sjoberg and Nett (1997) the two may be compatible, but often they are not. Actual norms often develop informally to guide data collection and analysis. Moreover, they "may arise from inconsistencies with the scientific enterprise" (Sjoberg & Nett, 1997:73). In addition, actual norms may also develop because of the researcher's involvement with and adherence to the beliefs of certain groups (Sjoberg & Nett, 1997).

Researchers, especially in the case of applied research, may feel pressure from political organizations, funding organizations, and the like to support or contradict certain ideas with data. Likewise, due to the lack of financial resources, researchers may be unable to conduct the "ideal" research project. For instance, longitudinal projects and studies that involve simple random samples are often very expensive and time-consuming to conduct. Similarly, the research results are also potentially clouded by sampling bias. There is always the potential for certain groups to be under-represented in the sample due to errors in developing the sampling frame as well as refusal to participate.

And while most social scientists acknowledge the important role of theory in research, theory often becomes an after-thought in the research process. Furthermore, scientists, in their haste to produce scientific findings, may neglect to adequately consider the process of project development. Some factors that contribute to a less than "ideal" environment for conducting social research may be beyond the control of the researchers themselves. However, many factors are not. Indeed, the generalizability of research findings could be improved by increased attention to the process of project development. Moreover, the applicability and utility of the findings could be improved by greater attention to theory in the earlier stages of project development. In sum, theory is an important component in survey research design, but many social scientists do not use it to its full potential.

Discussion Questions

1. What parts of a survey research project are affected by one's choice of a guiding theory?

2. Why is it important to rely on theory for designing a survey research project?

3. What types of theories are most applicable for use in a survey research project?

4. What are the dangers of not using theory to guide the construction of a survey?

CHAPTER 7

Macro and Micro Research Approaches: Which Makes More Sense?

Julie C. Kunselman
University of West Florida

This chapter presents the debate between macro research and micro research. In general, macro research refers to the study of aggregates or large units, while micro research refers to the study of individuals or small units. Which is better suited for a certain research methodology? Where do the various stakeholders of research (e.g., practitioners, academics, funding agencies, and customers) stand in the debate of macro and micro research? More importantly, does it matter where one stands in the debate? These questions will be discussed in the context of the advantages and disadvantages of macro and micro research, in relation to associated policy and interpretation implications, and in discussions of how each has its "place" in research methodology.

Much of the controversy in research methodology traditionally has centered on differences between the physical and social sciences. For example, some individuals rely completely on physical science methodology suggesting that it was easier to accept results from controlled lab experiments where "precise" measurements are made and causality (arguably) more formally established. Meanwhile, social science methodology was viewed as "soft" science, where quantitative applications were sometimes replaced with qualitative observations, sometimes without mathematical structure (e.g., nonprobability sampling).

More recently, however, social science methodology has been given higher marks and due acceptance in the literature (Bailey, 1994; Miller & Tewksbury, 2001; Neuman & Wiegand, 2000; Rossi & Freeman, 1993; Shadish, Cook & Campbell, 2002). What followed from this acceptance is the movement of methodological controversy from an *interscience* debate to an *intrascience* debate. That is, social scientists now question the utility and efficiency of specific social science methods (see Bailey, 1994:34-35). For example, Chapter 4 in this text focuses on the controversy surrounding the use of quantitative methods versus qualitative methods and Chapter 5 discusses the debate of substantive significance vs. statistical significance. In these chapters, the authors discuss the advantages and disadvantages of each method or analysis, in addition to the utility of each given the definition of the research question. Similarly, this chapter discusses the controversy of using macro methods vs. micro methods in social science research. Again, discussion will focus on the advantages and disadvantages of each method, and the utility of each depending on how the research question is framed.

What Is Macro Research?

Macro research refers to the study of aggregates or large units. The research may focus on large units of people (groups or a population), an abstract concept (social structure), or a system (higher education). Because macro research focuses on studying large units researchers evaluate the aggregate "system" or "population" by operationalizing the research question for interpretation at the macro-level. Thus, macro studies seek to interpret or analyze the "big picture," whether it is an aggregate system, social context, or population; and, in most instances macro studies utilize sub-unit analyses in order to conceptualize the macro measurement model. These sub-unit analyses are of macro-level data. For example, overall crime for a city may be measured using macro-level data of city crime rates, including aggregate data of arrests, charges, and convictions.

Macro theorists focus holistically on society (e.g., societal norms or social life). For example, conflict and strain theories may be used as underlying theoretical propositions in macro research. Specifically, Blau and Blau (1982) conducted a study of urban criminal violence by operationalizing differences in urban criminal violence using macro-level measurements (or macro-level theoretical propositions). That is, the authors used data from 125 of America's largest cities to analyze whether "inequalities in metropolitan structure" are correlates of urban criminal violence (Blau & Blau, 1982). In this sense, urban criminal violence is a macro-issue measurement model. The Blaus (1982:120) operationalized or measured urban criminal violence, the dependent variable, using major violent crime rates (e.g., murder, forcible rape, aggravated assault, and robbery). The independent variables in this macro-level analysis, which must also be measured at the macro-level, included "population size, percent black, percent poor, geographical region, income inequality, percent divorced, and racial socioeconomic inequality" (Blau & Blau, 1982:120).

The inclusion of Blau and Blau's study is important to present the relationship between the dependent and independent variables in a macro-level study. "Macro level refer[s] to social forces operating across a society or relations among major parts of a society as a whole" (Neuman & Wiegand, 2000:110). Thus, in the above study, one should note that both the dependent variable (urban criminal violence) and independent variables (population size, . . ., socioeconomic inequality) are operationalized or measured at the macro level. Specifically, urban criminal violence is operationalized using violent crime rates and each independent variable is measured at the city or aggregate (macro) level.

A second example of macro research is presented using a structural equation model for measuring customer satisfaction of facility services as presented in Figure 1. Customer satisfaction of services obtained from a juvenile counseling department is the macro-issue to be measured and is conceptualized by latent variables labeled "satisfaction of facility" and "satisfaction of personnel." Latent variables (e.g., customer satisfaction, intellectual ability, criminality) are simply factors or constructs that are defined or measured using some number of observed or measurable variables (Kline, 1998). Latent variables, therefore, are represented by measurable variables. For example, urban criminal violence is a construct that might be represented or measured by numerous variables; Blau and Blau (1982) utilize the Part I violent crimes from the *Uniform Crime Reports*, namely murder, aggravated assault, forcible rape, and robbery. In the current example, both "satisfaction of facility" and "satisfaction of personnel" are latent variables which are analyzed using observed measures. The analysis, however, is not based on individual measures. That is, there are no measures of the individuals working at the facility or attending sessions at the facility, but simply measures of facility services. For example, "satisfaction of facility" is represented by the measures of "convenience of office hours," "condition of facilities," "convenience of location," "friendliness of staff," and "opportunity to explore facilities and resources." Such latent variable analyses might serve as macro-level research measurement models.

The determination of what measures to include in macro research depends on the research question presented. This is a question of research design and units of analysis. A researcher first develops research questions, theoretical perspectives, and obtains adequate resources, and from these he develops a research design (Bickman & Rog, 1998). The design serves as a contextual model for "answering" the research questions and therefore focuses on identifying the data, data analysis, and research management (Bickman & Rog, 1998). Once the research questions are defined, the units of analysis are outlined to complement each specific research question. Units of analysis are simply "whom" or "what" is being studied in terms of defining the appropriate level of measurement for the study (Babbie, 1998). That is, selection of the units of analysis really *determines* whether a study is completed at the macro or micro level. Therefore, the selection of a macro or micro study depends on the research questions, the underlying theoretical constructs, and simply how the researcher operationalizes the study issue in terms of selecting units of analysis.

Figure 1
Customer Satisfaction with Facility Services*

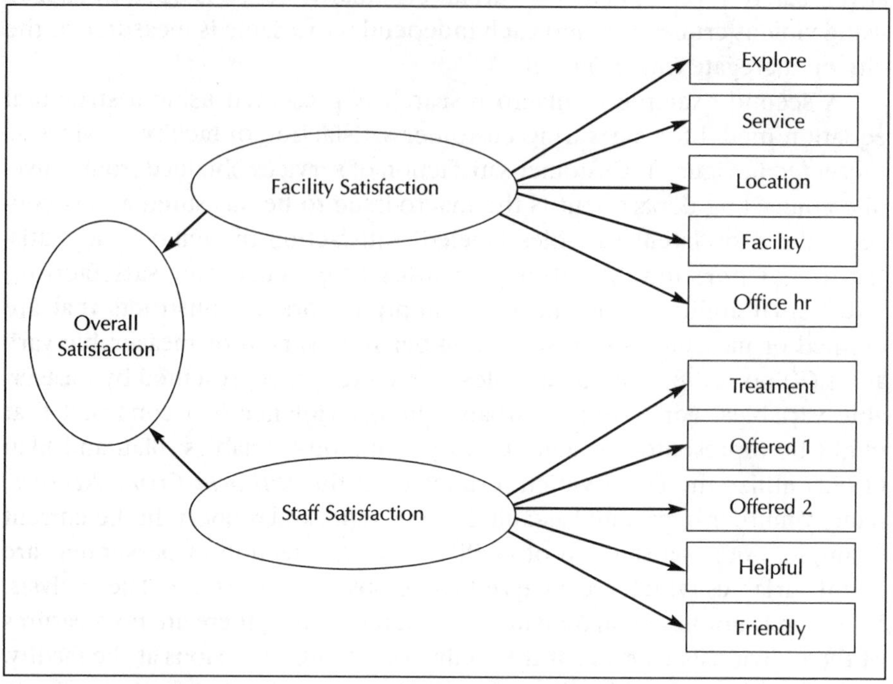

*Note: In a structure equation model, each observed variable would also have an error component.

Thus, defining the units of analysis is important, as the units of analysis serve to limit the boundaries of a study (Bickman & Rog, 1998), as well as having the boundaries of the study (i.e., the research questions) limiting them (Neuman & Wiegand, 2000). Specifically, the units of analysis define the level of unit for measurement, as well as determine how variables will be measured (Neuman & Wiegand, 2000). The main issue involved in defining units of analysis is related to the need for the researcher to choose the unit of analysis that appropriately and correctly answers the research question.

Exhibit 1 presents an overview of a macro research study of racial profiling undertaken by reporters at a local newspaper; also included are both supportive and critical comments of the newspaper's methodology. The news reporters conducted this study of racial profiling in an attempt to determine whether city police were engaging in racial or bias profiling in making traffic stops.

Exhibit 1
Racial Profiling Study by a Local Newspaper

A local newspaper undertook a racial profile study designed to determine whether a local police department was engaging in bias profiling. The newspaper compared two sets of city police records. One set was computerized dispatch records of more than 6,200 traffic stops city officers made on the 30 days. The 30 days were randomly selected from a 12-month period between 1999 and 2000. Total number of traffic stops for the 12-month period was 79,805. The other record was a set of handwritten logs kept by dispatchers, listing all the people officers requested checks for arrest warrants or invalid driver's licenses. These handwritten records included race.

By comparing the traffic stop reports with the handwritten logs, the newspaper was able to identify the race of people stopped by city police in 1,647 of the 6,211 stops that occurred on the 30 days studied. Thus, race was identified in 1,647/6,211 (26.7%) of the stops occurring on the 30 days randomly selected; this represents only 2.1 percent of the aggregate stops made in the 12-month period.

According to the newspaper article, many studies of racial profiling, including most news media studies, utilize information from traffic tickets or arrests. In this study, therefore, it seems the newspaper's traffic stop data were broader in that the data included some people who were not cited at all.

Discussion Question: Given the above information, would you consider this study to be an example of macro or micro research? Explain your answer. Discuss whether macro or micro research is better suited for this type of research. Further, discuss whether this is an issue of individualistic or ecological fallacy.

Source: Adapted from J. Adams, "Study: Police Stopped Blacks Twice as Often as Whites. Louisville Chief Says Traffic Survey Is Flawed." *The Courier-Journal*, October 29, 2000. Available online at: http://www.courier-journal.com/localnews/2000/0010/29/001029dwb_prof.html

Discussion of whether or not the case study presented in Exhibit 1 is a macro or micro study centers on how the newspaper study defined its research question as well as the selection of units of analysis.

First, one might question whether racial profiling is completely conceptualized (as a macro issue) using only traffic stops because traffic enforcement represents only one sub-unit of law enforcement duties. Some researchers suggest traffic stops adequately "measure" racial or bias profiling by agencies (see Adams, 2000a, 2000b). However, and more importantly, when engaging in a macro study on racial profiling in a city police department there is a need to complement the data obtained via traffic stops with additional data, both qualitative and quantitative. For example, aggregate crime data may be utilized to analyze arrests, charges, and convictions across race; average response time across area addresses might also be utilized, coupled with complaint and complimentary data obtained from addresses and/or police substations across the jurisdiction. In macro studies researchers are interested in the big picture, for example racial profiling *as a department* as opposed to whether a particular police officer stops motorists in a racially biased manner, and so utilization of aggregate level data (e.g., collected at the department or jurisdiction level) is appropriate.

Second, selection of units of analysis must complement the research question. For example, simply utilizing a random sampling of traffic stops and discerning whether a license check or arrest warrant check was made by individual officers who made the stop *does not* adequately represent the entire department. Generalizing in this matter, from an individual representative of a group to the aggregate group, is a common pitfall for some individuals when interpreting data. This is known as *fallacy of nonequivalence* or *individualistic fallacy*. Specifically, individualistic fallacy is a problem when a researcher utilizes individual-level or disaggregated data to generalize to a larger group.

There are at least three "units of analysis" or individualistic fallacy problems to consider from the racial profiling case study presented in Exhibit 1. Again, the newspaper study utilized traffic stops completed on 30 randomly selected days of which all traffic stops made on those days were selected for inclusion in the study. The problem with this is the "stratification" of the sampling process from individual traffic stops into days of stops. Specifically, a local professor suggested that "rather than studying 30 randomly selected days over a year's time, the newspaper should have selected individual stops randomly from the 'whole population of stops over a period of a year'" (Adams, 2000a). In essence, the newspaper study was negligent in not maintaining the appropriate unit of analysis in the study. That is, the unit of analysis should have remained "traffic stops" and this was lost in the sampling process because "a sample of days" was used to "'generalize' about stops" (Adams, 2000a).

Suppose one poses a question about why crime occurs; would this be a macro- or a micro-level study? Determining the level of analysis for the question "why crime occurs" depends on how the researcher operationalizes the question in terms of units of analysis. For example, a researcher might operationalize the question by asking why some cities have higher crime rates than others (Blau & Blau, 1982), or he might ask why some individuals commit crime more than others (Toch, 1969, as cited in Blau & Blau, 1982). The original question of "why crime occurs," therefore, might be operationalized at either the macro- or micro-level. The macro-level analysis might be generated by the question of why some cities have higher crime rates than others. At the macro-level, the units of analysis would focus on city-level data, again as outlined by Blau and Blau (1982), this might include violent crime rates, population size, racial composition, and income inequality.

Macro-level studies encompass description, analysis, and interpretation of aggregate level data. In this sense, it is important for the researcher to operationalize a research question using appropriate (macro-level) units of analysis. Again, this is evident from the above discussion about "why crime occurs" in terms of how the researcher defines the research question.

Therefore, the importance of macro-level research is not so much a question of its utility, but hinges in the ability of the researcher to select this method as appropriate for a given research question.

What Is Micro Research?

Micro research refers to the study of individuals or small units. The research may focus on small units of people (individuals or small groups), limited or specific time periods (certain hours or days), or limited observations (individual behaviors or counts). Neuman and Wiegand define micro research as dealing with "small slices of time, space, or numbers of people" where the "concepts are usually not very abstract" (2000:46). Because micro research focuses on studying small units, researchers evaluate and interpret by operationalizing the research question at the micro-level. Bailey suggests that groups comprised of one to four individuals might be considered a micro-level study, but that "there is no consensus on the borderline between micro and macro" (1994:36). Neuman and Wiegand state that what makes a micro-level analysis is a "study's attention to norms and social interaction within a relatively small group" (2000:109). Thus, micro studies seek to interpret or analyze the small units, whether it be individual people, a group of people, or particular behaviors within a group.

As with macro studies, the selection of units of analysis must complement the research question in micro research. For example, simply utilizing aggregate citizen perceptions or attitudes regarding law enforcement in their community *does not* adequately allow interpretation of an individual citizen's perception and/or perceptions focused at an individual officer. Utilizing data gathered at a group level to make inferences about individual representatives of the group (e.g., behaviors) is known as *ecological fallacy*. Specifically, ecological fallacy is a problem when a researcher utilizes large group or aggregated data to generalize to individual level or disaggregated data (Neuman & Wiegand, 2000).

Hagan (1993:366) suggests that "much" of the early research in the field of criminal justice is "plagued by shifts" in units of analysis which has led to inaccurate interpretations, namely ecological fallacies. For example, most recently news media[1] have covered incidents of several fraternities "condoning" the wearing blackface or Klu Klux Klan garb during fraternity events; while this is a problem for these fraternities and respective members, one must be careful not to make assumptions about *all* individual fraternity members in general. Meanwhile, Neuman and Wiegand (2000) discuss the "dangers" of both ecological and individualistic fallacy when interpreting data, such that the macro unit is formulated from individual micro units. For example, they suggest (2000:113):

---

[1]   E-mail correspondence received from the Higher Education Center listserve (higheredctr@edc.org) utilizing cite from the *Mobile Register*, November 11, 2001.

> [I]t is easy to slide into using the causes or behavior of micro units, such as individuals, to explain the actions of macro units, such as social institutions. What happens among units at one level does not necessarily hold for different units of analysis. . . . [Furthermore], the causes, forces, structures, and processes that exist among macro-level units cannot be reduced to individual behavior.

This suggests that micro units may not be utilized to provide accurate description, analysis, or interpretation of a macro unit. Arguably, media accounts of individual school violence or hate crime incidents, when sensationalized and presented as the "norm" rather than an "exception to the norm" are examples of inaccurate descriptions or interpretations of school violence and hate crime (in general) across the United States. The problem of description and interpretation as it relates to a macro analysis of school violence is highlighted by Schiraldi in "Hyping School Violence," when he suggests: "It (school violence) doesn't happen anyplace, and it rarely happens at all. . . . Young people are being assaulted in schools today at the same rate as in 1976. . . . 99% of kids' deaths are away from school" (1998:A15). In the same newspaper article Schiraldi discusses the problem with "hyping" the individual incidents of school violence as it relates to generalizing or turning these individual incidents into macro-level meaning (1998:A15):

> The media's linking of these shootings as a 'trend' has exacerbated people's fear about safety of their children in schools. The result has been that misdirected public policy is being generated to safeguard schools, even though the real threat lies elsewhere.

Again, this suggests that micro units may not be utilized to provide accurate description, analysis, or interpretation of a macro unit.

Suppose one returns to the question about why crime occurs and whether it is a macro- or a micro-level study. As outlined above, this question might be operationalized at either the macro- or micro-level, depending on how the researcher operationalizes the question in terms of units of analysis. For example, a researcher might operationalize the question by asking why some cities have higher crime rates than others if he were interested in a macro-level analysis. However, a micro-level analysis might be generated by the question of why some individuals commit crime more than others. Thus, at the micro-level, the units of analysis would focus on individual-level data, for example, demographics, friendship networks, criminal and family history, and deviant behavior. It is important to recognize the differences between the macro- and micro-level definitions of "why crime occurs" in terms of how each research question is operationalized. Specifically, one should recognize the differences in variable selection in terms of units of analysis for measurement (i.e., macro-level analysis utilizes macro-level measurable variables, while micro-level analysis includes individual-level measurable variables).

Micro-level studies encompass description, analysis, and interpretation of individual level data. As is the case in macro-level studies, it is important for the researcher to operationalize a research question using appropriate (micro-level) units of analysis. For example, in the discussion of "why some individuals commit more crime than others," it is evident that the researcher operationalizes the research question with variables defined at the individual or micro level. Again, as discussed in the section of macro-level research, the importance of micro-level research is not so much a question of its utility, but hinges on the ability of the researcher to select this method as appropriate for a given research question.

Selecting a Macro or Micro Design

Selecting a type of study, either macro or micro, depends on (1) what the research question is, (2) what theory the study is couched in, and (3) how the research question is defined (Bickman & Rog, 1998). Senese suggests that (1) units of analysis, (2) levels of measurement, (3) variables, and (4) theoretical concepts are specific concepts that "need to be considered when selecting study subjects or groups as well as for determining the most appropriate techniques of analysis of the collected data" (1997:30).

Rossi and Freeman (1993:63) discuss the implications involved in designing a study or evaluation regardless of whether the study engages a macro or micro perspective. Specifically, the authors discuss the complexity and large amount of information that is needed for a "social problem" to be identified and defined. Furthermore, Rossi and Freeman note that once the problem is identified, it is often described as a "complex mix of related conditions" by evaluators. Such complexity may stem from the inclusion of definitional propositions from each stakeholder in the evaluation. The policy implications related to such a decision include "critical consideration in the explication of problem definitions" such that there is:

> Fit between what is popularly considered to be the problem and the implicit or explicit definitions in the legislative proposals. . . . [The purpose] is to examine how the problem has been formulated and to delineate as clearly as possible the set of policy alternatives that are, realistically, likely to be considered (Rossi & Freeman, 1993:62).

The goal, therefore, of researchers and evaluators is to provide policymakers and decisionmakers with a general definition and alternative definitions of a social problem, such that the definition may be inclusive of the macro-policy strategy (e.g., decrease the city's juvenile crime rate) or may be inclusive of micro-policy strategies (e.g., a curfew that pertains to youth). Research problems, and hence research designs whether macro or micro, must be empirically grounded as well as "clearly and specifically articulated" (Frankfort-Nachmias & Nachmias, 1996:53)

Researchers, practitioners, and policymakers engage in macro-research studies for different reasons. For example, a "naturalist approach" might be warranted so that both researchers and practitioners gain entrée in the research population (Tewksbury & Gagné, 1997). Specifically, working with "people for long periods of time in their natural setting" allows the researcher to conduct research "in the native environment to see people and their behavior given all the real-world incentives and constraints" (Bickman & Rog, 1998:479). This might include the researcher or (undercover) practitioner doing fieldwork for an extensive period of time.

Researchers also engage in macro research in order to explain macro concepts that might be more abstract (Neuman & Wiegand, 2000). For example, macro research may be used in researching operation of social institutions, entire cultural systems, and whole societies (Neuman & Wiegand, 2000:47). Furthermore, macro-level analyses may be used by researchers and policymakers or decisionmakers to "emphasize cultural and social structural differences between [two] societies" (Neuman & Wiegand, 2000:109). For example, researchers or policymakers may engage in explanatory studies aimed at discovering "social dynamics operating within a population" in order to determine social restructuring or policy implications (Babbie, 1998:93).

Studies might also be conducted at either the micro- or the macro-level. For example, ethnographic studies range from the micro to macro level, as do both descriptive and inferential studies. Babbie suggests that descriptive studies usually utilize individuals as the unit of analysis and such cases would be considered micro studies (1998:93). However, studies may be initiated as either macro or micro research depending on whether a research question is defined at the macro or micro level, when exploratory studies have no underlying or grounded theory, when the researcher is "breaking new ground," or when insights are needed into developing a research methodology (Babbie, 1998:91).

A researcher may also use theoretical perspectives to define his level of research design. That is, because units of analysis are defined to operationalize measurement, they are also "loosely" related to the level of analysis (Neuman & Wiegand, 2000:110). Neuman and Wiegand suggest, therefore, that:

> Social-psychological or micro levels of analysis fit with the individual as a unit of analysis, whereas macro levels of analysis fit with the social category or institution as a unit (2000:110).

The need to test theoretical propositions also focuses or limits the level of a research study (Bickman & Rog, 1998). For example, all stakeholders in a research project may want to utilize a single case study to test a theoretical proposition (Bickman & Rog, 1998), which might include both macro- and micro-level analyses. Riley, Hermalin, and Rosero-Bixby (1993) utilize a case study of Costa Rica to analyze both micro- and macro-level factors associated with desired family size. The authors utilized macro-level indicators such as "aggregate level of fertility," and micro-level indicators such as "individual cognitive skills" in this study (Riley et al., 1993). Neuman and Wiegand present an example of trying to explain street crime using theory in their textbook; specifically, they discuss the use of routine activities theory (a micro-level theory) to study robbery (2000:46). By defining the study using a micro-level theory, the authors *operationalized* street crime using micro-level measures. For example, they explain that the daily "routines" of taxi drivers (i.e., handling money, being alone, and transporting strangers) might be correlated with criminal victimization (Neuman & Wiegand, 2000:46). Thus, by operationalizing street crime using a micro-theory, the authors "measure" street crime using individual-level variables or interactions among individuals (Neuman & Wiegand, 2000:110).

Individuals using research methods such as survey or experimental research are most often conducting micro studies (Neuman & Wiegand, 2000:110). Such studies may include "when crime statistics are used to compare individuals or households, towns or cities, states, regions of the country, or even countries" (Neuman & Wiegand, 2000:110). Micro studies or micro research methods include focus groups, individual interviews, and observation (Bailey, 1994). Practitioners, politicians, or corporate managers interested in analyzing organizational theory engage in micro research. Most research conducted by policymakers and decisionmakers as well as practitioners, is conducted using individual units of analysis and are, hence, micro studies (Neuman & Wiegand, 2000:110).

Researchers, policymakers, and practitioners may utilize both macro and micro research to analyze public policy. For example, research may focus on trends in the effectiveness of drug interdiction or eradication processes. Again, the study may be conducted at either the macro or micro level depending on how the research question is defined. Aggregate or macro level data may include arrests for drug trafficking, aggregate number of plants eradicated, or total number of drug seizures. Meanwhile, micro-level research may focus on the measurement of illicit drug use by individuals or groups of individuals (e.g., juveniles). Public policies can be defined or evaluated using either a macro- or micro-level research design.

Summary

The decision to commence in either a macro or micro research project is limited not only by how the research question is defined, but also by availability of resources. For example, a research project might be limited by time restraints, personnel restraints or monetary restraints. Further, the project is limited in how various stakeholders *define* the research question. For example, some research projects have a hierarchical structure of stakeholders, where the highest-level individual is interested in the ability to replicate this study at a state or national level, whereas the lowest-level individual is simply interested in keeping his program running. Utilizing stakeholder input, the researcher must determine the level of analysis to use and then successfully operationalize the research question using the appropriate units of analysis.

Further, in determining whether a macro or micro study is feasible, decisionmaking must include both theoretical priorities and consideration of both practicality and feasibility (Bickman & Rog, 1998). Again, a research project might not have appropriate funding support to engage in a macro-level analysis (e.g., funding not available for data collection), whereas limited personnel and research assistance might not enable one to engage in a successful micro-level analysis (e.g., gang infiltration to study the life of a gang member). Furthermore, the importance of determining whether to engage in macro- or micro-level research is not a question of utility as each method is rooted in theoretical and methodological applications.

The purpose of this chapter has been to analyze and dismantle the controversy surrounding macro and micro research. The importance of recognizing the type of research design one should employ is dependent on the defining research question, as well as the available resources. Discussion in this chapter should point out that the controversy of whether to use macro or micro research is really *noncontroversial* in the fact that researchers should select the method that is appropriate for the given research question. Furthermore, both methods have an important role in social science research.

Discussion Questions

1. What are the differences between macro and micro approaches to criminal justice research?

2. What types of questions can best be answered by macro or micro approaches to criminal justice research?

3. What types of data collection are most appropriate for macro and micro approaches to criminal justice research?

4. Which "makes more sense," macro or micro approaches to criminal justice research? Why?

CHAPTER 8

Getting In and Getting On: Entrée Strategies and the Importance of Trust and Rapport in Qualitative Research

Patricia Gagné
University of Louisville

Introduction

In October 1995, as part of a larger study of transsexuals and cross-dressers, I found myself participating in and observing a national, organized lobbying campaign, located in Washington, DC. My time at "Transgender Lobby Days," as the event was known, included spending several days and evenings with members of the transgender community, attending training sessions, observing as they spoke with congressional representatives, and eating meals and riding with them on the DC Metro. As a nontransgendered woman, my ability to attend the event and later interview many of the people I met there, was dependent on my ability to do two things: to gain entrée to the group and to establish and maintain rapport with them once I was in the field. Indeed, all qualitative research is, to a greater or lesser degree, dependent upon these two factors.

In the pages that follow, I draw upon the experiences of qualitative methodologists far more skilled than myself, as well as on my own successes and failures, to explain and illustrate some of the ways that entrée to the field may be gained and why it is so vitally important to establish and maintain rapport with those one wishes to study. In the end, we will see that qualitative research is an undertaking that depends as much upon the good will and cooperation of those we wish to study as on our own ability to garner their support.

Research Design and Qualitative Methods

Qualitative methods consist of a number of techniques that may be used to gather data. These include conducting participant observation, interviews, and focus groups, as well as gathering archival data, such as transcripts, letters, meeting minutes, or e-mail exchanges on a group list. Although the number of methods is limited, there is a great deal of variety in the way each may be carried out. For example, studies may be conducted as ethnographic field work, which involves participating with, observing, and recording notes on research subjects in the settings where they are naturally found. To do this, researchers may study a group to which they already belong, or they may get permission to study a population as one who is there strictly to observe (Lofland & Lofland, 1995). In the field, interviews may be carried out as conversations, with the researcher jotting notes afterward, or they may be structured, in-depth, and tape-recorded, which ideally requires a quiet setting, away from the activities of the group under investigation. Another important part of field research may include gathering archival data that can provide a more detailed record of the group being studied. Qualitative methods may also be employed without the researcher using participant observation. Rather than living with the group being studied, one may solicit a sample in a number of ways that do not require daily interaction with members of the population. No matter what combination of methods one uses, the ability of investigators to build rapport and win the trust of those they are studying will enhance the quality and quantity of data that are made available.

Research Strategies and Flexibility in the Field

Before beginning a study, researchers must determine the type or combination of methods to be used, but they must also be flexible enough to adapt to conditions in the field. For example, in their study of people who live in recreational vehicles (RVs), Dorothy Ayers Counts and David Counts (1992) planned to augment their participant observational research by distributing surveys among the people living in the RV communities they encountered. In a very short time, the Counts discovered that an important aspect of the RV community was a strong norm of reciprocity. For that reason, most of the people they asked to complete a survey refused, even though they were willing to verbally answer all the questions the researchers posed. The key was to interview people conversationally, with an easy exchange of information between the interviewers and their research subjects. Without a willingness to be flexible and a working knowledge of how to substitute one method for another, the Counts would likely have failed in what was ultimately a successful research project.

The methods most appropriate to any study will depend on the research question, the group to be studied, the location(s) where the project will take place, and whether the investigation will be conducted openly or covertly. Flexibility in the field is important, but before research can be carried out, one must gain entrée to the group to be studied.

Getting in Covertly

In field research, gaining entrée to a particular population is relatively easy if the research is to be conducted covertly. Covert research is carried out without the knowledge or consent of the subject population. For that reason, it consists primarily of participant observation and interviews carried out as informal conversations. Typically, the researcher observes for a period of time and then secretly records key observations by going into a relatively private location, such as a restroom. Field notes, as those scribbled records are called, are later transcribed into a more complete recollection of what occurred, with the key observations used to spur a memories of a fuller account.

Lofland and Lofland (1995:32) argue that gaining entrée is rarely an issue in covert research and that it is so easy, "You simply take up or continue playing a role in the setting and begin logging data 'on the sly'." Sometimes it really is that simple, particularly if the researcher is observing routine, legal, unstigmatized behaviors in a public setting. Even then, investigators' ability to enter and remain in the field will be enhanced if they adopt a self-presentation that offers an easily observed explanation for being there and if they use "props" appropriate to the setting. For example, in my research on violence and control of women in Appalachia (Gagné, 1992), I spent time observing interactions among women and men in bars. Typically, I took a seat in a booth and sat with one or two friends who knew I was doing research. They conversed while I watched people. With a notepad on my lap, and with friends and a bottle of beer as props, I was able to study interactions among women and men in such public settings without their knowledge. This approach can be modified in any number of ways, depending on the locale where activities are being observed.

In public settings, especially when outdoors, the nonverbal cues and the props researchers use can simply entail those that indicate they are "hanging out." Indeed, this is the approach that Thomas Calhoun (1992) was using to observe male street prostitutes when he was approached by one of his subjects who was trying to "turn a trick." Calhoun responded by telling the young man who he was and why he was there. Although Calhoun's cover was blown, the researcher's flexibility in the field, his rapid assessment of the situation, and his spontaneous judgment that he should reveal his research agenda to the hustler paid off when the young man introduced him to other male prostitutes. One quick decision made it possible for Calhoun to interview a number of young male prostitutes about how they got into that line of work.

Calhoun's advantage in initiating his research covertly was that he was observing in a public setting. As researchers move into more private settings and make an effort to observe deviant, stigmatized, or illegal behavior, the development of a convincing cover becomes imperative. One may question whether covertly observing groups in private settings is ethical. Those issues are discussed in Chapter 10. Whether ethical or not, sometimes the only way one can gather data that will address a particular research question is to do so covertly and in private settings. For example, we frequently hear it said that racism in the United States still exists, although often in more subtle forms. Moreover, middle-class professional people of color often feel marginalized among white professionals, as well as in the ethnic cultures to which individual professionals belong. To better understand the cultural roots of such feelings, Lawrence Otis Graham (1995) took a job bussing tables in an exclusive country club, where he worked openly as a busboy and covertly as a researcher. While serving affluent white members of the club, he was able to hear and later record the comments they made about people of color, even while he—an African-American—filled their water glasses and cleared away their dishes. Without his cover as a busboy, it is highly unlikely that the "very white" clientele would have spoken as openly in his presence or that he would have been given permission to study the racial attitudes of club members. Similarly, Judith Rollins (1985), in an effort to understand how relations between women are affected by race and class, sought jobs cleaning the homes of affluent white women. It is very improbable that she would have been hired if she had revealed to her employers that she was conducting research. If they knew she was a graduate student at a prestigious east coast university, it is even less likely that they would have treated her as they would any other domestic employee.

Not all covert research involves taking a new job or pretending to be someone else. But in every research setting where participant observation is to be used, investigators must determine, before they enter the field, what role and presentation-of-self they will adopt. In some instances, they may decide to pass as a member or potential member of the group they are studying. For example, in his study of female impersonators and their audiences, J. Brian Brown (2001) posed as a fellow patron, mingling among audience members and later recording their comments in a stall in the men's restroom.[1] Similarly, Barbara Ehrenreich (2001) accepted a number of low-wage, entry-level jobs in her study of how people make ends meet by working full-time, year-round for poverty-level wages. None of her employers or co-workers suspected that she was collecting data for a book. Those Ehrenreich spent time with assumed she was one of them, an assumption that makes it possible for researchers to study people as they actually live, work, and play.

---

[1]   Personal communication with the author.

Of course, there are limits to what each of us is able to convincingly portray in the field. The decision to pass as an insider or to adopt the role of an outsider whose presence is either necessary or can be tolerated will depend upon a number of salient factors, such as one's age, race, gender, and social class background. For example, in his report of the research conducted at the exclusive country club discussed above, Graham would have preferred to mingle freely among club members as an equal. But, he explains, "Quite frankly, I got into this country club the only way that a black man like me could—as a $7-an-hour busboy"(1996:1). Although he had better professional and academic credentials than many of the club's members, as an African-American, it was impossible for him to become a member of the club or to have a presence in it in any other way. Ironically, his research was more successful because he worked in a role in which he was socially invisible to those he studied. They simply acted as if he was not there as they carried on their conversations. To successfully pass in the field, researchers must realistically evaluate their ability to pass in the role they decide to play, just as they must also assess how the role they have chosen will give them access to some data, while restricting their ability to gather other information. The key is to maximize the former, while minimizing the latter.

Passing in the field presumes that investigators understand the norms, manners, and styles of the setting and that they are capable of assuming a presentation-of-self that convincingly accounts for their presence. When covertly observing and passing as a member in relatively private settings where stigmatizing behaviors occur, it is especially important to adopt the mannerisms of those present and to be aware of and adhere to the norms of the situation. Frequently, the only way to learn those norms and manners is to enter the field, pay close attention to what others are doing, and imitate what you see. Just as a novice to fine dining will often look to others to determine which fork to use, the covert researcher must adjust and adapt on the spot. Unlike those experiencing fine dining, there often is no book of etiquette that could have been consulted before entering the field. For example, as part of his graduate training in qualitative methods, Richard Tewksbury (1990) conducted covert participant observation in adult bookstores where, he quickly learned, men not only sought sexually explicit materials, but on-site anonymous sexual activity with one another, as well. Having had no previous experience in an adult bookstore and lacking any research that might have educated him on how a patron of pornography should comport himself, Tewksbury was left to wing it. The first time he went to observe interactions at an adult bookstore, he noted and followed the norms of the setting: He remained silent and avoided eye contact, except to communicate potential interest in another man or to reject the nonverbal signals being communicated to him by others. As his research progressed, he learned, by watching other men, how to posture himself to facilitate or avoid interactions. Although he never participated in the sexual activities that were initiated or consummated by many men, he was able to remain in the setting and continue his research by acting as if he would be willing to do so, if he found the right partner. By adopting a presentation-of-self that indicated that he was potentially interested in the activities taking place on the premises, he was able to log more than 50 hours in the field.[2] Furthermore, he did so without arousing the suspicion of store personnel.

Passing in the field is central to successful covert research. Having one's cover blown, particularly in a private setting, is likely to result in distrust, a breakdown of any rapport that has been built, and expulsion of the observer from the group. For that reason alone, researchers must carefully consider whether their research is best conducted openly or covertly. Moreover, they must determine ahead of time what role they will play in the field and make an honest assessment of whether or not they are capable of passing in the role they wish to play. Furthermore, it is important for researchers to think ahead about how they will respond if they are confronted in the field. Revealing oneself as an investigator, if done at the right time and in the right way as, for example, Calhoun (1992) did, can result in greater success than one originally anticipated. Failure to properly handle being revealed can result in a prematurely terminated project.

Because of the ethical dilemmas and methodological limitations imposed by covert research, many social scientists opt instead to conduct their qualitative research openly. When conducting noncovert research, investigators are first faced with the challenge of gaining access to the population they wish to research. Moreover, because their role as a researcher is known, these investigators must work harder than covert observers to win their subjects' trust, establish rapport with them, and maintain that trust and rapport over time. In the next section, I discuss methods researchers can use to gain entrée to the population they wish to study, as well as the pros and cons involved in selecting one method over another.

Getting in Openly

Conducting research openly presents the possibility of conducting in-depth interviews and focus groups, in addition to participant observation and short, informal interviews. Noncovert research includes ethnographic research in naturalistic settings, where people are found going about their daily lives. It also includes recruiting volunteers to participate in interviews or focus groups either in or independent of ethnographic research settings.

---

[2]   Personal communication with the author.

Getting Past the Gatekeeper

Investigators often first must obtain permission to enter the field when conducting open ethnographic research. With some populations, it is necessary to gain permission from someone in a position of authority over them. These gatekeepers often hold the power to determine whether one's research will or will not go forward. To get permission from these authorities, researchers must present themselves as responsible, trustworthy, and knowledgeable about the field or group they wish to study. Few gatekeepers, such as prison administrators, nursing home managers, or recreation coordinators, will grant permission to investigators who appear not to know what they are doing or not to take their work seriously.

To gain permission, it is often helpful if one begins by sending a letter to the gatekeeper, on university or other official letter head, stating the purpose and duration of the study, that clearance from one's institutional review board has been or will be attained before the research begins, what will be required from the gatekeeper and from research participants, any known risks or benefits the study poses to the population being studied, how the research findings will be disseminated, and whether individual and organizational confidentiality will be maintained. The letter should also include a time frame in which the researcher will call to answer any questions and to set an appointment to further discuss the project. A professional demeanor on the phone and in meetings with the gatekeeper, together with a willingness to answer questions and to discuss the study, will help to facilitate entrée to the setting and the population. Of course, little details, such as calling back within the time frame noted in the initial contact letter, showing up on time for any scheduled meetings, being prepared, and dressing in an appropriately professional manner will help to convey that one is a serious and trustworthy scholar.

Getting in with a Guide

Although negotiating permission from a gatekeeper may be necessary to gain access to certain populations, investigators must recognize that this strategy often carries with it certain limitations that may impede access to particular members of a population. For example, in her study of survival strategies in a poor, urban, African-American community, Carol Stack (a white anthropologist) chose to go against the advice of her colleagues to enter the community through "the older black establishment" (1974:xi). Instead, she worked with a guide, whose role was to provide initial introductions to families the guide had known while growing up in the community. Stack explains, "In time I knew enough people well who were closely related so that after any family scene, gathering, or fight, I could put together interpretations of the events from the viewpoints of different individuals. . ." (1974:xi). In this way, Stack was able to observe the way average members of the community lived and survived, rather than studying those members of the community whom gatekeepers thought might represent a more respectable public image of the community. Stack's goal in using the entrée method was to debunk certain myths by revealing the various strategies poor, urban, African-Americans used to survive and to explain how those strategies sometimes ensured short-term survival while ensnaring community members in long-term poverty.

Gaining Entrée from Research Subjects

Once researchers gain entrée to the field, they must then win the trust and permission of those they wish to study. For example, in his study of homeless women, Eliot Liebow (1993) tells his readers that, after retiring from his job as an anthropologist, he began doing volunteer work with homeless women. He continues, "Seduced by the courage and the humor of the women, and by the pleasure of their company, I started going to the shelter four and sometimes five days a week. . . .Probably because it was something I was trained to do, or perhaps out of plain habit, I decided to take notes" (Liebow, 1993:ix). Liebow easily gained permission from the shelter director and from most of the women he wanted to study. "All except Regina. Her acceptance was conditional. 'Only if you promise not to publish before I do,' she said (1993:ix)." He commenced his research, but kept his promise to Regina by getting her permission to publish his book before she published anything. As one of the most successful ethnographers in the twentieth century, Liebow recognized that building trust and rapport among those he wanted to study depended, above all else, upon keeping his word. If you promise your research subjects you will do something, do it; and if you cannot or do not intend to make good on a promise, do not give your word, even if it makes matters more tense or awkward at the moment.

Getting Along in the Field

Once initial access to a population has been granted, researchers must adopt a demeanor that will help to "keep the flow of information coming" (Lofland & Lofland, 1995:55). Whether in the field or while conducting interviews or focus groups, this presentation is one that is nonthreatening, nonjudgmental, nonconfrontational, and non-argumentative. It is a demeanor that conveys honesty, interest, empathy, and even support for the group under investigation. In most types of qualitative research, and particularly when relying upon participant observation, one must bear in mind that the investigator is the research instrument. It is one's demeanor and ability to build trust and rapport in the field that will open (or close) opportunities to observe and listen to those being studied. Getting along in the field will ultimately determine what data become available and which remain hidden.

Ironically, the competent professional demeanor that is most likely to gain entrée through gatekeepers or with a guide may be at odds with the image in the field that is most likely to facilitate data gathering. Specifically, Lofland and Lofland (1995) argue that "acceptable incompetence" (1995:56) may facilitate the flow of data more easily than any other role the qualitative researcher can assume. Specifically, whether conducting formal interviews or conversing with subjects in the field, researchers who play the role of one who is acceptably incompetent, but otherwise cordial and empathetic, present themselves as people who need to be taught. Rather than always indicating an immediate understanding of what subjects are explaining or describing, researchers who act as if information is completely new are likely to hear and learn more because greater detail is required of the "teacher."

For example, in my research on motorcycling culture (Gagné & Austin, 2002), I frequently attended rallies, club meetings, and other events. I have always been more interested in the culture of motorcycling than in the technology of motorcycles or the physics of riding. In conversations with other riders, I was commonly inundated with highly technical language about bikes of a certain make or vintage or with an analysis of the physics of riding. My standard response was that I was new to such intricacies but was very interested in whatever it was I was being told. This reaction elicited more data than I could possibly record. For example, one man who rode the same make and model motorcycle I owned gave me a detailed explanation of the electrical system and later took me to his bike to show me all the spare parts he kept in his saddle bags. Admittedly, I learned and was able to retain only a little of the technical information he offered. But by playing the role of the interested student, I learned the significance that serious touring riders place on self-reliance and being prepared. If I had acted as if I understood everything my "teacher" was telling me, it is possible he would not have taken me to his motorcycle to show me his spare diode board, voltage regulator, fuses, and other parts. It would have taken me much longer to acquire the information I learned that day.

Although playing the learner can facilitate the flow of data, it is a role that must be managed very carefully, particularly in research where a certain level of knowledge or competence is required to maintain rapport in the field. Success in qualitative field research requires managing the delicate balance between demonstrating enough competence to be respected and enough incompetence to keep the flow of data going. Over the past nine years, I have established competence as a touring motorcycle rider, capable of riding hundreds of miles in a single day. But when I am conducting research at rallies and other events, I am not readily observable in a way that conveys my membership in the community of riders. As part of my ongoing research on motorcycling culture, in March 2001 I attended Bike Week in Daytona, Florida and camped with hundreds of other motorcyclists. My collaborator, D. Mark Austin, and I distributed surveys at many locations throughout Daytona, including at the campground where we were staying. One morning at an open shelter where coffee was available, my colleague overheard three male riders comment that they "Bet that female researcher wouldn't know the first thing about a motorcycle." Recognizing the potential of such a rumor to become "fact," Austin introduced himself as one of the investigators in the study. As he engaged the men in conversation, he casually mentioned that I had ridden with him to Bike Week from Louisville, Kentucky, thus re-establishing the two of us as competent members of the group. It is possible that even if this particular incident had gone unchallenged, we would have continued to gain the trust and cooperation of members of the touring motorcycling community. But one should not underestimate the potential of rumors to become accepted as facts and the danger such myths can pose to efforts to establish and maintain rapport in the field.

Staying Centered and Out of the Middle

Conducting field research is different from any other type of scientific endeavor. It requires us to live among, yet remain separate from, those we study. To be successful in the field, it is essential not to become embroiled in disagreements and arguments or to become associated with one faction over another or to give the impression that one is taking sides. This generally requires keeping one's opinions to oneself and mandates that researchers make an effort to spend time with all group members, even when one's natural inclination is to like some better than others.

One experience in the field quickly taught me how easy it is to get caught in the middle. After I had completed a number of interviews with transsexuals and cross-dressers (Gagné, Tewksbury & McGaughey, 1997; Gagné & Tewksbury, 1998; 1999), the former president of a support group who had played an important role in helping me find subjects, asked me to attend a meeting and give a presentation of my preliminary findings. I arrived at the meeting with a research assistant whose role it was to observe and make mental notes, to be recorded later. We arrived early and were invited to share refreshments and to mingle with people informally. I enjoyed chatting with many of the people I had interviewed and was introduced by them to other members of the group. At some point, early in the evening, one of my new acquaintances invited me to go out with them after the meeting. My field work in other groups had taught me that this type of socializing was common, and I accepted the invitation. After the meeting was over and my presentation completed, another individual approached me and asked me to go out with them. I said I was planning on going and that so-and-so had invited me. To this, the individual replied, "Oh, so you're going with them. Well, perhaps another time then." Suspecting that I had done something wrong, but not knowing what, I explained that I was sorry that I did not know that there were two groups that went out separately, but that I had already accepted the first invitation. I thought I had taken care of things until my assistant and I arrived at the home of the first individual who had invited us to go out. The rest of the evening was spent listening to this small group gossip maliciously about people who were not present. After about an hour, we were able to express our thanks and make a polite exit. The next day, I immediately e-mailed the second individual who had invited us out, and once again expressed my apologies for not being able to accept her invitation. I suggested that perhaps I could come back later in the year and make another presentation, at which time I would be happy to go out with her group of friends.

I do not know the extent of damage that was done by my being erroneously associated with one faction over another. I suspect that if I had been in the process of collecting data, I would have had a great deal of work to do to overcome the perceived slight. Fortunately, I was finished with my data collection, although I was sorry to have offended people who had been instrumental in helping me find subjects to interview. What I learned from this valuable experience is just how easily one can lose her center and get caught in the middle between warring factions, and how difficult it is to undo damage that has already been done.

Establishing Trust and Rapport in Interviews and Focus Groups

Not all qualitative research involves participant-observational field work. Nonetheless, when conducting research on a population that is not situated in a particular location, it is still important to win the trust of research subjects and to maintain rapport with them. This is particularly true when investigating sensitive topics or examining stigmatized populations. Even when researchers interact with subjects for only short periods of time, say during one interview or one focus group session, they are likely to come away with richer, more complete data if those they are studying trust them.

In the course of a two-hour interaction, how then can trust be won and rapport be established? Just as in field research, it is important to maintain a demeanor that conveys interest, empathy, and even support for the group being studied. Before beginning an interview or focus group, researchers should take the time to chat or make small talk with their subjects. In a focus group setting, this can be done by welcoming people to the setting, offering them refreshments, and helping them get comfortable. Rather than simply letting individuals sit and wait for others to arrive, focus group facilitators and their assistants should ask nonthreatening questions and, in exchange, offer information about themselves. For example, while conducting focus group research on the support networks and survival strategies of pregnant teenagers (Logsdon & Gagné, 2002), I greeted each young woman as she entered the room. While an assistant offered soft drinks and pizza, I asked each of them about when her baby was due, how she was feeling, whether or not she knew the child's sex, what she thought she would name the child, and where she planned to deliver. As the young women offered information, I told them equivalent things about my grandchildren, in a style that facilitated conversation. As each new member joined the group, I included her in the conversation by introducing myself and the other young women and summarizing what we were talking about. Once the group was assembled, we all knew a little something about the others and were accustomed to talking amongst ourselves. At that point, it was an easy transition to explain to them the purpose of the study and, in the process, to convey my empathy for their difficulties as pregnant, unmarried teenage women. Before an interview or focus group begins, it is also important for the researcher to answer any questions subjects might have about the study.

Similar methods can be used to set the stage for interviews. In my research with battered women who had killed or assaulted abusive husbands or boyfriends (Gagné, 1996; 1998), I never started the interview as soon as we met. Rather, I thanked them for making the time to talk with me and going through the trouble to meet with me. I asked how things were going and expressed empathy for the difficulties they had lived through during the relationship, their trials, in prison, and since incarceration. I explained that the goal in my research was to help other people understand what battered women live with and what they endure when they defend themselves from abuse and that it was my hope that, by telling their stories in their own words, perhaps life would be better for other women facing similar difficulties.

Whether in interviews, focus groups, or participant observation, it is important to convey to those we wish to study that we are not there to judge them, but instead are there in an effort to understand and to convey to others why individuals were motivated to do what they did. In my own research on sensitive topics, I have found that empathy goes a long way in helping individuals relax and tell their stories openly. During the interview or focus group itself, empathy can be conveyed by repeating back or summarizing what subjects have just said. In my research on transsexuals (Gagné, Tewksbury & McGaughey, 1997; Gagné & Tewksbury, 1998; 1999), I initially had great difficulty understanding why individuals would undergo a gender transformation that often ultimately led to loss of homes, jobs, family, and friends. But I found that by saying, "It sounds as if your life had become unbearable," or "It sounds as if you are much more at ease with yourself today," my subjects would relax because they knew I was not making a judgment about their decisions. In subsequent questions, they were more open and went into greater depth to help me understand their experiences. In addition, body language that says "I'm interested in everything you have to say" can encourage subjects to go into greater detail about their experiences. Leaning forward, maintaining appropriate eye contact, and waiting patiently while subjects find the right words or compose themselves when they become upset are likely to help them feel more comfortable and thus to trust the researcher more.

Summary and Conclusion

Gaining entrée and building trust and rapport with those we wish to study are dependent upon many of the same interpersonal skills that can help us make and maintain good friendships. People are more likely to accept those who "fit in" among them. In covert and open research, this means adopting a demeanor and self-presentation that will explain our presence in the field and make others comfortable sharing time and space with us. In open research, one demeanor may be appropriate with gatekeepers, while another will work better in the field. Moreover, in open research, it is vitally important to treat people respectfully, to be honest with them, and to make good on the promises and commitments one makes and to avoid making promises one cannot or does not intend to keep. Demonstrating an honest interest in those we wish to study and showing a nonjudgmental attitude or empathetic attitude toward them will open countless doors. Once entrée has been gained, keeping confidences and avoiding malicious gossip and the appearance of taking sides or playing favorites will keep those doors open until one is ready to leave the field.

Discussion Questions

1. Why is it important to think about how to gain trust and rapport with qualitative research subjects?

2. What are the methods of building trust and rapport with research subjects?

3. What are the dangers of not gaining trust and rapport with research subjects?

4. How does a qualitative researcher decide what methods to use to try to build trust and rapport with research subjects?

CHAPTER 9

Interviews as a Data Collection Method: But, Which Type Should I Use?

Kathrine Johnson
University of West Florida

Overview

The interview is an alternative, complementary, and flexible method of collecting self-administered survey and observational data. Interviews allow researchers to gather data about their respondents' experiences, opinions, attitudes, beliefs, behaviors, and values. In an interview, researchers gather data in a face-to-face setting (or by telephone) by asking questions of respondents, rather than by distributing a survey or questionnaire to be completed (self-administered) by the respondent and returned to the researcher. Interviews can also be used to complement participant observations in that a researcher can ask questions (e.g., for clarification) about the situations or events being observed.

Fitzgerald and Cox (1994) suggest that an interviewer "must be concerned with three things: (1) establishing good rapport with respondents; (2) determining the meaning and truthfulness of their responses; and (3) using the type of questioning that will elicit the required information" (1994:99). Establishing rapport is a critical component of effective qualitative research. If an interviewer is unable to create an atmosphere where the respondent feels comfortable enough to provide honest and open responses to the questions, the entire research project may be in danger. For example, respondents may refuse to participate. Or, perhaps worse, they may simply create responses that they think the interviewer wants to hear or what they think they should say.

The second concern for interviewers, determining the meaning and truthfulness of responses, addresses one of the inherent problems of using interviews as a data collection method. Determining the legitimacy of responses can be a difficult task for an interviewer. What does the response suggest? Is the response obtained valid? By first establishing rapport, an interviewer improves the likelihood that respondents will be truthful. Informing respondents that the information they provide will remain confidential may also encourage truthfulness. Further, the interviewer must remain neutral and make sure that personal attitudes are not shared with the respondent. It is equally important that the interviewer maintain neutral body language. An offhand comment or body language suggestive of disapproval may impact responses. For example, if an interviewer collecting data on the use of club drugs begins to fidget in her chair when a respondent admits he has slipped Ecstasy into the drink of an unsuspecting person, the respondent may be less likely to be forthcoming in answering the remaining questions.

The final concern for interviewers is determining what types of questions will elicit the desired information. Determining the types of questions that will yield the "best" responses, however, is predicated on determining whether interviewing (as a data collection method) is appropriate for the given type of research. Berg (1989) argues that "when investigators are interested in understanding the perceptions of participants, or learning how participants come to attach certain meanings to phenomena or events, interviewing provides a useful means of access" (1989:19). For example, suppose a researcher wanted to know *how often* college students use club drugs. A self-administered questionnaire or survey is sufficient to obtain this information. However, if the researcher wants to *understand* the experience of using club drugs, conducting an interview provides more complete and meaningful data.

The remainder of this chapter discusses in detail the four primary types of interviews: structured, semi-structured, unstructured, and focus groups. The primary difference among the types of interviews is the extent to which the researcher identifies and articulates the interview questions prior to conducting the interview. The reader is offered a brief outline of how each type of interview works, including the types of research questions that are best suited to each, the advantages and disadvantages of each type, and examples of how that type of interview has been used in the criminal justice/deviance literature.

Structured Interviews

A structured, formal, or standardized interview is desirable when the researcher wants to "offer each subject approximately the same stimulus so that responses to the questions, ideally, may be comparable" (Berg, 1989:15). Structured interviews are used when the researcher has an all-inclusive foundation for identifying the appropriate questions that will elicit the desired information in the interview. That is, the researcher identifies/includes the questions in the interview that "are sufficiently comprehensive to solicit from subjects all (or nearly all) information relevant to the study's topic(s)" (Berg, 1989:15). Structured interviews do not leave room for either the interviewer or the respondent to express his/her own feelings, attitudes, opinions, or biases. "It is very much a matter of squeezing oneself into one of a predetermined number of boxes which may or may not be appropriate" (Jupp, 1989:63).

As discussed above, structured interviews can use the same questions as a traditional self-administered survey or questionnaire with the exception that they are conducted orally, either in person or over the telephone. That being the case, the format is fixed and inflexible, just as it is for a pen-and-paper survey. Structured interviews offer no leeway for either the interviewer or respondent to ad-lib questions or responses. Each question is asked in exactly the same manner (and order) to each respondent who then identifies the best/most appropriate response (Fitzgerald & Cox, 1994; Patton, 1987). The goal is to make sure that each question is answered in the exact same manner so that the responses can be easily identified and analyzed. Exhibit 1 illustrates a partial example of a structured interview asking about club drug use by college students. Note the types of questions being asked. Each respondent will be asked the same question, in the same order, and in some questions, the respondent will be provided appropriate response categories. All answers will be recorded by the interviewer. However, one of the basic assumptions of structured interviews is that each respondent understands each question and interprets its meaning in exactly the same way. As Berg (1989) suggests, these assumptions are largely based on faith.

Because structured interviews utilize a predetermined list of questions, the interviewer is not able to gain any additional insight into the respondent's answers by asking additional or clarifying questions. While this may seem like a severe limitation to using such interviews, it does serve to increase the consistency of responses. Patton (1987) argues that structured interviews are to be "used when it is important to minimize variation in the questions posed to interviewees. It may be particularly appropriate when several people are to conduct interviews. . . . (L)eft to themselves, different interviewers will ask questions on the same topic in different ways" (1987:113). Further, if the researcher anticipates that certain questions may need clarification, the clarification is written directly into the interview. The same is true for potential probing questions (Babbie, 2002; Patton, 1987). In fact, Babbie (2002) suggests that if a respondent provides an inappropriate response to a question, it is acceptable to probe. For example, an interviewer may ask the question: "During a typical week, how many times do you use club drugs" and the possible answer choices are: 0, 1-2, 3-4, 5-6, or more than six. The respondent replies, "Oh, maybe 4 or 5." The interviewer could

---

Exhibit 1
Structured Interviews: Exploring Drug Use Among College Students

---

The interviewer will ask each participant the following questions and record all answers. In some cases, the appropriate underlined word will simply be circled. This interview will *not* be tape-recorded.

Confidentiality Number: _____

Birth date: _____

Sex: _____

Race: _____

Have you ever used any illicit drugs?   ☐ Yes   ☐ No

Have you ever used:

Marijuana	☐ Yes	☐ No	Where did exposure occur? _____
Ecstasy	☐ Yes	☐ No	Where did exposure occur? _____
Speed	☐ Yes	☐ No	Where did exposure occur? _____
GHB	☐ Yes	☐ No	Where did exposure occur? _____

. . . . continued list

List age when first used the above drugs. (Write the age to the left of the drug.)

Have you ever given illicit drugs to someone? Have you ever sold illicit drugs?

Have you ever been given drugs without knowing it?

Have you ever given someone drugs without their knowledge? Explain.

Have you ever used alcohol to facilitate sex? Explain.

Have you ever gotten someone else drunk to have sex? Explain.

Have you ever used a "date rape" drug on someone to have sex with them? Explain.

Source: Adapted from Johnson, K.A. & J.C. Kunselman. (Current Study). "Club Drug Use by College Students: A Trend Analysis." Summer Research Grant funded by the University of West Florida.

(and probably should) use a probing question like, "Would you say that 4 or 5 is more typical because it is necessary for me to check one of the answer categories." If the respondent cannot make the distinction between 4 or 5 (or refuses to do so), the interviewer should simply write down that the respondent indicated 4 or 5 times. Exhibit 2 illustrates a slightly different format for a structured interview. Notice that these questions seem to be less structured, in appearance, yet note the probing questions and the written comments that are included in case a question needs clarification.

Research projects where the interviewer is able to identify all of the relevant questions to be asked are amenable to using a structured interview. Of course, it is important that considerable attention is paid to the wording and ordering of questions and that great care is taken to ensure that the respondents will be able to clearly understand what is being asked of them. Some of the advantages and disadvantages of structured interviews are discussed below.

Exhibit 2
Structured Interview: Male Strippers

Background

Where are you from? *(Probe: where born, lived, live now)*

Family? Parents' occupations? How do you interact with family:

Still see them regularly?

How do they react to dancing?

Schooling   When? Where? What?

What other jobs currently? In past?

Other performing jobs/activities?

How long have you been dancing? *(Probe: career, this town, this location)*

How did you start in this field? *(Clarify response: friends, money, desire?)*

Do you intend to continue with this? How long? Why/why not?

How often do you dance? *(Get idea of daily, weekly etc.)* Where? *(city, club name)*

Income:

Good/bad? Vary by locations? What do you do to improve tips? *(Probe for specifics)*

Different techniques for different locations/audiences? *(Clarify how do you know)*

When working an audience, how can you tell if someone will tip? *(Probe for specifics)*

Describe a "typical" audience in five words.

In terms of performance, do you see yourself as a "sex symbol"? *(has it always been?)*

Do you believe your performance is sexually stimulating? *(Clarify for whom)*

Do you feel stimulated by your performance?

Source: Adapted from (a) Tewksbury, R. (1994). "A Dramaturgical Analysis of Male Strippers." *Journal of Men's Studies*, 2(4):325-342; (b) Tewksbury, R. (1993). "Male Strippers: Men Objectifying Men." In *Doing 'Women's Work': Men in Nontraditional Occupations*, edited by Christine L. Williams. Newbury Park, CA: Sage Publications.

Advantages

Structured interviews offer a number of advantages over self-administered surveys or questionnaires. First, an interview will likely result in a higher response rate than a mail survey. Babbie (2002) argues that "A properly designed and executed interview . . . ought to achieve a completion rate of at least 80-85 percent. Respondents seem more reluctant to turn down an interviewer standing on their doorstep than to throw away a mailed questionnaire" (2002:261). Second, when being asked a specific question, respondents are less likely to reply with "I don't know" or "Not applicable." Again, Babbie (2002) suggests the advantage of using probing questions to minimize the "no answers" during an interview, which are not possible when conducting a self-administered survey or questionnaire ("If you had to pick one of the answers, which do you think would come closest to your feelings?") (2002:262). Third, if a respondent clearly does not understand the meaning of the question, the interviewer is able to clarify the meaning (within a very limited scope) of the question. Finally, because the interviewer is present, he or she is able to observe the respondents as they answer the questions. This allows the interviewer to note any situational variables during the interview. Returning to the club drug example, if an interviewer is conducting an interview in a respondent's home, he or she is able to observe the conditions of the residence, including any drugs or drug related paraphernalia in plain view (e.g., posters, glow sticks, pipes, or rolling papers). The interviewer is also able to get a general "feel" for the respondent's reactions to the questions (Babbie, 2002). While the presence of an interviewer can improve the quality of the interview, it is important to remember that the presence of an interviewer must not have any impact on the respondent or the answers provided. "In other words, the interviewer should be a neutral medium through which questions and answers are transmitted" (Babbie, 2002:262).

Structured interviews also are advantageous on their own merit. First, other researchers are able to easily replicate the study when they can use the same interview with a different sample. These researchers will know precisely what was asked (and, what was not asked) in the previous study. Second, interviews are appropriate for almost any kind of respondent, including those who cannot read or write. This is especially important considering that many of the groups that criminal justice researchers want information about (e.g., prisoners, juveniles), may have reading and writing skills that are sufficiently deficient. Interviews are one of only a few methods of obtaining data from these populations (see the discussion on Focus Groups below). Third, because the format is structured (standardized), a researcher can employ a number of trained assistants to conduct the interviews without being too concerned about variations across interviewers or in responses, thereby minimizing interviewer effects (Patton, 1987). Finally, because of the structured question/response format, data coding and analysis is much easier than it is with other types of interviewing. Coding is accomplished by simply associating a numerical value with each of the responses and entering those numbers into a database. Typically, the analyses of these type data are quantitative and can be completed much more quickly than having to read through pages and pages of written narrative-type responses.

Disadvantages

One primary disadvantage of structured interviews is that because they are so structured and there is no room for elaboration, "it restricts the pursuit of topics or issues that were not anticipated when the interview was written" (Patton, 1987:114). In addition, it does not allow an interviewer to use different wording or slightly different questions with different respondents, based on the needs of the respondents. For example, when interviewing college students about club drug use (college students are assumed to be both literate and be able to understand most terminology related to drug use), the interviewer asks if the student has ever used a nutritional supplement. If the respondent does not fully understand what constitutes a nutritional supplement, it can result in a misleading or misinformed response. It is important to note that the researcher *should* build into the interview examples of nutritional supplements in case this question arises. Clearly, using a standardized interview format has the potential to mask individual differences and circumstances between respondents (Patton, 1987). A second disadvantage is the high cost of conducting a large-scale interview study. If a researcher wants to interview either a large number of people or wants to conduct interviews with a smaller number of respondents, but over a long period of time, the costs can be considerable.

Examples of Structured Interviews

One interesting study used structured phone interviews not only to obtain information regarding the respondents' sexual behavior, but also to attempt to determine the truthfulness of the response (Catania, Binson, Canchola, Pollack, Hauck & Coates, 1996). Because adults typically underreport their sexual behavior, the researchers anticipated that the respondents would be even less forthcoming when being asked about "questionable" sexual behavior. The authors used a standard survey that was based on established AIDS and human sexuality studies. While the use of a structured interview was necessary to obtain the data, the focus of the research was to find out how to encourage truthful responses.

Some of the respondents were given the option of having an interviewer from the same or the opposite gender. The others were randomly assigned to one or the other. This was done in order to eliminate any interviewer effect on the honesty of the respondent. In addition, the respondents were randomly assigned to receive either the "standard" or "enhanced" item questions. A standard question (asked of heterosexual men) reads:

Have you ever had sex of any kind with another male?

An enhanced question (also asked of heterosexual men) reads:

In past surveys, many men have reported that at some point in their life they have had some type of sexual experience with another male. This could have happened before adolescence, during adolescence, or as an adult. Have you ever had sex of any kind with a male at some point in your life?

Results indicated that regardless of the gender of the interviewer, 3.3 percent of the men answered "yes" to the standard question whereas 6.2 percent answered "yes" to the enhanced question. With respect to possible interviewer effects based on gender, 5.9 percent of men responded "yes" to male interviewers and only 3.6 percent of the men responded "yes" to a female interviewer, regardless of whether it was the standard or enhanced question. The results of this research illustrate the importance of the wording of interview questions, especially when addressing what some would see as questionable sexual behavior. In this case, it would seem that using an enhanced question would result in "more truthful" responses. This study also emphasizes the need to recognize that the gender of an interviewer may play a role in gaining truthful responses. Depending on the sensitivity of the topic to be studied, it may be beneficial to make sure that the interviewer and the interviewee are the same gender.

Grella, Chaiken, and Anglin (1995) also employed a structured interview as a "screening process" to determine who was a suitable candidate for a methadone treatment program. They anticipated that because many of their potential candidates would be desperate to obtain free methadone treatments, many of them would lie in order to meet the eligibility requirements. In order to be eligible, the candidate had to be either: HIV positive, a gay/bisexual male, a prostitute, or a sex partner of one of these persons. Built into the interview were specific questions designed to verify their eligibility. For example, those who claimed to be HIV positive were required to produce medical documentation. Those who said they were prostitutes were asked about the number of "dates" they had per week and about how much money they made. Any responses outside the norm were further screened. In some cases, especially for those who claimed to be a sex partner only, candidates were asked to bring their partner in for additional questioning.

They found that almost one-third of the potential candidates had falsified at least some of the information they provided. Two-thirds of these "liars" did not meet any of the eligibility requirements, while the remaining one-third were eligible even without lying about it. Clearly, the use of the structured interview allowed the researchers to identify those who were legitimately eligible for the program. Perhaps more importantly, the use of the structured interview in this situation demonstrated that information obtained through an interview methodology can in fact be "tested for truthfulness."

Catania et al. (1996) were able to use a structured interview in such a way that they were able to test some degree of both interviewer effects and truthfulness of respondents. Grella et al. (1995) specifically tested the truthfulness of respondents. Note, however, that the level of desperation to obtain free methadone may be a powerful force and that these individuals may really be "truthful" people. Not all structured interviews offer such an opportunity, but the recognition of the diversity of structured interviews is important. The results of these research projects also shed considerable light on the importance of preparing quality interviews and recognizing that even with a structured interview, there can be situations (e.g., interviewer effects, truthfulness) that challenge the validity of the findings.

Semi-Structured Interviews

A semi-structured or semi-standardized interview, as the title implies, includes some structure to the interview, but allows more freedom for the interviewer and the respondent to interject additional questions, comments, and answers throughout the interview process. According to Williamson, Karp, and Dalphin (1977), this type of interview permits the interviewer to collect some types of data that are consistent across respondents (e.g., age, gender, race, marital status) "as well as other data derived from questions tailored to take advantage of the unique experiences and perspectives of each individual" (1977:176). Such semi-structured interviews contain specific topic areas to be asked about during the interview, but allow for additional input by both the interviewer and the respondent. This approach allows more flexibility in obtaining data and can provide the researcher with valuable information that would not have been available through a structured interview.

Instead of using a predetermined list of questions to be asked of each respondent without any variation, a semi-structured interview employs an interview guide. An interview guide is a list of questions or topics to be discussed during the course of the interview. By using the guide, the interviewer is able to systematically ask each respondent the same questions, but still has enough latitude to explore related areas. In fact, interviewers may be expected to use probing questions to explore beyond the interview guide (Berg, 1989; Patton, 1987).

The interview guide used in semi-structured interviewing can be more or less detailed and specific. The detail of the interview guide depends on how important it is to identify topics in advance, and the need to ask all of the questions in the same order (Patton, 1987). In fact, Patton suggests it is most important that the interviewer simply cover all the topics that are included in the interview guide, not necessarily that the questions be asked in a specific order or with the same words. That is, one benefit of the semi-structured interview is the ability to alter the wording and the order of the questions so that the flow of the conversation is natural.

For example, suppose a student athlete is being asked a question regarding her use of club drugs. During the course of the response, the student implies that she is also a member of a sorority. Membership in other university organizations or groups is a topic on the interview guide, but not at that point. At this time, however, the interviewer should explore the student's views on how her membership in a sorority is related to club drug use instead of waiting until the topic is listed on the interview guide. Exhibit 3 provides an example of an interview guide created to obtain data from people who are HIV positive. Note how many of the questions complement each other with regard to content, and therefore might be answered with a similar or interconnected response (e.g., how life has changed and the state of health). It is imperative that the interviewer be able to alter wording or question order in an attempt to keep a conversational flow to the interview. This natural conversational flow allows the interviewer to continuously gain valuable insight and also helps the interviewee feel more at ease; more like a discussion than an interview. Notice the opportunities throughout for the interviewer to delve for additional or confirmatory information.

Exhibit 3
Semi-Structured Interview Guide: Individuals with HIV

Confidentiality: Is it ok to tape?

When were you first diagnosed?
    When did you first learn you were HIV+?
    Why did you get tested?
    How did you react to the positive test result?
    Who did you tell?
    What were the reactions of the people you told?

How has your life changed since first testing positive?
    How has your life changed since being diagnosed?

What has been the general state of your health? (how has your illness progressed?)

What impact has there been on your social life?
    Family? Friends?
    Membership in groups/organizations? Political activism?
    Sex life?

Have you seen changes in how people interact with you since they have learned of your HIV status?

Do any of your friends also have AIDS?
    Were these friends from before your diagnosis?
    Have you made any new friends since, or because of, your diagnosis?

Why should people care?

What has been the *worst* thing about having AIDS?   . . . the *best* thing about having AIDS?

What is the one thing you would like to have others (people who do not have AIDS) know about the experience of having AIDS?

Source: Adapted from (a) Tewksbury, R. (1994). "'Speaking of Someone with AIDS. . .': Identity Constructions of Persons with HIV Disease." *Deviant Behavior*, 15(4):337-355; (b) Tewksbury, R. & D. McGaughey (1997). "Stigmatization of Persons with HIV Disease: Perceptions, Management and Consequences of AIDS." *Sociological Spectrum*, 17(1):49-70.

One way to explore a related topic is through the use of probing questions, or probes. Unlike the structured interview where probes are built into the interview, semi-structured interview guides do not necessarily have predetermined probes. Rather, the interviewer is responsible for recognizing the opportunity to draw out additional information from the respondent. As the respondent is talking, the interviewer must remain attentive to what is being said. If the interviewer wants to know more about that particular topic or wants to explore a related area, he or she should ask through the use of a probing question. Probing questions, such as "Could you tell me more about that?" or "How long have you been doing this?" allow the respondent to elaborate on a particular answer. It is also possible (perhaps critical) to probe topic areas that the respondent has not referenced. Lofland and Lofland (1984) suggest saying things like "Did ____ happen?" or "Was ____ a consequence?" (1984:56).

It is important to remember that probing questions must be neutral in themselves. They must not lead the respondent to answer in a particular manner nor should they add information to questions or answers already discussed (Berg, 1989; Babbie, 2002). While not necessary, in some cases it is useful to provide some suggested probes for items in the interview guide. According to Babbie (2002) providing probes for the interviewer has two important advantages. "First, you'll have more time to devise the best, most neutral probes. Second, all interviewers will use the same probes whenever they're needed. Thus, even if the probe isn't perfectly neutral, all respondents will be presented with the same stimulus" (2002:264).

Advantages

Like structured interviews, semi-structured interviews typically have a higher response rate and fewer "no answers" than a self-administered paper-and-pen survey. Further, because the interviewer is present, he or she can clarify any questions the respondent may have, as well as make observations about the location. In fact, there is benefit in the additional flexibility of semi-structured interviews to clarify questions and answers. Consider again, for example, the researcher who is interviewing the college student about club drug use. In response to a question about a "typical weekend," the student mentions "going fishing." The interviewer does not understand how that fits into club drugs. A semi-structured format allows the interviewer to ask about the specific meaning of that statement. By clarifying the response, the interviewer now knows that "going fishing" means looking for drugs rather than taking out a rod and reel and heading for the lake!

Another advantage of the semi-structured format is that, because it is more conversational than the structured interview, the interviewer and the respondent typically establish a closer rapport with each other. In that way, the interviewer is more likely to get accurate responses to sensitive or personal topics. Further, because of the flexibility of the semi-structured interview, sensitive questions can be addressed from a variety of different perspectives rather than being asked verbatim. Finally, if during the course of the interview, the interviewer gets the sense that the respondent is not being completely truthful, the interviewer can ask a question or questions that can be used to test the truthfulness of the original answer.

Disadvantages

There are several disadvantages to using a semi-structured interview, all of which relate to its "flexibility" in questioning. First, it is difficult, if not impossible, to replicate a study that uses this method. This is problematic in the respect that replication of research projects serves to validate information across time, geographic location, and study populations. Second, because each interview is conducted on an individual basis, the consistency of questions and responses may vary greatly across interviews thereby making it difficult to derive meaningful analyses from the data. However, this may not be a major problem when the interview data are used in concert with other data collection methods (e.g., participant observation) or when the data elaborate or supplement other data (e.g., a questionnaire). Finally, because a semi-structured interview is less formal than its structured counterpart, there is the possibility that the interview will get "off track." It is up to the interviewer to make sure the interview guide is followed. Therefore, it is critical that interviewers are trained properly.

Examples of Semi-Structured Interviews

Iliffe and Steed (2000) used a semi-structured interview to explore an area that is typically ignored in the research on domestic violence. They wanted to know about counselors' experiences in working with offenders and victims of domestic violence. The use of a semi-structured interview allowed the researchers to gather common data from respondents (age, years of working experience, caseload size, and amount of training). The interviews also provided the researchers with rich descriptive data regarding the experience of the counselors.

Their results indicated that counselors often feel a loss of confidence when beginning work with domestic violence clients. In addition, even though they knew they were not responsible for their clients' situations, they felt more responsible than they did with other clients. Their feelings about the trauma experienced by the clients were more intense than for other clients, they often felt less secure in their own lives, they saw the domestic violence clients as more challenging, experienced burnout more quickly, and often felt powerless. This information likely would not have come to light had a different methodology been used.

Decker (1996) conducted a three-year study of gang activity in St. Louis. Prior to beginning the study, a series of unstructured interviews were conducted (to be discussed in the next section) in order to gain enough information to create a semi-structured interview. During these unstructured interviews, the respondents were asked for information about joining the gang, the nature of gang organization, illegal activities (especially violence), legal activities, links to other gangs, and ties to traditional institutions. Common information across respondents was also gathered. For example, they were able to identify the age, race, and gender of the gang member, how long he or she had been an active gang member, and how long the gang had existed. In addition, by using a semi-structured interview, information about gang structure and organization, the amount of violent activity (gang and nongang related) in which gang members engage, how each member defined the term "gang," violence related to joining and leaving the gang, and turf could also be obtained.

Both of these studies offer insight into worlds previously left unstudied. Iliffe and Steed (2000) used semi-structured interviews to explore the impact that working with domestic violence offenders and victims has on the counselors. This information can be used to develop coping strategies and make sure that the counselors have adequate support networks available. Decker (1996) was able to empirically illustrate gang life in such a way that the knowledge gained by his research allows law enforcement, social services, and academics to understand the complex dynamics of gang life. While violence is a core component of gang life, it is necessary to see the larger perspective if there is any hope of trying to reduce or eliminate gang violence. Using semi-structured interviews was critical to gaining the quality and depth of information provided in these studies. Structured interviews would not have allowed the researchers to gain insight into areas previously ignored in the literature.

Unstructured Interviews

Unstructured, informal, unstandardized, or intensive interviews are much more flexible than either the structured or semi-structured interview. They typically have some type of general framework from which the interviewer will operate. Both the interviewer and the respondent are free to ad-lib questions and responses. An unstructured interview is more like a guided conversation from which the interviewer gleans rich, detailed information.

Informal interviews are often used when a researcher is conducting an exploratory study or when the researcher needs detailed information that cannot be obtained using any other method. Often, questions asked during an unstructured interview are open-ended and the exact order of the questions may not be predetermined. "Rather, the interviewer explores preselected general question areas, follows up on particular responses, and pursues additional topics suggested by the respondent" (Fitzgerald & Cox, 1994:99).

Unstructured interviews begin with a different set of assumptions about the nature of the interview. The researcher realizes that there is no way to know, in advance, exactly what questions, or even what kinds of questions should be asked (Berg, 1989; Patton, 1987). Therefore, it is impossible to create a detailed and specific (or all inclusive) interview guide. Further, given the nature of the research topic, it is likely that not all of the respondents will understand the meaning of the questions in the same way as the researcher understands them (a requirement for structured interviews). This is especially the case when the interviewer and the respondent come from "different worlds." For example, a researcher may be unfamiliar with the respondent's lifestyle, religious or ethnic background, culture, or customs and therefore the "interviewers must develop, adapt, and generate questions and follow-up probes appropriate to the given situation . . . This results in appropriate and relevant questions arising from the process of interactions during the interview itself" (Berg, 1989:17).

Exhibit 4 is an example of the types of ideas that one interviewer wanted to discuss with men concerning their use of personal ads to "pick up" other men. Notice the difference in structure and form from the structured and semi-structured interview guides. Here, the researcher simply outlines five distinct areas or issues to cover, and leaves the remainder of the interview to "unstructured conversation" where the researcher generates questions relevant to each specific interview.

Exhibit 4
Unstructured Interview: Men and Personal Ads

When did you start using ads? Why?

What type of men do you meet with ads?

Why do men use personal ads?

What makes a "good" ad? (Or, what is it that determines the ads to which you respond?)

What are the advantages/disadvantages of meeting men this way? Explain.

Source: Tewksbury, R. (Current study). "Experiences of Men Seeking Men via Personal Ads."

The unstructured interview is similar to an informal conversation in that the interaction is generated by the natural and often spontaneous question-and-answer dialogue between the interviewer and respondent. Unstructured interviews can take place as part of an ongoing participant observation (Berg, 1989; Patton, 1987), but may also be conducted as a stand-alone research project. In this case, the respondent may not even realize that he or she is being interviewed. Rather, it will be perceived as a conversation that takes place in the course of the observation.

This conversational type of interview allows both the interviewer and the respondent to discover the important topics of interest as they talk. It also allows the researcher to gain additional information that cannot be gleaned from observation alone. In fact, Patton (1987) argues that such interviews are useful when there are things that cannot be observed directly. "We cannot observe feelings, thoughts, and intentions. We cannot observe behaviors that took place at some previous point in time. We cannot observe situations that preclude the presence of an observer. We cannot observe how people have organized the world and the meanings they attach to what goes on in the world" (1987:109). Although more structured interviews could be used in these cases, unstructured interviews provide a situation for the interviewer to gain in-depth and information rich responses.

Because each interview develops with the conversation, the data gathered during unstructured interviews will be different for each person interviewed. If an unstructured interview is being used to complement an observation (either participant or nonparticipant), it may be possible to interview the same person on several different occasions. That way, it is not necessary to try to collect all of the information during a single discussion. Take, for example, a life history interview. Imagine how difficult it would be to get someone's entire life-history in one sitting. Instead, the researcher is able to adapt interview questions over time, and build upon preceding ones, thereby "expanding information that was picked up previously, moving in new directions, seeking elucidations and elaborations from various respondents in their own terms" (Patton, 1987:110).

Advantages

The primary advantage of the unstructured interview is that it allows the interviewer to adapt to individual differences and situations as they arise. Therefore, the interviewer is able to individualize the questions to the respondent in such a way that personal and in-depth data can be obtained (Patton, 1987). Truly rich, qualitative data that is often more extensive and insightful than quantitative data can be obtained through this type of interviewing. In addition, unstructured interviews are beneficial when the researcher does not know everything to ask, in advance, and can therefore explore situations and topics as they arise. For example, life histories offer a complete and comprehensive glimpse into the world of people who might otherwise go unnoticed. It would be impossible to know, in advance, every possible question to be asked of a madam, a professional fence, female street hustlers, or a professional thief. However, unstructured interviews can elaborate on the life histories of these individuals and provide researchers with incredibly valuable information that perhaps they did not even know they wanted.

Disadvantages

One disadvantage to unstructured interviews is that they are time- and labor-intensive. As discussed above, they are often included as part of an observational methodology (also time and labor intensive). In addition, the amount of time it takes to transcribe field notes and/or audiotape recordings and analyze the data is significant.

Clearly, this type of interview is subject to interviewer effects to a greater degree than either the structured or semi-structured format. Patton (1987) offers that unstructured interviews are highly dependent upon the ability of the interviewer to carry on a conversation. In this vein, it is critical that the interviewer be one who can "interact easily with people in a variety of settings, must be able to generate rapid insights, to formulate questions quickly and smoothly, and to guard against asking questions that impose interpretations on the situation by the structure of the questions" (1987:111).

Examples of Unstructured Interviews

Hopper and Moore (1990) have conducted research on outlaw motorcycle gangs for almost two decades and their study of female bikers is groundbreaking. Their research included both participant-observation and unstructured interviews, a frequent combination.

Having participated in "biker life" for many years, the researchers were able to identify the characteristics of the women involved in motorcycle gangs. In addition to their observations, the researchers conducted unstructured interviews with motorcycle gang members throughout their years of studying them. They report that women were reluctant to speak to them when men were present. Although the men did not instruct the women to remain quiet, it was understood that women played a subservient role and frequently "did not know" anything when asked in the presence of men. However, when the men were absent, the women spoke frequently, articulately, and intelligently. The women "belonged" to men and were often passed around for sexual favors. By and large, the women did not see anything wrong with this behavior and accepted that role.

Perhaps the only method acceptable to get a clear and comprehensive picture of life in an outlaw motorcycle gang is unstructured interviews. Clearly, it is highly unlikely that bikers will take time to fill out questionnaires or to allow their lives to be recorded on videotape or audiotape. In fact, Hopper and Moore (1990) report that it was extremely difficult to gain the trust of this group so it is also unlikely that they would submit to semi-structured interviews. Also, to have access to such a small and hard-to-find group adds significant value to the information they report. Further, because of the length of their study and their use of unstructured interviews, Hopper and Moore (1990) were able to chronicle how female bikers have changed over time.

Crimmins, Langley, Brownstein, and Spunt (1997) conducted life history interviews with 42 women who were incarcerated for killing a child, in most cases, their own child or children. They wanted to understand the experiences and the inner perspectives of these women. Were they too "damaged" to care for their children? Why did they resort to such acts? What factors influenced their lives and their development? The only way to obtain such information is through unstructured life-history interviews. The characteristics of these women indicated that many of them were "motherless" mothers, there was a history of drug/alcohol abuse in the family as well as a history of their own drug use, and many were victims of abuse as children and that cycle continued into adulthood. This means that not only did the women enter into abusive relationships, but they also were abusive to their children and to themselves. Clearly, these women experienced a number of situations that "damaged" them to the point that they were unable to care for their own children.

One of the key purposes for conducting this research was to get a more comprehensive picture of these women. Unstructured interviews would allow the researchers to explore who and what these women are, not just label them "bad" or "mad" as had been done in previous research. The women in this study were asked what kinds of programs or assistance would be valuable for women like them. Almost one-half of them suggested programming that would improve their self-esteem. They felt like they must be in charge of their own lives and not rely on a dysfunctional relationship. They stated that their own feelings of worthlessness put themselves and their children in danger. Further, because they were in prison for killing children, they were ostracized by the other women. Therefore, they sought programs or assistance that would help them deal with the loss of their children, because they were not likely to receive that support from the other female prisoners. Other methodologies, including structured and semi-structured interviews, could not have produced the rich, qualitative data obtained by unstructured interviews.

Both of these research projects sought out a group of women who had been ignored in the research. Through the use of unstructured interviews, the researchers were able to create an illustration of who these women are. Hopper and Moore (1990) highlighted what it is like to be a female outlaw biker. While outsiders typically think that the women are being mistreated and used as property, the biker women do not see any mistreatment and, in fact, enjoy belonging to "their man" and doing whatever he says, regardless of how it is perceived by those who are not members of the motorcycle gang. Crimmins et al. (1997) focused their research on a group of women who had killed their children in order to illuminate the dynamics that resulted in such violence. Society is quick to write off these women as evil or crazy, and is unable to comprehend what could drive a woman to kill a child, especially her own. As a result of this research, there is a better understanding of the complex processes that have driven these women. Further, the research offers suggestions for programs and assistance to help women before they get to the breaking point as well as for those whose lives have already been eternally altered.

Focus Groups

Focus groups or group in-depth interviews have become an increasingly popular research method for those studying criminal justice. Although focus groups have been used commonly by market researchers, social scientists are finding them more and more useful (Krueger, 1994). According to Stewart and Shamdasani (1990), a focus group is "an interview among a number of interacting individuals having a community of interest that is limited to a small number of issues" (1990:10). Most focus groups consist of 8-12 people and a moderator (interviewer) who come together to discuss a particular topic. It is important to make sure that the focus group is not too small or too large. If there are too few people, it is likely that the discussion will be dominated by only a couple of the members. If the group gets too large, it is difficult to control and may stray from the topic (Krueger, 1994; Stewart & Shamdasani, 1990).

Most focus groups last anywhere from one to two and one-half hours and are most often conducted in a variety of locations including homes, offices, or even via conference call. However, under *ideal* circumstances, a focus group will be conducted in a location specifically set up for such a purpose. This location provides "one-way mirrors . . . , viewing rooms where observers unobtrusively may observe the interview in progress. . . . equipment for audiotaping or videotaping of the interview and perhaps even a small transmitter for the moderator to wear so that observers may have input into the interviews" (Stewart & Shamdasani, 1990:10). It is important to note, however, that most social scientists do not have such facilities. Often, the focus group will take place around a conference table with one person being the moderator and another operating a tape recorder and taking notes.

The moderator is responsible for making sure the group stays focused on the topics to be discussed. Therefore, he or she must be well trained both in interviewing and in group dynamics. The moderator typically does not get overly involved in the discussion, rather he or she lets the discussion take its own course, as long as it remains related to the topic of interest (Krueger, 1994; Stewart & Shamdasani, 1990). The general idea is that the participants will respond to and expand upon each other's comments. Exhibit 5 provides a basic outline to be used by one moderator during a focus group.

Focus groups can be used as a way of obtaining information that can later be used to create a questionnaire or survey. Specifically, a researcher can employ a focus group in order to discern what topics are important to ask in a survey, structured, or semi-structured interview. For example, prior to creating an interview guide to study college students' use of club drugs, it might be advisable for the researcher to conduct a focus group. By guiding a discussion about club drug use, the researcher should be able to identify the salient issues (as the students see them), understand the context in which students talk about club drugs, and identify a variety of categories for closed-ended survey items. Without using a focus group to ascertain this kind of information, it would be very difficult for a researcher to design a survey or an interview guide that is relevant to college student club drug use.

Exhibit 5
Focus Group: Residents of Housing Authority

Purpose: Gain an understanding of issues affecting quality of life in communities.

First name and how long lived here:

What are the most common problems in this community?

Common belief is that public housing is "full of crime"; is this true here?

Are drugs common here?

What other crimes are common in this community?

How often are Bright Leaf County police in the community?

What are interactions with Housing Authority of Bright Leaf County staff like?

Do you like living here? Why/why not?

Source: Adapted from Walsh, W.F., F.V. Gennaro, R. Tewksbury & G.P. Wilson (2000). "Fighting Back in Bright Leaf: Community Policing and Drug Trafficking in Public Housing." *American Journal of Criminal Justice*, 25(1):77-92.

In addition to using focus groups as a method of gaining information for future research, they can also be used to confirm or elaborate on data already gathered (Krueger, 1994). Suppose, for example, a researcher has conducted a self-administered questionnaire asking students their opinions about club drug use in general. Much of the data are quantitative in nature and the researcher wants to get a more in-depth understanding about these drugs. The researcher could facilitate a focus group that includes participants who are demographically similar to those who completed the questionnaire in an attempt to gain a greater understanding of the complex nature of club drug use.

Stewart and Shamdasani (1990) identify the following as common uses of focus groups:

1. Obtaining general background information about a topic of interest;

2. Generating research hypotheses that can be submitted to further research and testing using more quantitative approaches;

3. Stimulating new ideas and creative concepts;

4. Diagnosing the potential for problems with a new program, service, or product;

5. Generating impressions of products, programs, services, institutions, or other objects of interest;

6. Learning how respondents talk about the phenomenon of interest. This, in turn, may facilitate the design of questionnaires, survey instruments, or other research tools that might be employed in more quantitative research; and

7. Interpreting previously obtained quantitative results (1990:15).

Advantages

Focus groups are widely used because they provide qualitative information and offer the researcher a number of advantages. First, focus groups are a relatively quick and inexpensive way of gathering data on just about any topic from just about any group of people (Krueger, 1994). Compare, for example, the time and financial costs of conducting a focus group to interviewing 8-12 people individually. Further, like interviews in general, focus groups are one method that is conducive to obtaining data from those who are unable to read and/or write.

Like the semi-structured and unstructured interviews discussed above, focus groups provide the opportunity for the group members to clarify their responses, for the moderator to ask follow-up questions and to probe for additional information (Krueger, 1994). Similarly, because the interviewer (moderator, in this case) is present, he or she is able to note observations about nonverbal communications among the group members. For example, "gestures, smiles, frowns, and so forth, which may carry information that supplements (and, on occasion, even contradicts) the verbal response" (Stewart & Shamdasani, 1990:16).

Further, focus groups usually result in large amounts of rich, qualitative data generated by the group members themselves. Again, the semi-structured and unstructured interviews offer the same type of advantage in that the researcher can often gain a more complete and comprehensive picture than is created by a more quantitative approach (e.g., a structured interview or self-administered survey). Finally, the group setting allows for the creation of group dynamics. In other words, one member's response may piggyback a previous response and "this synergistic effect of the group setting may result in the production of data or ideas that might not have been uncovered in individual interviews" (Stewart & Shamdasani, 1990:16). In this way, focus groups have an advantage over all types of interviews in that the participants are cultivating their contributions from each other's ideas; thereby expanding the pool of topics and information that can be obtained.

Disadvantages

One primary disadvantage of focus groups is the fact that they are conducted using a small group. In addition, the group is usually made up of a convenience sample. Both of these facts make the generalizability of results difficult. In fact, Stewart and Shamdasani (1990) suggest that people who are willing to participate (especially when it involves travel) in a two-hour focus group may be very different from the general population.

Similar to the semi-structured and unstructured interviews, the vast amount of data, often qualitative in nature, makes it difficult to code, analyze, and interpret. Also, the moderator may create interviewer effects if he or she shows any bias or models any behavior that either encourages or discourages particular types of responses (Krueger, 1994).

Although the interaction between the group members (including the moderator) can serve as an advantage, there are also disadvantages associated with such interaction. Because group member B may respond to a comment made by group member A, group member B's response may not be a response to the topic raised by the moderator. Rather, it is a response to member A. This may further affect the generalizability of results. Also, if the focus group contains one or more dominant or highly vocal members, the results may be biased in that those who have different ideas or opinions may not offer them (Stewart & Shamdasani, 1990).

Because responses are coming from "live people" and not presented as statistically significant findings, Stewart and Shamdasani (1990) suggest that the researcher may be inclined to have more faith in and see the results as being more credible than they actually are. It is important to remember that people lie, they say what they think others want to hear, they are disgruntled, and they may simply be misinformed. Therefore, researchers must keep in proper perspective the credibility of a focus group discussion.

Examples of Focus Groups

Short, McMahon, Chervin, and Shelley (2000) conducted focus groups of women who were survivors of intimate partner violence. In fact, one of the requirements for participation in the focus group was that the women could no longer be in an abusive relationship. The moderator probed the areas interest which included early warning signs of violence, reasons for staying in the abusive relationship, the process of ending the relationship, and those factors that would help these women continue to live lives without interpersonal violence.

The results of the focus group revealed that early warning signs included knowledge about the abuser's history of family violence or actually witnessing such violence, a whirlwind romance, extreme charm on the part of the abuser, his jealousy and efforts to control her. The women stated that they stayed in the abusive relationships out of love, commitment to wedding vows, desire to keep the family together, lack of financial resources, emotional dependence, fear, shame, hopelessness, and/or because they hoped things would change. The major benefit of this research is that it provides a wealth of information and strategies from women who have, somehow, found the strength and support to leave abusive relationships. By employing a focus group design, the researchers were able to obtain information from a group of women who likely felt more comfortable in a group setting (given their circumstances and the purpose of this research). Therefore, it is possible that they provided more information than they would have had individual interviews been conducted.

Using focus groups from a slightly different perspective, Wortz (1999) discusses their value for understanding how potential jurors will view medical negligence cases. Attorneys frequently use mock jurors and simulated deliberations to help decide how "real" jurors might act in a given case. A focus group application is simply a formalization of their earlier processes. This focus group was convened to try and discover what jurors think doctors "could" have done vs. what they "should" have done, what they think of medical care in general, who would be to blame if the victim is a child (the doctor or the parents), what jurors think the role monetary rewards are, and what impact their own personal experiences have on their decision-making processes.

While medical negligence is a complicated area, the results of this focus group study were used to identify the areas where attorneys should be especially prepared at trial. For example, during the opening statement, attorneys should focus only on the basic medical issues, and let the experts discuss medical facts. Time-lines and glossaries are extremely useful exhibits during trial. Brevity is also critical if the attorney wants to avoid intimidating the jurors. Attorneys should ensure that key terminology (e.g., standard of care) is fully and completely understood, both from the hospital's policy and the medical experts who will testify. Finally, jurors have little tolerance for lack of, or poor, communication and sloppy record-keeping. Minimize the use of evidence that demonstrates either of these situations. It is difficult to imagine gaining this type of insight into jury behavior through any other research design. In fact, it is likely that the only other way to obtain this type of information would be through retrospective studies of previous jury members. Sometimes, after-the-fact, is too late.

Obviously, focus groups can be used for many different research topics, as demonstrated by these two highly divergent projects. On the one hand, Short et al. (2000) proffer insight into the complex processes of interpersonal violence. In addition, the data provided by the women in the focus group offer hope to other women who may be struggling to remove themselves from abusive situations. Social service agencies can also benefit from the program and assistance suggestions provided by these women. Wortz (1999), on the other hand, employed a focus group in order to understand what and how people (e.g., potential jurors) view medical negligence situations. Gaining this knowledge will help ensure that attorneys are prepared to offer the type of information that jurors understand and believe is important. In the long run, it is hoped that juries for medical negligence trials will be presented with the evidence in such a way that they can make an informed (and legal) decision.

Summary

This chapter has outlined the basic types of interviews: structured, semi-structured, unstructured, and focus groups. Each type is designed to elicit certain types of information. Further, interviews are appropriate for a wide variety of research topics. In some cases, interviews may be the only way to gain information from a specific group of interest (e.g., gang members). In other cases, interviews can be used in concert with other methods (e.g., participant observation).

Structured interviews offer consistency among interviewers and ease in data collection and analysis. They typically result in higher completion rates and fewer "not applicable" responses than questionnaires or other survey methods. Because the interviewer is present, he or she is able to observe the environment and gain a general feel for the interviewee's reactions to questions. Further, because the interviewee is being asked questions, it is not imperative that he or she be able to read or write (a requirement for completing a questionnaire). Structured interviews can be easily replicated and also, because of their structure, the researcher can employ a number of trained interviewers to assist in the data collection.

Of course, the structure can also be somewhat problematic. Because there is very little room for deviating from the exact interview, the researcher must make sure, in advance, that the questions are worded clearly and precisely; that the topic of study is completely covered in the questions; and that the interviewees will understand the terminology and questions being asked of them. It is also important to recognize that conducting structured interviews on a large-scale basis can be expensive. These problem areas can easily be overcome if the researcher is diligent in developing the structured interview and keeps the research project on a reasonable scale.

In fact, semi-structured and unstructured interviews allow the researcher to overcome the inflexibility problems of structured interviews. Both of these interview types allow the researcher to explore areas of interest as they develop. Because there is more flexibility in the topics to be discussed and greater latitude for the respondents to share their thoughts, the interviewer and interviewee are often able to establish rapport. This conversational type interview becomes more of a discussion which may lead to more complete, in depth, and truthful responses.

Because of the qualitative nature of such interviews, data collection and analysis can be time consuming and labor intensive if the researcher relies on reading and analyzing the data. However, with the assistance of computer software, qualitative analysis is not as painstakingly slow and tedious as it once was. A critical area of concern for semi-structured and unstructured interviews is the quality of the interviewers. The interviewer must: make sure to remain neutral in all discussions, make sure that the interview stays "on track," be able to interact easily with others, and adapt questions and probes quickly. Careful selection and training of the interviewer can reduce or eliminate these concerns.

Focus groups provide researchers the opportunity to gather information on a topic that they may not understand completely. Focus groups can be used as either a preparatory or confirmatory tool. They are relatively easy and inexpensive to conduct. However, because the group is small and often made up of a convenience sample, the information provided may not be generalizable beyond that study. Because focus groups are often used as a basis for future research (e.g., to determine what kinds of questions to ask) or in combination with a questionnaire or interview (e.g., to gain additional insight into data already collected), the concern about generalizability is lessened. It is important to note that the quality and training of the moderator of a focus group is just as critical as it is for a semi-structured or unstructured interviewer in that the moderator must not taint or influence the course of the discussion.

The criminal justice and deviance literature indicates widespread acceptance of interviewing as a respectable research methodology. In fact, if used properly, interviews can provide reliable and valid data regarding a variety of complex social processes that would otherwise be unattainable by researchers.

Discussion Questions

1. What are the different types of interview structures that a researcher can use? What are the advantages and disadvantages of each?

2. How does a researcher decide which type of interview is best suited for a particular research project?

3. How does a researcher's personal qualities influence the type of interview they select for a research project?

4. What types of research questions are best answered using each type of interview?

CHAPTER 10

Validity of Participant-Observational Data/Research

Alexis J. Miller
Middle Tennessee State University

Introduction

A researcher who engages himself or herself in direct observation and/or participation and observation of the people or group being researched gathers participant-observational data. Essentially, this is when the researcher becomes a part of the group or event in some way, through observation, membership and/or participation in the group's activities. This type of research, as with other methods employed by researchers, is advantageous in certain settings where gathering information may not be accessible by other, more common methods. Furthermore, observational data allows researchers to obtain information that may not be known already or as readily available through interviews or surveys of the group's members due to the secretive nature of the group.

The validity of observational data is an ethical argument that researchers tend to either agree or disagree with entirely. Participant-observational data is one of the most controversial of research methods available. The argument about the validity of data gathered through observation, either direct observation or covert or overt participation, provokes some authors to spend very little time addressing the rationale behind observation research and the way to implement this research.

The lack of discussion concerning participant-observational research is due to the controversy surrounding the validity of participant-observational research. The basic issues of validity surrounding observational data centers on the questions: Is the data gathered by researchers participating, either with the party's knowledge or without, truly unbiased and objective data? The argument for, or against, this type of research comes at several levels. The different levels of the argument are based on the different ways you can implement participant-observational research. Some researchers argue that it is impossible to become involved with a group and remain objective, while others, primarily those conducting this type of research, stand firm on the notion that observational data is valid and can be accomplished objectively. Those conducting participant-observational research often will provide examples of their own research to show that observation research deserves and demands a chapter and discussion within research methods courses and textbooks. As with other types of research, observational research has its own set of limitations, which often bring the validity question of objectivity to the surface.

Of the limitations or problems associated with participant-observational research, the issue of researchers going native is one of the most prevalent ethical issues. Going native refers to the researcher who completely immerses himself/herself into the program of study, and begins to identify as a member of the group (Patton, 1990). Instead of just accessing the group for information through observation, the researcher who goes native sees himself or herself as a full-fledged member of the group or organization. When researchers go native it becomes difficult for them to remain unbiased, which hurts their ability to gain meaningful knowledge of the program or organization they are observing. Going native can be a very significant problem for certain types of participant observers, as will be discussed later in the chapter.

This chapter will address the validity of participant-observational data. First, the different methods of gathering observational data will be introduced followed by a discussion on the advantages and limitations to this unique type of research. Finally, particular types of research that call for observational methods will be presented.

Methods of Collecting Participant-Observational Data

There are several different ways of conducting participant-observational research. There is no one set of terms used by researchers to explain the methods of collecting participant-observational data. In fact, most authors develop their own version of the different labels to explain the process of observational research. Commonly, those conducting this type of research fall into one of three categories. Some terms previously used, and that will be used in this chapter, to describe these researchers are the "complete observer, participant as observer and observer as participant" (McCall & Simmons, 1969; Fitzgerald & Cox, 1994). Each method has its own set of limitations and reasoning. This section will discuss the three different types of observational research and when it is appropriate to use such methods.

Complete Observer

The complete observer is probably the least controversial of the three types of participant-observational research; however, it still has its criticisms. This is essentially the act of only observing. There is no social interaction between the researcher and the participants. The participants do not have knowledge of the researcher and the researcher does not participate in the activities being researched. This researcher may be present during the group's activities; however, he or she is not participating, only observing and listening. Where one of the other types of participant-observers may make notes during the observation, this will usually be difficult for the complete observer. The complete observer should not act any different from the participants, in an effort to keep from giving up their role as observer.

There are only certain situations in which a complete observer role is appropriate. Such as, if the researcher wants to determine what type of patron visits a particular establishment. The researcher could go to the establishment and sit and visually take in different aspects of the patrons. For instance, are there men or women patronizing the establishment and what are the topics of conversation between the patrons? It will be difficult for the researcher to make notes while at the establishment, however there are ways to handle that situation. Erickson and Tewksbury (2000) reviewed the problem of who attends strip clubs and what activities occur there. They found that when taking notes within the establishments' open areas was a problem, they could go into a bathroom stall and jot down information on either fliers provided within the establishment or a small notebook or card that could then be concealed.

There are several limitations; however, to this type of research. The most notable limitation is the possibility of misunderstanding what the researcher has observed during the observation. This problem is more susceptible when the researcher is conducting cross-cultural (or subcultural) research and may not understand some of the behaviors or languages used by those being observed. Furthermore, there is the ethical question of observing and analyzing people without getting permission from them. Some researchers feel that under no circumstances should a participant be observed or used in research without their knowledge and consent. While those who conduct this type of research find ways to deal with problems of consent and identity, they also do not agree with the ethical argument against this type of research. Preventing the identities of the participants from being acknowledged and giving them the same protection that is demanded by more mainstream types of research can be done by concealing the names and identities of the participants and the exact locations of where their research was conducted.

There is also the potential problem of ethnocentrism. According to McCall (1969), ethnocentrism is when the researcher "will not or cannot interact meaningfully with the informants" (1969:37). This happens in settings where the researcher may not have the ability to understand the comments or behaviors of those being observed and thus, simply rejects them as unimportant. Therefore, the researcher may believe they have observed a behavior or comment that is not important, when in reality that comment or behavior may define reasons for what they are observing.

Participant as Observer

Participant-observational researchers completely immerse themselves into the research at hand by participating in the group's activities. However, their role as researcher is not disguised. They announce their objectives and reasons for being present to the participants. Furthermore, they gain informed consent and follow the appropriate channels of permission to conduct the observation. An example of when this approach may be used would be a researcher who wants to gain an understanding of the participants in a new drug rehabilitation program; choosing to act as a participant observer would be a productive research approach. In doing so, they would attend all meetings and assume the role of a participant in the rehabilitation program. This type of research becomes an important tool in programs or topics that are under-researched. Participating in the program allows the researcher to gain insight as to how the program works, while interviews and surveys will allow the researcher to gain knowledge of how the program influences particular participants.

Strict quantitative researchers often look down on this type of research as less than worthy; however, participant-observational research, as all other types of study, has its place in social science research. Participant-observational research allows researchers to conduct inductive research. For instance, a researcher may not have the appropriate knowledge of how a newly developed program operates, the concepts of the group or the special vocabulary used by the participants. This lack of understanding will make it difficult for the researcher to develop an appropriate survey for evaluation. Thus, participant-as-observer techniques will lend the researcher the capacity to understand how the program operates, the written and assumed goals of the program, and how to obtain those goals through social interaction. This newly discovered information would subsequently assist the researcher in developing an appropriate survey for evaluation of the program.

As with participant observation, the participant-as-observer technique has its limitations. First, it is difficult for some researchers after announcing their role and agenda as a researcher to then develop a trusting relationship or rapport with the subjects while observing and participating in the group's activities. Many participant-observational researchers find themselves in a group situation that will not lend itself to gaining information. Either distrust among the program participants and/or the researcher's inability to relate to the membership roles of the program participants can greatly affect the amount and credibility of data obtained. One way to overcome some of these issues is for researchers to demonstrate the similarities between themselves and the observed. An example of how this can be done is seen in Fleisher's (1989) book *Warehousing Violence*. In this research Fleisher looks at the life of inmates and correctional officers inside of the United States Penitentiary at Lompoc. Fleisher demonstrated the problems he had with gaining trust of correctional officers at Lompoc. It was not until Fleisher assisted staff in a serious assault by inmates against the officers that he started to see a change. "Staffers who hadn't said anything to me before this, and staffers who hadn't before called me by name, now began paying attention to me" (1989:109). By helping the correctional officers regain control of a cellblock after a violent episode, Fleisher gained respect and rapport with many of the officers that earlier found little reason to even acknowledge his presence. This rapport allowed him to gain insight about the officer's attitudes and experiences within the prison.

Tewksbury shows similar tactics with gaining trust and respect during interview research with HIV positive individuals (see Tewksbury & Gagné, 1997). When conducting this research, Tewksbury was often offered a glass of water or food as a way for interviewees to "test" his comfort and knowledge of HIV. After establishing a level of trust with the interviewees, they may assume that the similarities between the researcher and themselves are even greater than in reality. During this same research, it was often assumed by the participants that Tewksbury too was HIV positive, without either affirmation or denial by Tewksbury. By focusing on the similar physical and social traits and establishing trust with the participants, one can gain a better understanding of what is being observed. The management of the researcher's identity with the participants is an ongoing process. This is a task with which participant researchers will continually contend in regard to both new and continuing participants. Through time and practice researchers can improve their abilities to establish trust and obtain credible data. (See also Chapter 8.)

Another limitation to the participant-as-observer technique is when the researcher does gain membership or entry into the group and becomes too closely identified with the group. Becoming sympathetic or losing your agenda as a researcher can affect the quality and amount of information available. Furthermore, as one becomes over-identified with the group, there is the problem of going native and losing perspective of the research. Going native is an issue with overt observation because often the role of the researcher inside the group will adjust and grow during the process of research. As one begins their role as the overt researcher, they may soon find themselves much more emerged in the activities of the group. Referring again to Fleisher (1989), he speaks of this problem during his research at Lompoc. Fleisher refers to a time during his study when he "lost objectivity." Specifically he says he "lost touch with my role as research anthropologist and began to think of myself as a correctional worker" (1989:112). It will take an avid researcher, aware of their objective, to step back from the research and rethink their role as the participant-observer researcher. Or, sometimes even further intervention from a colleague may be needed, as in the case of Fleisher, when a close friend and anthropologist helped him regain his perspective and reason for being in the prison. This limitation, though, is not exclusive to overt observation. The participant-as-observer research has many more limitations similar to these problems; however, they too have their place in social science research.

Observer as Participant

The observer-as-participant researcher is the secret or disguised observer. They are sometimes referred to as the "complete participant." Those being studied never know the researcher's true identity and purpose, as is also the case with participant observers. However, rather than just observing the group, the observer as participant is also participating with the group as a group member, although choosing not to reveal to the group their reason for becoming a participant. They may interact as a normal member, participating in any and all behaviors and activities with the group. For instance, a researcher that wants to gain knowledge of the initiation techniques for a gang may participate in the process themself to gain this knowledge without ever revealing to the other members of the gang their true reason for being there.

Complete participation observation can also be accomplished with a method referred to as the "potential participant" (Tewksbury, 2001). The potential participant becomes involved with the setting just like the covert observer; however they do not participate in all of the activities as the observed. In other words, there are some limits to the involvement in which the researcher will partake. Tewksbury (2001) explains how such a research approach would be conducted in regard to sexualized settings and subcultures. Whereas some researchers conducting research in sexual settings have actively become involved in the sexual behaviors to gain insights (Goode, 1999; Styles, 1979), Tewksbury found that by acting as a potential participant he was able to gain as much information, but without violating ethical standards. For instance, the potential participant will frequent the settings (bath houses, adult bookstores, or gay bars) and while there, act as a patron, present himself as someone potentially interested in all activities of the setting, but not actually participate in all that goes on in the setting.

As one can assume, there are many potential ethical problems associated with this type of research. As in the above example, activities that a complete participant observer may have to participate in could be risk-taking and/or criminal activities. This raises the question of how far the researcher should go to gain knowledge of the behaviors. Assuming the role as the complete participant means that the researcher has to first weigh moral and ethical dilemmas of possibly participating in criminal activities, while also considering the possible legal sanctions of those activities.

How far a researcher will go to obtain information about participants is a question that is best answered by the researcher; however, there are examples of researchers that have gone too far in their quest for information. For instance, during Laud Humphreys' (1970) research about sex in public bathrooms he decided that he would further his knowledge of participants by tracing the license plates of certain participants after viewing their sexual acts in public bathrooms. He then proceeded to contact a random sample of these men through their license plates and interview them. Even more disturbing, at the time of his public bathroom study, Humphreys was asked to develop a social health survey for another study. With permission from the director of that research project, Humphreys used it as a means to approach the individuals he observed in the public bathrooms and conduct an interview. Humphreys received much criticism for methods used in his study and he faced criminal charges for failing to report the illegal sexual behavior. Since the publication of the original study, Humphreys has addressed and recognized that the methods he used were unethical. There is no one correct answer that dictates how far a researcher should go to obtain information from their participants. Rather, researchers themselves will have to consider this dilemma and make their own decisions.

In addition to the problems associated with possible criminal activity for the observer as participant, once again there is the problem of "going native." As discussed earlier, going native refers to when researchers step too far into the group or entity they are observing and begin to identify themselves as true members of the group. As for the example regarding the gang initiation, going native would be when the researcher incorporates the role of the gang member into his or her own self-identity. They are no longer acting as the researcher; rather they identify themselves as a gang member. Going native is one of the most pressing of the limitations regarding this type of research and the most dangerous of the ethical arguments.

The pretend role the complete participant is assuming is another limitation to this type of research. The fact that they are participating with the group, in group activities, unlike the complete observer, and have not revealed their identity or purpose for being a participant, like the participant as observer, adds to the ethical problems associated with this type of research. They have to continually remind themselves that they are not true gang members, to keep from going native. This may hinder their ability to gain true knowledge of the initiation techniques, because they constantly have to remind themselves of the nature of their research. It has been advised that complete participant take time to withdraw from the research and/or take breaks from the observation. This will assist the researcher in what has been called "information overload" (Miller, 1995). Skeptics of this type of research believe that the limitations researchers will encounter of constantly reminding themselves of their role and keeping from information overload will make it difficult for them to gain valid data and information about their topic of study without going native.

Finally, like the complete observer, complete participant researchers have to deal with further problems surrounding their misrepresentation and deception. They will not have permission from the subjects to participate in the study. The lack of informed consent and the possibility of causing harm to the subjects is often the most criticized of the limitations to covert observation. One has to weigh the moral and ethical aspects of traditional social science research and that of a democratic society (Miller, 1995). Along the same lines as the complete observer, the complete participant researcher will need to find innovative ways of keeping notes. Jotting information down in a bathroom stall may be increasingly dangerous for this researcher, thus techniques like body wires and small, hidden tape recorders may be more appropriate (Miller, 1995).

Insights that Can Be Gained Only via Observation

There are several insights that can be gained only through observation methods. For instance, if a researcher wants to conduct a study about a subject that they know very little about or that is under-researched, they may have a difficult time developing a survey that accurately assesses the behaviors they are trying to understand. Observational research allows researchers to conduct an inductive study. This is when a researcher enters a setting without any preconceived hypotheses regarding the behaviors they are studying. Through inductive research the researcher is able to gain a more in-depth understanding of the participants' behaviors, thus allowing for a more appropriate survey to be developed regarding these behaviors. Finally, observational research further allows us to escape some of the problems associated with the Hawthorne effect. The Hawthorne effect is when participants in a study change their behavior based on their knowledge that they are being studied. Observation research allows researchers to enter the research setting without acknowledging their reason for being there, thus reducing this risk substantially.

The use of observational data to subsequently develop a research survey can be seen in the work of Myers (1992), who was interested in the motivations for body modification, such as body piercing and tattoos. Myers was looking to identify what social and personal reasons individuals might have to modify their body. Specifically, he was looking for the reasons beyond what had already been identified by the mental health community—the suggestion that deficiencies in mental health lead people to get tattoos, piercings, and other body modifications. What Myers' observational research revealed was an understanding of the rites of passage surrounding ritual symbolism on the body and how body piercing can function as a language for that symbolism. Without the information revealed through observational research, how could a researcher develop an appropriate survey to distribute to those who engage in body piercing? Would the survey pinpoint the true nature of the symbolism, or would the researcher lack the ability to put into words why someone might participate in such an activity? Do only psychopaths mutilate their bodies, or is there more to body piercing? When there are no direct answers to particular questions, often observational research will allow us to obtain this knowledge through immersion in groups that participate in the behaviors in which we are interested.

Very simply, it is through inductive research that we gain these understandings. Sometimes when conducting inductive analysis we have no understanding about the setting or participants. It is often through this type of research that we gain a concept or path to follow with further, deductive research. For instance, Myers' (1992) research involving body piercing revealed that the participants in the study were conventional, sane individuals. If this researcher approached this study in a deductive manner, the study would have begun with the assumption that those engaging in body piercing are disturbed, because that is what earlier psychological studies had suggested. Instead, Myers approached this research with an inductive analysis, trust was established with the participants, and the researcher was able to gain insights and knowledge to the rationale behind Western-world body modification.

When researchers conduct complete observational or complete participation research, they are also reducing the likelihood of the problems associated with the Hawthorne effect. By not acknowledging the existence of the study, the researcher or the process to the participants, those being observed will be unlikely to change their behavior just because of the study. For instance, when students know they are being watched during an exam, they do not cheat; however, if the professor leaves the room, their behavior may change and become deviant. Thus, any observations and data to emerge from the research would be more likely to be considered valid.

The Limitations of Interview and Survey Data

The validity of observation research is constantly questioned. Whether the observer can accurately take in and record the behaviors of participants while acting as the complete participant is a pressing question. One cannot argue that there are limitations to strict observational research, as has been noted in this chapter; however, there are also limitations to traditional survey and interview data-collection strategies.

When a researcher is using surveys to gain insights to particular research questions, they must have knowledge of that behavior or group to produce a valid and reliable instrument to use as a questionnaire. If that knowledge is not available, any questionnaire used will only gain insights within the boundaries of the questions. For instance, if a researcher is attempting to gain an understanding of a particular group that uses a form of slang to verbalize their behavior, it will be difficult for the researcher to obtain that knowledge without asking the questions in a way that includes the slang. Observational research permits us to participate within the group and gain an understanding of the particular behaviors and language that may be used by the group. By understanding the language used within the group's activities, researchers can devise an appropriate survey or questionnaire to find out what else that participant may personally be able to add in regard to the group.

While surveys and interviewing have a place in the research world, so does observation research. Both open-ended and structured interviews will allow researchers to gain further knowledge of the behaviors of those they study; however, some settings do not allow for a researcher to come in with surveys to distribute. For instance, if the researcher is attempting to gain information from a group that is known for low literacy skills, such as prison inmates, distributing a survey and expecting them to be able to read or understand it is useless. Furthermore, some settings do not allow the researcher to schedule interviews with participants. As mentioned earlier, if the researcher is attempting to gain knowledge of the techniques for gang initiation, they will be unable to approach the gang or its members and expect that by scheduling an interview with them they will obtain any valid data. Often the techniques used to become a member of a gang will involve criminal activity, thus most members will not offer this information to just anyone who happens to ask. Rather, this information is best obtained through complete participation or complete observational research.

Research Questions that Necessitate Observational Data

As can be seen, observational research is an important tool when conducting certain types of social science studies. In this section, other types of studies and research questions that not only can benefit from, but that actually call for the use of, observational research will be reviewed.

When participants are a part of groups that are unlikely to willingly participate in research—such as criminal groups—the need for complete participation research is evident. In addition, when there simply is not a great deal of research in a particular area of interest, observational research can provide a foundation to carry out more sophisticated studies, whether they are quantitative or qualitative. For instance, research regarding the behavior of patrons in gay bathhouses has been largely ignored since the 1980s, according to Tewksbury (2002). Thus, observational data could provide a basis for information regarding these patrons and their behaviors in these establishments.

Furthermore, in regard to research about gay bathhouses, some researchers simply walked into gay bathhouses and distributed questionnaires to the patrons (McKusick, Horstram & Coates, 1985; Richwald, Morisky, Kyle, Kristal, Gerber & Friedland, 1988). However, the findings of these studies may be viewed as suspect, because of low response rates of the patrons. In such situations observation data could provide the researcher with the information they are pursuing, without the limitations surveys provide. This can be seen with Tewksbury's (2002) study regarding gay bathhouses. For this research Tewksbury patronized gay bathhouses acting as the potential participant. He participated with the patrons in all areas without participating in sexual acts. Observational research like this is capable of contributing knowledge regarding all types of behaviors within establishments. For instance, Tewksbury (2002) was able not only to provide when, where, and what types of sexual acts are displayed in gay bathhouses, but he was also able to distinguish the different ways that nonverbal communication was employed, without participating in sexual acts. If survey or interview data were used to facilitate this research, then it would be limited within the boundaries of the questions as to the amount and type of information it could provide. On the other hand, Styles (1979) argues that there is no way to truly understand gay bathhouses without actively participating in all of the activities with the patrons, including sexual acts; however, as can be seen there are several ethical questions involved with such behaviors and the problem of potentially going native.

There are also other uses for observational research within government and private programs. For instance, when new drug rehabilitation programs are developed, the need for observational research is great and is best suited as the first step in attempting a program evaluation. How can the researchers devise a survey or interview guide when little or no information is available about the program? Observation research would allow the researcher to first get an understanding of the program so as to devise an interview guide. Interviews could then allow for further information regarding the personal aspects of the program that observational research may not provide.

Other types of groups and behaviors that are taboo in society will also call for observational research. In 1990, Hopper and Moore provided information about women in motorcycle gangs. Their study provided data through both participant observation and interviews. They were included in motorcycle gangs parties, cookouts, and other events. By observing these events, they were better prepared to ask questions during the personal interviews with the women members. Language barriers were overcome by observing behaviors during events. For instance, during one event the researchers learned that when bikers refer to something being 'legal' they are speaking in terms of their gang's bylaws, not societal law. One can see how difficult it may be to devise a survey without prior knowledge of the different meanings of certain slang words within particular groups or gangs.

This type of complete-participation research is also necessary in settings where the behavior is criminal. Undercover police officers often behave very similarly to the complete-participant researcher. They are attempting to detect illegal behavior in an effort to gain knowledge of additional illegal activities. Complete-participant researchers are attempting to understand and gain knowledge of the illegal activity in an effort to expand our knowledge of the behavior or discover unknowns regarding the behavior without prompting arrest. When attempting research that involves criminal behavior very often covert methods, either as the complete participant or potential observer, is the best way to obtain this knowledge.

Conclusions

Observational research provides researchers with an avenue to discover new and unexplored cultures. This type of research is an important tool for social scientists to learn because in many settings it is the most, and sometimes only, appropriate way to gather data. As has been seen in this chapter, there are several limitations to when and how one should use observational research; however, there are also limitations and problems with strict quantitative research. The introduction to the types and problems associated with observational research should be discussed in the classroom and included in research methods textbooks. The different types of observational research, complete observer, participant-as-observer or observer-as-participant and the potential participant need to be differentiated for students. More importantly, the differences between the types of observational research need to be discussed and decided on when venturing into this type of research by social scientists. There are, of course, situations that do not warrant observational research as a method, but in many cases, without observational research, we would be incapable of constructing a valid instrument to measure behaviors quantitatively if we did not have inductive research that is provided by participant-observational research.

Discussion Questions

1. What are the different approaches to conducting observational research?

2. What types of research questions are best answered using each of the different forms of observational research methods?

3. How do we know whether a research project drawing on observational data is valid?

4. When would it not be appropriate to use an observational research method in criminal justice?

CHAPTER 11

Utility of Case Studies

Kim Davies
Augusta State University

A brief examination of any of the major criminal justice and criminology journals would indicate the present importance of quantitative methods for those of us who study criminal justice. As other chapters in this book indicate, there are excellent arguments for the use of quantitative methods. However, in spite of the seeming dominance of statistical analyses in criminal justice and criminology, I would bet that most academics that study crime and criminal justice could tell you that Stanley, Chick, and Vincent are the subjects of the *Jack Roller*, *Street Corner Society*, and *The Professional Fence*, respectively. For many of us, the case studies by Clifford Shaw, William Whyte, Carl Klockars, and others brought criminal justice studies to life during our days in college. Many of us loved the idea of learning from "criminals" and believed that this was a good way to learn about crime. Even now, it is the case studies mentioned above and more recent studies such as Patricia Adler's study of Dave, a drug smuggler, and Claire Sterk's study of women crack users in an Atlanta neighborhood that bring crime and criminal justice to life for my students and others across the United States.

Despite the appeal of the case-study method to many of us because of the simplicity in understanding case studies in contrast with some statistical criminological research, case studies are less frequently found today at least partly because of arguments about their generalizability. In the following pages, I will discuss not only the importance of generalizability for case studies, but the value of understanding individual cases as well as theoretical and policy contributions of case studies. I will also discuss the case study method as a foundation for future research. However, we first must understand what a case study is; so I will begin with a discussion of what is meant by a case-study approach.

What Is the Case Study Method?

The case-study method is an approach to research that involves an intensive study of a single case or very few cases. A case study can be an in-depth examination of an organization, a community or even a whole country. William Foote Whyte (1955), for instance studied an Italian community he called "Cornerville" in his widely read *Street Corner Society*. However, in criminal justice research, the *case* studied is often an individual person such as Stanley, the young juvenile offender in Shaw's (1930) *The Jack Roller* or a small number of people involved in the same activity such as Cressey's 1953 study of embezzlers or Polsky's 1969 study of pool hustlers.

Regardless of the individual case studied, the goal of case studies is to study a "phenomenon within its real-life context" (Yin, 1989:23). Yin (1989) argues that case studies are a practical choice when seeking answers to "why" or "how" questions, when one has little control over events and when focusing on "contemporary phenomenon within some real-life context" (Yin, 1989:13). Unlike most experiments that examine a phenomenon in an artificial setting, the investigator who uses the case-study method can learn how an individual really acts or how a phenomenon actually occurs. Instead of manipulating individuals as a way of producing a response or situation in a false environment, the researcher who uses a case-study method observes and learns about how individuals act in real-life, nonresearcher constructed situations. This is particularly useful in the field of criminal justice where oftentimes we are interested in illegal or deviant activities that may be inappropriate for experiments. As a case in point, it would be difficult to learn about how addicted pregnant women deal with their pregnancies without actually studying women in this actual situation.

Furthermore, a case-study approach allows one to take into consideration dynamics that might not be easily captured with survey research. Survey research is restricted to information collected on a limited number of variables that can be garnered with questions (and often multiple-choice questions) on a questionnaire. Case studies can lead us to different information and allow a greater range of possible variables than survey research. Though, it is important to note that case studies may be useful for generating survey questions.

You may have noticed that I defined the case-study method as an approach. This is because researchers who make use of case studies to investigate the world of crime and criminal justice do not employ a single technique (Berg, 1998, Hamel, Dufour & Fortin, 1993). Rarely, in fact, would a researcher rely on one technique to complete a case study. Instead, they often use various research practices to obtain an inclusive depiction of the person or group they are studying. For instance, a researcher using a case-study approach to learn about women who use heroin may do what Marsha Rosenbaum did and interview women who are heroin users while also accompanying addicted women "on their rounds in their communities, including treatment facilities, 'scoring' places, and 'shooting galleries'" (Rosenbaum, 1988:11). Case studies may also involve analyzing personal documents and official records as well as interviewing others involved with the subject of the case study. For instance, before he even began interviewing Vincent, *The Professional Fence*, Carl Klockars (1974) interviewed police, lawyers, crime reporters, security agents and anyone else he could think of who might come into contact with thieves as part of their occupations. Finally, case studies may also involve quantitative research approaches as well as the many qualitative approaches for which case studies are known. Recently, for instance Bromley and Cochran (1999) studied community-oriented policing at a single Southern Sheriff's Office through the use of a self-administered questionnaire given to all the officers and an analysis of the officers' responses.

Nevertheless, because case studies usually seek to understand a single case in as much depth as possible, case studies usually rely on at least some qualitative methods. Case studies that are well done give the reader the opportunity to know deeply about a particular individual or event. Through case studies, we can gain rich details that may contribute to our understanding of similar cases or help us generate theoretical understanding of crime and criminal justice events. For instance, Sutherland (1947) relied on case studies to support his differential association theory.

Another benefit attributed to cases studies and other qualitative methodology is that they are seen as giving individuals voice to their own stories (Sullivan, 2001). If a researcher uses interviewing, observation or, even analyses of documents as part of their case study approach; *verstehen* is more possible than when we rely on existing databases. An example from my own work highlights how much more real individuals can be for the researchers and the readers when using the case study approach. For my dissertation research, I learned a great deal about situations in which women killed using the Supplemental Homicide Report data to test various theories of women's involvement in crime (Davies, 1996). Using this data, I was able to find out how many women killed their intimates or their children, what weapons they used and the overall context in which they killed such as whether the homicide occurred in the context of another felony or resulted from an argument. However, I was not able to obtain richer detail such as what a woman who killed her partner may have been arguing about before she killed him. In contrast, when a colleague and I constructed individual cases histories of incidents in which women killed another person using police arrest and incident reports, victim's assistance files, trial transcripts, and newspaper accounts, the cases came alive (Scott & Davies, 2000). Learning about how an individual white woman suffered abuse at the hands of her father and how the two had argued about her dating an African-American man before she fatally stabbed him with a knife made the incident more real than including it as one of several cases in which a woman killed her parent with a knife in the context of an argument. Clearly, we can learn much from either type of study, but immersing ourselves in individual cases brings more life to our studies.

The Importance of Generalizability

When I was first invited to write this chapter, I laughed to myself as I thought back to a seminar course I took in graduate school. My professor was making the point that locking up kids was not always a good idea and he was using Stanley, the subject of Clifford Shaw's *The Jack Roller*, as a case in point. We had just read *The Jack Roller,* and my professor was noting that Stanley gained more knowledge about committing delinquency while he was locked up in an institution for young delinquents. I interjected that Shaw had an "N of one" and asked how we could generalize from Stanley, a single case to all other youngsters locked up in institutions across the United States. As noted by Yin (1989), I was expressing a common concern about the case study method, the problem of generalizability. In other words, can we study a single case or a few cases and apply our conclusions about it or them to others similarly situated? My question, while undoubtedly annoying to my professor, is not an uncommon one and one that I was trained to ask as a graduate student at a major research institution that emphasized the importance of quantitative methods.

While Yin (1989) and others (Guba & Lincoln, 1981) note that the question about generalizations in case studies does not have a simple answer, they make the point that the purpose of case studies is not "statistical generalization" but "analytic generalization" (Yin, 1989:21). In other words, the goal of case studies is to learn about social actors in their natural habitat, to learn all that can be gleaned about how individuals interpret and perhaps even create their realities. Researchers who use the case study method are more often concerned with expanding and generating theories, rather than testing hypotheses and finding correlations among a few variables.

Another answer to give those who criticize the case study approach based on generalizability was noted more than 30 years ago by Polsky (1969). In his book, *Hustlers, Beats, and Others,* Polsky pointed out that we will fall short in our examination of those who do crime if we rely on skewed samples, "studied in non-natural surroundings (anti-crime settings), providing mostly data recollected long after the event" (1969:115). Indeed, we can learn a lot about crime from data sources such as the Uniform Crime Reports, the Supplementary Homicide Reports, and the National Crime Victimization Surveys, and even from surveys of incarcerated populations, but to get a truly complete picture, we also need case studies of individuals and groups of offenders. We need case studies to help us learn not just what kind of crime is being done (which the UCR and NCVS may give us some hints at), but the social context in which the crimes are being done.

Likewise, it is important to have data on crime to know what the police may be busy doing, but in reality, any good police officer or criminal justice researcher knows that crime data does not give us the full picture. Case studies are a valuable resource that we need to use to get the more complete picture of crime. Take the case of Mandy (a pseudonym) who I often use as an illustration in my teaching. Mandy was a young woman who was arrested for prostitution in the late 1980s in a midwestern city. The inclusion of her arrest in the crime statistics might at first seem to indicate that she was, in fact, working as a prostitute and that the police were simply doing their job by arresting her. However, because I know more about Mandy's particular case, I know there is actually a different story to explain Mandy's arrest. Granted, Mandy was working at a club where women gave lap dances to men who paid money for this service, but Mandy had never, and was not at the time, accepting money in exchange for sexual acts. In fact, because of an injury, Mandy was not even performing lap dances the night she was arrested for prostitution. Instead, she was working the front counter of the "lap-dancing establishment" when undercover police officers came in to purchase a lap dance as part of a sting operation. After accepting their money and taking their order, Mandy accidentally touched one of the undercover officers at the base of his throat as she examined his necklace that had caught her eye because of her penchant for turquoise jewelry. Because the technicality of the law stipulated that the women working as lap dancers could not touch the customers, Mandy was arrested for prostitution. Furthermore, because she was the one who accepted the money and made the arrangements at the front desk, she was charged with running a brothel. This whole incident took place as the local sheriff was embroiled in a battle for re-election. Thus, it seems, he had pushed his officers to make arrests to look like he was cleaning up the city. Eventually, he was re-elected and the charges against Mandy were dropped. Cases such as Mandy's or a case study of a police officer or a police organization such as that done by David Simon (1991) a journalist who studied the Baltimore Police Department's homicide unit for an entire year, could provide one with a more inclusive description of what police really do in their day-to-day world, as well as shed some light on those accused of criminal behavior. While we must be careful about generalizing cases like Mandy's to every case, or Simon's findings to every homicide unit, their cases do open additional lines of inquiry for the criminal justice researcher.

Another point made by those in the criminal justice field is that all deviance or crime does not come to the attention of police. As Sutherland (1945) pointed out, deviance by upper-class individuals, especially in the context of their occupations, is not always thought of as criminal and this type of misconduct is not often or always brought to our attention. Because of the secretive nature of such deviance/crime and the little attention it has traditionally received from police agencies, the case study approach has been important for expanding our knowledge about white-collar and occupational crime. In fact, through case studies such as Gilbert Geis' (1967) study of heavy electrical equipment antitrust cases and Lee and Ermann's (1999) case study about the Ford Pinto, we have begun to learn about how organizational structure can contribute to deviance in the workplace.

Finally, another criticism launched at case studies has to do with the reliability of the method. Research is considered reliable when the same or another researcher is able to obtain the same results using the same research instrument. Critics make the argument that different researchers, using the case study method may come to different conclusions or even learn different "facts" because of the interactions between those studying and those being studied or because of different researchers' idiosyncrasies or personal biases. While reliability may at times be an issue with the case study method, there are a few answers for those who criticize the case study method on these grounds. First, as noted by Orum, Feagin, and Sjoberg (1991), there are ways to make one's study more reliable. For instance, one could have a team of researchers study a phenomena as a way to compare observations and interpretations. One can also involve the subject(s) of the case study as a check on interpretation as Clifford Shaw does with Stanley in *The Jack Roller* and Whyte (1955) did with Chick in his study of Cornerville. Checking one's "facts" against several sources and reporting where there are differences is also an important tenet of those who use the case study method. The case study method allows, and perhaps even demands, that the researcher check official documents such as arrest records and newspaper reports in addition to observing and interviewing individuals. Some, in fact, argue that this triangulation of sources (Denzin, 1989)—the ability to have many different measures or observations of a phenomenon— is an important strength of the case study method (Orum, Feagin & Sjoberg, 1991). Finally, Sjoberg, Williams, Vaughan, and Sjoberg (1991) also make the point that all researchers, no matter what methods they use, cannot divorce themselves from their sociocultural setting and become objective even if they claim they are. The most ethical approach to any research is to state your biases and explain your research methods honestly and fully.

The Value of Understanding Individual Cases/Instances

As Simpson and Piquero (2000) noted in a discussion of their case study of the Archer Daniels Midland 1996 anti-trust case, case studies are:

> A useful tool to assess what is known about a phenomenon, to develop empirical generalizations, form observations that may be explored by others, to inform theory, and to identify new areas of research (2000:187).

Indeed, case studies, while not always generalizable to every other case, have and will continue to offer much to the study of criminal justice. Becker (1966), for instance, noted that life history case studies might help to disprove hypotheses and introduce variables that are overlooked in other work (Geis, 1991). In this way, they serve to stimulate more research, as Geis (1991) argues Thrasher's study of gangs did in 1927.

While Kimball Young noted that case studies such as *The Jack Roller* focus on the conditions and stories of individuals and thus deflect attention away from important socio-structural explanations for their behavior (quoted in Geis, 1991), this is not constituent of case studies. If we are cautious and attentive to the impact of social forces and the effects of structural constraints on the individuals we study using the case study method, we have the potential to gain much that may be generalizable to other similar cases, as well as less similar cases. For instance, from Diane Vaughan's intense revisionist study of NASA's 1986 fatal decision to launch the Space Shuttle *Challenger*, we learned about how the environment of an organization can unintentionally normalize decisions that lead to deviant outcomes (Vaughan, 2001). In fact, the case study method may be better than other methods at getting at the social context that is so important in understanding the interactions and actions of humans—whether acting as individuals, groups, organizations, or even nations.

Another benefit to the case study method noted by Maguire (2000) is that this approach is intrinsically more longitudinal than other approaches that take one snapshot in time, such as a survey. Using a case study method, a researcher can discover how an individual's behavior and beliefs change or transform over time and within different social contexts. Using observational and interview techniques, a researcher can gain an understanding as to how and why people change as they observe how they react to situations that either change or stay stagnant.

Theoretical Contributions of Case Studies

Orum, Feagin, and Sjoberg (1991) argue that the case study method is one of the best methods for generating theory and generalizations. They go as far as arguing that "significant new theoretical innovations and generalizations" are more likely when using qualitative methods such as a case study approach than when using quantitative methods (Orum, Feagin & Sjoberg, 1991:13-14). Indeed, the goals of quantitative research are not often theory generalization but hypothesis testing while the case study approach is often more open to grounded theory (Glaser & Strauss, 1967), especially when several cases are employed to learn about some phenomena. In a recent study for instance, Jody Miller (2001) studied several young women who were involved in gang life in St. Louis, Missouri and Columbus, Ohio. Miller's study helped to move feminist studies of women and crime forward by looking at gender and more importantly, how young women often have agency in their criminal activity—they are not always or simply victims, but in some cases active offenders themselves.

Because one of the goals of the case study method is to understand how people live their everyday lives including their involvement in deviance, crime, or criminal justice, case studies can help the criminal justice researcher both empirically and theoretically. Case studies allow one to examine how the "complex web of social interactions" that occur in all our lives impact on individual decisions whether they be about making arrests, making judicial decisions, or deciding to shoot another human being (Orum, Feagin & Sjoberg, 1991:9). Through her 1998 study of women in the Central California Women's Facility, for instance, Barbara Owen, learned how and why some women joined in "the mix" (the continuation of behavior that led to imprisonment such as drug use and lawbreaking) and others stayed away from it.

Policy Contributions of Case Studies

The case study method is also an extremely valuable method for generating and evaluating policy. If care is taken in determining whom to study and to what or whom generalizations can be made, the case study approach has much to contribute to policy because of the holistic approach taken in the case study method. For instance, studies of women's use of crack cocaine such as that by Inciardi, Lockwood, and Pottieger (1993) and Claire Sterk (1999) helped make clear the challenges faced by communities or cities attempting to stop the devastation caused by crack cocaine. Through these case studies of women and communities deeply affected by crack cocaine, we learn how gender interplays with addiction to lead some women to drugs and how difficult it is for women addicted to crack to see a future that leads them out of drug use and addiction. Inciardi and his colleagues were some of the first to really show us how difficult it was for women to get drug counseling, especially if they were pregnant or had children. Now, we see more programs that counsel and help addicted, pregnant women—although laws allowing drug-addicted women to be prosecuted for injuring their unborn babies show how important it is to find a wider audience for such studies.

Furthermore, Yin (1989) notes that case studies have "distinctive place" in evaluation research. A case study can explain and describe the real-life consequences and causal links involved in interventions that are too complex for survey or experimental strategies to capture. Finally, a case study approach can be used to explore situations in which there is no clear or single set of outcomes in an intervention (Yin, 1989).

Case Studies as a Foundation for Future Research

The rich detail data obtained through a good quality case study may lead to the development of a "solid empirical basis for specific concepts and generalizations" (Orum, Feagin & Sjoberg, 1991:7). In this way, case studies can set the stage for future research. Unlike many other types of research, case studies permit the researchers to analyze human activities and actions as they actually occur. There is not the artificiality of the experimental laboratory or a reliance on individuals to predict what they would do or tell what they have done as often occurs with survey research. Instead, case study research, because it often relies on observations and in-depth discussions with the actors, allows the researcher to observe how individuals or organizations actually do act and react. Case-study methods, like much qualitative research, also give voice to the subject of the case studies. We can learn about drug dealers and smugglers as Adler (1985) learned about Dave—from Dave's perspective as well as from probation officers, police officers, or other criminal justice workers who are often, because of their positions, purposely not told some information by those who participate in crime. Case study research can open the door to questions that criminal justice researchers can pursue with other methods. Once we read Ralph Weisheit's (1991) study about domestic marijuana cultivation, we may ask different questions concerning criminal motivation than we did before—especially with regard to those who grow or manufacture illegal drugs. Instead of assuming that individuals involve themselves in drug sales because of the possible financial rewards, we may also include questions regarding possible spiritual, social, intrinsic, and other rewards.

Conclusion

While the case-study approach holds much promise, it is something that not everyone can do well. First, one has to have the drive and determination to seek out and find cases worth studying. Second, one needs to have good research and people skills. A case study done poorly is just that a poor case study. However, a case study, in which one gleans important information and works at getting the whole story from different sources is much more likely to contribute to our understanding of individuals and social phenomena of interest. Lastly, there is some risk to the case-study method within the field of criminal justice. One may find themselves in situations that are ethically questionable or even dangerous. Patricia Adler (1995), for instance, discusses an occasion in which she and Peter Adler felt they had to escape their house in the middle of the night with their transcripts and tapes while they were studying drug smugglers and dealers. Adler reports that at various times she and Peter felt threatened by people in the drug business who became suspicious of them. In order to protect their research and ensure confidentiality of their taped informants they met up with someone who could guard their tapes. Similarly, Klockars (1974) noted that a police officer promised to track down his killer if he were killed in his quest to learn about professional fences.

Clearly, we have much to learn about crime, those who do crime, and those who work to prevent or stop it and case studies remain an important method for helping us learn. There will remain certain types of crime, like white-collar crime that are particularly amenable to the case study approach. Moreover, case studies about career criminals in their natural setting are an important contribution to the understanding of crime, criminals, and criminal justice. Different research questions call for different types of research approaches, and in criminal justice we still have questions that case studies can best answer. In 1969, Polsky, argued that there was no way around it—the study of "uncaught" criminals as they "normally go about their work and play" was absolutely necessary for understanding crime (Polsky, 1969:115-116). And it still is.

A Selective List of Case Studies

Frederick Thrasher	1927	*The Gang*
Edwin Sutherland	1937	*The Professional Thief*
Clifford Shaw	1930	*The Jack Roller*
Clifford Shaw	1938	*Brothers in Crime*
Clifford Shaw	1931	*The Natural History of a Delinquent Career*
Jon Snodgrass	1982	*Jack Roller at 70*
Darrell Steffensmeier	1986	*The Fence*
William Whyte	1943	*Street Corner Society*
Stanley Liebow	1967	*Tally's Corner*
Ned Polsky	1972	*Folk Devils and Moral Panics*
Carl Klockars	1975	*The Professional Fence*
Richard Wright & Scott Decker	1994	*Burglars on the Job*

Discusion Questions

1. In what ways does case study research differ from other criminal justice research methods?

2. What types of research questions are best answered using a case study method?

3. How can a case study be used for making decisions about social policies?

4. What special skills does a researcher need to have to successfully complete a case study research project?

Conclusion

Throughout all of the chapters of this book you have seen how even one of the more mundane, and supposedly straightforward aspects of the social sciences—research methods—can be characterized by debates and disagreements. In each of the chapters of this book, you have read about how researchers have different views about some of the very basic issues that are involved in how and why research is done. Many of the controversies you have read about are probably not issues you had ever thought were "problems" or things that could be debated. Many of the controversial issues discussed in this book are probably issues that you never really thought about before. That is expected, though. The issues and controversies that are discussed in this book are not necessarily ideas and issues that most people think about very often. But, one thing that you should see pretty clearly now is that, although many people may not be familiar with these controversial, scientific issues, they are pretty important.

Some readers may still be wondering how and why the issues discussed in this book are called "controversies." After all, the ways that the authors of each of the chapters have presented the varying beliefs and different views on their issues do not focus on how researchers argue about what is right and wrong, or even what is best or worst. Instead, what you have seen is that, in each of the chapters, the authors have focused on showing you what some of the different interpretations of various processes or approaches are, and how decisions that a researcher makes can impact the way that their research is carried out and the results of their research endeavors. We are sure that many readers are not going to get fired up and go out to protest about any of the controversies that are highlighted in the discussions in this book. But, for readers who are (or who plan to become) serious and devoted practitioners and/or consumers of research, the issues that you have read about are very important. And, believe it or not, some of us actually do get a bit emotional about these issues.

As a research consumer, it really is important for you to know that these are issues and ideas that have several sides to them. If you know that researchers care deeply about these types of issues, and that decisions researchers make are carefully thought out, and usually based on a set of assumptions and beliefs, you are in a much better position to understand the research to which you are exposed. Yes, we are talking about scientific research, social scientific research. There are social (and political and economic and personal) issues involved in how research is done. Social science is based on social beings interacting in social settings to study social worlds and events. There are simply a lot of different ways research questions, processes, and outcomes can be approached and understood. Perhaps this is the most important idea to take away from this book: social science is not an all-or-nothing, right-or-wrong enterprise. Yes, there are obviously appropriate ways to do things, and definitely some wrong ways to do just about every step of the research process. But, there are a number of acceptable (or, "correct") ways that research can be done. The range of options on each of the specific decisions that a researcher has available to choose between, and that you as a research consumer can make in regard to interpreting and understanding a research project, are just that, choices.

Some of the controversies in social science research methods are about the very foundational issues of social science. Should theory guide how we do research? And, if so, how can it help us structure our projects? What makes a good research report/article? We hear all the time that criminal justice research is important for setting social policies, but does it really? In fact, how can it? When we do research in criminal justice, what should we focus on, the big picture, or specific instances of behavior? And, is it possible to combine different approaches to get closer to answering some of our basic questions?

Most of the controversies in criminal justice, and, in fact, all of social science research, are about how we should go about trying to answer our research questions, and what specific methods are the most effective means to obtain our answers. In quantitative research, this may mean asking questions about how to incorporate theory to surveys. Or, it could be asking questions about whether it is better to go out and gather your own original data, or to locate already existing data that you can use to answer your research questions. In qualitative criminal justice research, controversial issues include questions of how researchers can go about gaining access to, and earning the trust of, people they study. And, how close should we get with those whom we study? Or, if we plan to conduct our research by talking to people or observing them, how should we go about actually talking with them (or watching them?) Is there anything we can learn from studying specific individuals or instances of behavior, or do we need to gather a large number of pieces of data in order to understand how something "really" happens?

No, these are not ideas and debates that many people find exciting and worthy of a conversation with family and friends. Some of us do, and sometimes some of us will devote a large part of our professional lives to advocating our positions on one or more of these issues. But, we do not expect many readers to get that excited about these issues. We do hope that readers will remember that there are choices to be made, and researchers have some very strong views on what the outcomes of the results should be. What choices a researcher makes directly, and strongly, influences the way research is done, and perhaps what the results of the research say.

And for those of us who are not going to become professional researchers, we still need to understand these issues. As consumers of research, it is important to understand what the decisions are that researchers make as well as why they decide the way they do. In order to be an informed consumer of research, we need to be able to evaluate the research to which we are exposed. For example, say you are reading *USA Today* and you come upon an article that outlines some new research about the effectiveness of the death penalty. It would be helpful and important to be able to read the article and evaluate the research undertaken. Perhaps the research is shoddy and should not be viewed as an important influence on policy. Perhaps the research was well done and should be taken seriously. Perhaps the researchers (or those providing the funding for the research to be conducted) are biased toward a particular conclusion. Perhaps there are political implications of the research. The point is, we do not have to take research that is reported as gospel. And the more effectively we can evaluate research on our own, the more informed and knowledgeable we can become.

References

Ackoff, R.L., S.V. Gupta & J.S. Minas (1962). *Scientific Method: Optimizing Applied Research Decisions*. New York, NY: John Wiley & Sons.

Adams, J. (October 29, 2000). "Methodology of Traffic Study Criticized." *The Courier-Journal*. Online: http://www.courier-journal.com/localnews/2000/0010/29/001029dwb_traf. html.

Adams, J. (October 29, 2000). "Study: Police Stopped Blacks Twice as Often as Whites; Louisville Chief Says Traffic Survey Is Flawed." *The Courier-Journal*. Online: http://www. courier-journal.com/localnews/2000/0010/29/001029dwb_prof.html.

Adler, P.A. (1993). "Dealing Careers." In *Wheeling and Dealing: An Ethnography of an Upper-Level Drug Dealing and Smuggling Community*, Second Edition. New York, NY: Columbia University Press.

Adler, P. (1985). *Wheeling and Dealing*. New York, NY: Columbia University Press.

Agnew, R. (1995). "Controlling Delinquency: Recommendations from General Strain Theory." In H. Barlow (ed.) *Crime and Public Policy*. Boulder, CO: Westview Press.

Agnew, R. (1985). "A Revised Strain Theory of Delinquency." *Social Forces,* 64(1):151-67.

Akers, R. (2000). *Criminological Theories: Introduction and Evaluation*, Third Edition. Los Angeles, CA: Roxbury.

American Psychological Association (2001). *Publication Manual of the American Psychological Association*, Fifth Edition. Washington, DC: Author.

Andranovich, G.D. & G. Riposa (1993). *Doing Urban Research*. Thousand Oaks, CA: Sage.

Babbie, E. (2002). *The Basics of Social Research*, Second Edition. Belmont, CA: Wadsworth/Thomson Learning.

Babbie, E. (2001) *The Practice of Social Research*, Ninth Edition. Belmont, CA: Wadsworth.

Babbie, E. (1998). *The Practice of Social Research*, Eighth Edition. Belmont, CA: Wadsworth Publishing Company.

Bailey, K.D. (1994). *Methods of Social Research,* Fourth Edition. New York, NY: The Free Press.

Bailey, W.C. & R.D. Peterson (1999). "Capital Punishment, Homicide, and Deterrence: An Assessment of the Evidence and Extension to Female Homicide." In M.D. & M.A. Zahn (eds.) *Homicide: A Sourcebook of Social Research*. Thousand Oaks, CA: Sage Publications, Inc.

Beccaria, C. (1819 [1764]). *On Crimes and Punishment*. Translated by Edward D. Ingraham. Philadelphia, PA: Philip H. Nicklin.

Becker, H.S. (1966). *Introduction to the Jack Roller: A Delinquent Boy's Own Story*, by Clifford R. Shaw. Chicago, IL: University of Chicago Press.

Becker, H.S. (1963). *Outsiders: Studies in the Sociology of Deviance*. New York, NY: Free Press.

Berg, B. (1989). *Qualitative Research Methods for the Social Sciences*. Boston, MA: Allyn & Bacon.

Berg, B.L. (1998). *Qualitative Research Methods for the Social Sciences*. Boston, MA: Allyn & Bacon.

Berk, R. A. (1981). "On the Compatibility of Applied and Basic Sociological Research: An Effort in Marriage Counseling." *The American Sociologist*, 16(4):204-211.

Bickman, L. & D.J. Rog (eds.) (1998). *Handbook of Applied Social Research Methods*. Thousand Oaks, CA: Sage Publications.

Bierstadt, R. (1978). "Sociological Thought in the Eighteenth Century." In T. Bottomore & R. Nisbet (eds.) *A History of Sociological Analysis*, pp. 3-38. New York, NY: Basic Books.

Blau, J.R. & P.M. Blau (1982). "The Cost of Inequality: Metropolitan Structure and Violent Crime." *American Sociological Review*, 47(1):114-129.

Block, C.R. & R.L. Block (1997). *Homicides in Chicago, 1965-1995*, Third Edition [Computer file]. Illinois Criminal Justice Information Authority.

Blumer, M. (1992). "The Growth of Applied Sociology After 1945: The Prewar Establishment of the Postwar Infrastructure." In T.C. Halliday & M. Janowitz (eds.) *Sociology and Its Publics: The Forms and Fates of Disciplinary Organization*, pp. 317-346. Chicago, IL: The University of Chicago Press.

Bordens, K.S. & B.B. Abbott (1996). *Research Design and Methods: A Process Approach*, Third Edition. Mountain View, CA: Mayfield Publishing Company.

Bromley, M.L. & J.K. Cochran (1999). "A Case Study of Community Policing in a Southern Sheriff's Office." *Police Quarterly*, 2:36-56.

Brown, J.B. (2001). "Doing Drag: A Visual Case Study of Gender Performance and Gay Masculinities." *Visual Sociology*, 16(1):37-54.

Browne, M.N. & S. Keeley (2001). *Asking the Right Questions: A Guide to Critical Thinking*, Sixth Edition. Upper Saddle River, NJ: Prentice Hall, Inc.

Bullock, A. & O. Stallybrass (1977). *The Harper Dictionary of Modern Thought*. New York, NY: Harper & Row.

Burgess, R.G. (ed.) (1991). "Field Research: A Sourcebook and Field Manual." New York, NY: Routledge.

Campbell, D.T. & D.W. Fiske (1959). "Convergent and Discriminant Validation by the Multitrait-Multimethod Matrix." *Psychological Bulletin*, 56:81-105.

Campbell, R. (1995). "The Role of Work Experience and Individual Beliefs in Police Officers' Perceptions of Date Rape: An Integration of Quantitative and Qualitative Methods." *American Journal of Community Psychology*, 23(2):249-277.

Canada, S. (1994). *The 1993 General Social Survey—Cycle 8: Personal Risk Public Use Microdata File Documentation and User's Guide*. Statistics Canada.

Caporaso, J.A. (1995). "Research Design, Falsification, and the Qualitative-Quantitative Divide." *The American Political Science Review*, 89(2):457-460.

Carlson, R.G., H.A. Siegal, J. Wang & R.S. Falck (1996). "Attitudes Toward Needle 'Sharing' Among Injection Drug Users: Combining Qualitative and Quantitative Research Methods." *Human Organization*, 55(3):361-369.

Carmines, E.G. & R.A. Zeller (1979). *Reliability and Validity Assessment*. Thousand Oaks, CA: Sage Publications.

Catania, J., D. Binson, J. Canchola, L. Pollack, W. Hauck & T. Coates (1996). "Effects of Interviewer Gender, Interviewer Choice, and Item Wording on Responses to Questions Concerning Sexual Behavior." *Public Opinion Quarterly*, 60:345-375.

Chase, N.D. (ed.) (1999). *Burdened Children Theory, Research, and Treatment of Parentification*. Thousand Oaks, CA: Sage Publications.

Chelimsky, E. (1991). "On the Social Science Contribution to Governmental Decision-Making." *Science*, 254(5029):226-231.

Chew, K.S.Y., R. McCleary, M.A. Lew & J.C. Wang (1999). "The Epidemiology of Child Homicide in California, 1981-1990." *Homicide Studies*, 3(2):151-169.

Clayton, R.R., A. Cattarello & K.P. Walder (1991). "Sensation Seeking as a Potential Mediating Variable for School-Based Prevention Intervention: A Two-Year Follow-Up of DARE." *Health Communication*, 3(4):229-239.

Clear, T.R. & N.A. Frost (2001). "Criminology & Public Policy: A New Journal of The American Society of Criminology." *Criminology & Public Policy*, 1(1):1-3.

Cohen, L.E. & M. Felson (1979). "Social Change and Crime Rate Trends: A Routine Activity Approach." *American Sociological Review*, 44:588-608.

Counts, D.A. & D.R. Counts (1991). "'They're My Family Now': The Creation of Community Among RVers." *Anthropologica*, XXXIV, 153-182.

Cressey, D.R. (1978). "Criminological Theory, Social Science, and the Repression of Crime." *Criminology*, 16(2):171-191.

Cressey, D.R. (1953). *Other People's Money*. New York, NY: Free Press.

Crimmins, S., S. Langley, H. Brownstein & B. Spunt (1997). "Convicted Women Who Have Killed Children: A Self-Psychology Perspective." *Journal of Interpersonal Violence*, 12(1):49-69.

Dalley, L. (Forthcoming Spring, 2002). "Children of Imprisoned Mothers: What Does the Future Hold?" In J. Joseph (ed.) *Women, Race, and Criminal Justice Processing*. San Francisco, CA: Prentice Hall.

Davies, K. (1996). "Women as Victims and Perpetrators of Homicide: A Test of Existing Theories of Women's Involvement in Crime" Doctoral Dissertation, The Ohio State University.

Davis, J.A. & T.W. Smith (1996). *General Social Surveys, 1972-1996: [Cumulative File]* Chicago, IL: [[Computer file].]. National Opinion Research Center [producer], Ann Arbor, MI: Inter-university Consortium for Political and Social Research [distributor].

Death Penalty Information Center. *Race of Defendants Executed Since 1976*. Retrieved January 28, 2002 from www.deathpenaltyinfo.org/dpicrace.html.

Decker, S. (1996). "Collective and Normative Features of Gang Violence." *Justice Quarterly*, 13(2):243-264.

Denzin, N. (1989). *The Research Act*. Englewood Cliffs, NJ: Prentice Hall.

Denzin, N.K. & Y.S. Lincoln (1988). "Entering the Field of Qualitative Research." In N.K. Denzin & Y.S. Lincoln (eds.) *The Landscape of Qualitative Research*, pp. 1-34.

Department of Health and Human Services and the Office for Protection from Research Risks (2002) *Institutional Review Board Guidebook*. Rockville, MD: U.S. Government Printing Office. (ohrp.osophs.dhhs.gov/irb).

Department of Health and Human Services (2001). *Office of Research Integrity Annual Report*. U.S. Government Printing Office. Rockville, MD.

Durkheim, E. (1952 [1897]). *Suicide*. Translated by John Spaulding & George Simpson. New York, NY: Free Press.

Durkheim, E. (1951 [1897]). *Suicide: A Study in Sociology* (J.A. Spaulding, Trans.). New York, NY: Free Press.

Durkheim, E. (1933/1984). *The Division of Labor in Society*. New York, NY: Free Press.

Earls, F.J. & C.A. Visher (1997). *Project on Human Development In Chicago Neighborhoods: A Research Update*. National Institute of Justice Research in Brief, February. Washington, DC: United States Government Printing Office.

Elliott, D.S., D. Huizinga & S. Menard (1989). *Multiple Problem Youth: Delinquency, Substance Use, and Mental Health Problems*. New York, NY: Springer-Verlag.

Elliott, D.S., S.S. Ageton & R.J. Canter (1979). "An Integrated Theoretical Perspective on Delinquent Behavior." *Journal of Research in Crime and Delinquency*, 16:3-27.

Erickson, D.J. & R. Tewksbury (2000). "The 'Gentlemen' in the Club: A Typology of Strip Club Patrons." *Deviant Behavior*, 21:271-293.

Feeney, F. (1986). "Robbers as Decision Makers." In D.B. Cornish, & R.V. Clarke *The Reasoning Criminal: Rational Choice Perspectives on Offending*. Heidelberg, Germany: Springer-Verlag.

Felson, M. & R.V. Clarke (1995). "Routine Precautions, Criminology, and Crime Prevention." In H. Barlow (ed.) *Crime and Public Policy*. Boulder, CO: Westview Press.

Fisher, C.S. (2002). "From the Editor" *Contexts*, 1(1):iii.

Fischer, R.L. (2000). "Reading and Reviewing Research: Tips for the Informed Consumer." *Families in Society*, 81(2):211-213.

Fitzgerald, J.D. & S.M. Cox (1994). *Research Methods in Criminal Justice*, Second Edition. Chicago, IL: Nelson-Hall.

Fleisher, M.S. (1989). *Warehousing Violence*. Newbury Park, CA: Sage Publications.

Flynn, P. (2000). "The Changing Structure of the Social Science Industry and Some Implications for Practice." *American Behavioral Scientist*, 43(10):1578-1601.

Fox, J.A. (2001). Uniform Crime Reports [United States]: Supplementary Homicide Reports, 1976-1999. Ann Arbor, MI: Inter-University Consortium for Political and Social Research.

Frankfort-Nachmias, C. & D. Nachmias (1996). *Research Methods in the Social Sciences*, Fifth Edition. New York, NY: St. Martin's Press.

Frankfort-Nachmias, C. & D. Nachmias (1992). *Research Methods in the Social Sciences*, Fourth Edition. New York, NY: St. Martin's Press.

Gagné, P. (1998). *Battered Women's Justice: The Movement for Clemency and the Politics of Self-Defense*. New York, NY: Twayne.

Gagné, P. (1996.) "Identity, Strategy, and Feminist Politics: Clemency for Battered Women Who Kill." *Social Problems*, 43(1):77-93.

Gagné, P. (1992). "Appalachian Women: Violence and Social Control." *Journal of Contemporary Ethnography*, 20, 4(January):387-415.

Gagné, P. & D.M. Austin (2002). "Doing Gender and Negotiating Equity: Women Motorcyclists in a Male-Dominated Subculture." Vancouver, Canada (April) Pacific Sociological Association Meetings.

Gagné, P. & R. Tewksbury (1999). "Knowledge and Power, Body and Self: An Analysis of the Knowledge Systems and the Transgendered Self." *The Sociological Quarterly*, 40(1):59-83.

Gagné, P. & R. Tewksbury (1998). "Conformity Pressures and Gender Resistance Among Transgendered Individuals." *Social Problems*, 45(1):82-102.

Gagné, P., R. Tewksbury & D. McGaughey (1997). "Coming Out and Crossing Over: Identity Formation and Proclamation in a Transgender Community." *Gender & Society*, 11(4):478-508.

Geis, G. (1991). "The Case Study Method in Sociological Criminology." In J.R. Feagin, A.M. Orum & G. Sjoberg (eds.) *A Case for the Case Study*. North Carolina: North Carolina Press.

Geis, G. (1967). "White Collar Crime: The Heavy Electrical Equipment Antitrust Cases of 1961." In M.B. Clinard & R. Quinney (eds.) *Criminal Behavior Systems:A Typology*, pp. 139-151. New York, NY: Holt, Rinehart & Winston.

Gelfand, D.E. (1975). "The Challenge of Applied Sociology." *The American Sociologist*, 10(1):13-18.

Gilsinan, J.F. (1997). "Public Policy and Criminology: An Historical and Philosophical Reassessment." In B.W. Hancock & P.M. Sharp (eds.) *Public Policy, Crime, and Criminal Justice*. Upper Saddle River, NJ: Prentice-Hall, Inc.

Girden, E.R. (1996). *Evaluating Research Articles From Start to Finish*. Thousand Oaks, CA: Sage Publications, Inc.

Glaser, B. & A.L. Strauss (1967). *The Discovery of Grounded Theory: Strategies for Qualitative Research*. Chicago, IL: Aldine.

Glaser, D. (1956). "Criminality Theories and Behavioral Images." *American Journal of Sociology*, 61:433-44.

Goode, E. (1999). "Sex with Informants as Deviant Behavior: An Account and Commentary." *Deviant Behavior*, 20:301-324.

Graham, L.O. (1995). *Member of the Club: Reflections on Life in a Racially Polarized World*. New York, NY: HarperCollins Publishers.

Grella, C., S. Chaiken & M. Anglin (1995). "A Procedure for Assessing the Validity of Self-Report Data on High-Risk Sex Behaviors from Heroin Addicts Entering Free Methadone Treatment." *Journal of Drug Issues*, 25:723-733.

Guba, E.G. & Y.S. Lincoln (1981). *Effective Evaluation*. San Francisco, CA: Jossey-Bass.

Hagan, F.E. (2002). *Introduction to Criminology: Theories, Methods, and Criminal Behavior*. Belmont, CA: Wadsworth.

Hagan, F.E. (1993). *Research Methods in Criminal Justice and Criminology*, Third Edition. New York, NY: Macmillan Publishing Company.

Hallinan, M.T. (1996). "Bridging the Gap Between Research and Practice." *Sociology of Education*, 69(extra issue):131-134.

Hamel, J., S. Dufour & D. Fortin (1993). *Case Study Methods*. Newbury Park, CA: Sage.

Hancock, B.W. & P.M. Sharp (1997) "Introduction." In B.W. Hancock & P.M. Sharp (eds.) *Public Policy, Crime, and Criminal Justice*. Upper Saddle River, NJ: Prentice-Hall, Inc.

Haney, C., C. Banks & P.G. Zimbardo (1973). "Interpersonal Dynamics in a Simulated Prison." *International Journal of Criminology and Penology*, 1:69-97.

Harmon, M.A. (1993). "Reducing the Risk of Drug Involvement among Early Adolescents: An Evaluation of Drug Abuse Resistance Education (DARE)." *Evaluation Review*, 17 (April):221-239.

Hirschi, T. (1969). *Causes of Delinquency*. Berkeley, CA: University of California Press.

Hopper, C.B. & J. Moore (1990). "Women in Outlaw Motorcycle Gangs." *Journal of Contemporary Ethnography*, 18(4):383-387.

Humphreys, L. (1970 and 1975). *Tearoom Trade: Impersonal Sex in Public Places*. New York, NY: Aldine de Gruyter.

Iliffe, G. & L. Steed (2000). "Exploring the Counselor's Experience of Working with Perpetrators and Survivors of Domestic Violence." *Journal of Interpersonal Violence*, 15(4):393-412.

Inciardi, J.A., D. Lockwood & A. Pottieger (1993). *Women and Crack-Cocaine*. New York, NY: Macmillan Publishing Company.

Jacob, E. (1988). "Clarifying Qualitative Research: A Focus on Traditions." *Educational Researcher*, 17(1):16-24.

Jacob, E. (1987). "Qualitative Research Traditions: A Review." *Review of Educational Research*, 57:1-50.

Jang, S.J. & B.R. Johnson (2001). "Neighborhood Disorder, Individual Religiosity, and Adolescent Use of Illicit Drugs: A Test of Multilevel Hypotheses."*Criminology*, 39(1):109-144.

Jasinski, J.L. (2001). "Pregnancy and Violence Against Women: An Analysis of Longitudinal Data." *Journal of Interpersonal Violence*, 16(7):713-734.

Jupp, V. (1989). *Methods of Criminological Research*. London: Unwin Hyman.

Justice, U.D.O. (2001). *National Crime Victimization Survey, 1992-1999* [Computer file]. U.S. Dept. of Commerce, Bureau of the Census. 9th ICPSR ed. Ann Arbor, MI: Inter-university Consortium for Political and Social Research [producer and distributor].

Kalton, G. (1983). *Introduction to Survey Sampling*. Thousand Oaks, CA: Sage Publications.

Katzer, J., K.H. Cook & W.W. Crouch (1978). *Evaluating Information: A Guide For Users of Social Science Research*. Reading, MA: Addison-Wesley Publishing Company.

Kaufman Kantor, G., J. Jasinski & E. Aldarondo (1994). "Socioeconomic Status and Incidence of Marital Violence in Hispanic Families." *Violence and Victims, 9*, 207-222.

King, G., R.O. Keohane & S. Verba (1994). *Designing Social Inquiry*. Princeton, NJ: Princeton University Press.

Kline, R.B. (1998). *Principles and Practice of Structural Equation Modeling*. New York, NY: The Guilford Press.

Klockars, C. (1974). *The Professional Fence*. New York, NY: The Free Press.

Kritzer, H.M. (1996). "The Data Puzzle: The Nature of Interpretation in Quantitative Research." *American Journal of Political Science*, 40(1):1-32.

Krueger, R. (1994). *Focus Groups*, Second Edition. Thousand Oaks, CA: Sage.

Kuhn, T. (1962). *The Structure of Scientific Revolution*. Chicago, IL: University of Chicago Press.

Kvale, S. (1996). *Interviews: An Introduction to Qualitative Research Interviewing*. Thousand Oaks, CA: Sage Publications.

Lazersfeld, P.F. & J. Reitz (1975). *An Introduction to Applied Sociology*. New York, NY: Elsevier Scientific Publishing Company.

Lee, M.T. & M.D. Ermann (1999). "Pinto 'Madness' as a Flawed Landmark Narrative: An Organizational and Network Analysis." *Social Problems*, 46:30-47.

Leistritz, F.L. & B.L. Ekstrom (1986). *Social Impact Assessment and Management: An Annotated Bibliography*. New York, NY: Garland Publishing.

Liebow, E. (1993). *Tell Them Who I Am: The Lives of Homeless Women*. New York, NY: The Free Press.

Locke, L.F., S.J. Silverman & W.W. Spirduso (1998). *Reading and Understanding Research*. Thousand Oaks, CA: Sage Publications, Inc.

Lofland, J. & L.H. Lofland (1995). *Analyzing Social Settings: A Guide to Qualitative Observation and Analysis*, Third Edition. New York, NY: Wadsworth Publishing Company.

Lofland, J. & L. Lofland (1984). *Analyzing Social Settings*, Second Edition. Belmont, CA: Wadsworth.

Logsdon, M..C., P. Gagné, T. Hughes, J. Patterson & V. Leffler (2002). "Development of a Social Support Intervention with Pregnant Adolescents." American Psychological Association's Conference, Enhancing Outcomes in Women's Health: Translating Psychosocial and Behavioral Research into Primary Care, Community Interventions, and Health Policy Conference, Washington, DC. (February) American Psychological Association.

Lundman, R.J. (2001). *Prevention and Control of Juvenile Delinquency*. New York, NY: Oxford University Press.

Maguire, M. (2000). "Researching 'Street Criminals': A Neglected Art." In R.D. King & E. Wincup (eds.) *Doing Research on Crime and Justice*, pp. 121-152. New York, NY: Oxford University Press.

Majchrzak, A. (1984). *Methods for Policy Research*. Thousand Oaks, CA: Sage.

Malterud, K. (2001). "Qualitative Research: Standards, Challenges, and Guidelines." *Lancet*, 358:483-88.

Marshall, G. (1994). *The Concise Oxford Dictionary of Sociology*. Oxford: Oxford Press.

Martin, D.W. (1996). *Doing Psychological Experiments*, Fourth Edition. Pacific Grove, CA: Brooks/Cole Publishing Company.

Marx, K. ([1867]1967). *Capital*. New York, NY: International Publishers.

Matsueda, R.L. & K. Anderson (1998). "The Dynamics of Delinquent Peers and Delinquent Behavior." *Criminology*, 36:269-308.

Maxfield, M.G. & E. Babbie (2001). *Research Methods for Criminal Justice and Criminology*, Third Edition. Belmont, CA: Wadsworth/Thomson Learning.

Maxwell, J.A. (1996). *Qualitative Research Design: An Interactive Approach*. Thousand Oaks, CA: Sage Publications, Inc.

McCall, G.J. & J.L. Simmons (1969). *Issues in Participant Observation; A Text and Reader.* Reading, MA: Addison-Wesley Publications.

McKillip, J. (1987). *Need Analysis: Tools for the Human Services and Education*. Thousand Oaks, CA: Sage.

McKusick, L., W. Horstram & T.J. Coates (1985) "Reported Changes in the Sexual Behavior of Men at Risk for AIDS, San Francisco, 1982-84—The AIDS Behavior Research Project." *Public Health Reports*, 100:622-628.

Merriam-Webster Online: The Language Center. http://www.m-w.com.

Merton, R.K. (1973). *The Sociology of Science*. Chicago, IL: The University of Chicago Press.

Merton, R.K. (1957). "Priorities in Scientific Discovery." *American Sociological Review*, 22:635-659.

Merton, R.K. (1938). "Social Structure and Anomie." *American Sociological Review*, 3:672-682.

Merton, R.K. (1968). *Social Theory and Social Structure*. New York, NY: Free Press.

Miller, J. (2001). *One of the Guys: Girls, Gangs, and Gender*. New York, NY: Oxford University Press.

Miller, J.M. (1995). "Covert Participant Observation: Reconsidering the Least Used Method." *Journal of Contemporary Criminal Justice*, 11(2):97-105.

Miller, J.M. & R. Tewksbury (eds.) (2001). *Extreme Methods: Innovative Approaches to Social Science Research*. Boston, MA: Allyn & Bacon.

Monahan, J., H. Steadman, E. Silver, A. Appelbaum, P. Robbins, E. Mulvey, L. Roth, T. Grisso & S. Banks (2001). *Rethinking Risk Assessment: The MacArthur Study of Mental Disorder and Violence*. New York, NY: Oxford University Press.

Morgan, G.A., J.A. Gliner & R.J. Harmon (1999a). "Definition, Purposes, and Dimensions of Research." *Journal of the American Academy of Child and Adolescent Psychiatry*, 38(2):217-219.

Morgan, G.A., J.A. Gliner & R.J. Harmon (1999b). "Evaluating the Validity of a Research Study." *Journal of the American Academy of Child and Adolescent Psychiatry*, 38(4):480-485.

Murphy, C.M. & K.D. O'Leary (1994). "Research Paradigms, Values, and Spouse Abuse." *Journal of Interpersonal Violence*, 9(2):207-223.

Mustaine, E.E. & R. Tewksbury (1998). "Predicting Risks of Larceny Theft Victimization: A Routine Activity Analysis Using Refined Lifestyle Measures." *Criminology*, 36:829-857.

Myers, J. (1992). "Nonmainstream Body Modification: Genital Piercing, Branding, Burning and Cutting. *Journal of Contemporary Ethnography*, 21(3):267-306.

Neuman, W. L. (2000). "Dimensions of Research." *Social Research Methods: Qualitative and Quantitative Approaches*, 20-38. Needham Heights, MA: Allyn & Bacon.

Neuman, W.L. (1997). *Social Research Methods: Qualitative and Quantitative Approaches*, Third Edition. Boston, MA: Allyn & Bacon.

Neuman, W.L. & B. Wiegand (2000). *Criminal Justice Research Methods: Qualitative & Quantitative Approaches*. Boston, MA: Allyn & Bacon.

Office of Juvenile Justice and Delinquency Prevention. Overview: Causes and correlates of delinquency program. Retrieved January 29, 2002, from http://www.ojjdp.ncjrs.org/ccd/oview.html.

Oleson, K. C. & Arkin, R. M. (1996). "Reviewing and Evaluating a Research Article." In F.T.L. Leong & J.T. Austin (eds.) *The Psychology Research Handbook: A Guide for Graduate Students and Research Assistants*, pp. 40-55. Thousand Oaks, CA: Sage Publications, Inc.

Olsen, A.E. (1981). "The Future of Applied Sociology." In M.E. Olsen & M. Micklin (eds.) *Handbook of Applied Sociology: Frontiers of Contemporary Research*, pp. 561-581. New York, NY: Praeger.

Orum, An.M., J.R. Feagin & G. Sjoberg. (1991). "The Nature of the Case Study." In J.R. Feagin, A.M. Orum, & G. Sjoberg (eds.) *A Case for the Case Study*, pp. 1-25. North Carolina: North Carolina Press.

Owen, B. (1998). *"In the Mix:" Struggle and Survival in A Women's Prison*. Albany, NY: State University of New York Press

Parse, R.R. (2001). *Qualitative Inquiry: The Path of Sciencing*. Sudbury, CN: Jones and Barlett Publishers.

Patton, M.Q. (1990). *Qualitative Evaluation and Research Methods*, Second Edition. Newbury Park, CA: Sage Publications.

Patton, M.Q. (1987). *How to Use Qualitative Methods in Evaluation*. Thousand Oaks, CA: Sage Publications.

Polsky, N. (1969). *Hustlers, Beats, and Others*. New York, NY: Anchor Books.

Popper, K. (1968). *Conjectures and Refutations: The Growth of Scientific Knowledge*. New York, NY: Harper & Row.

Posavac, E.J. & R.G. Carey (1997). *Program Evaluation: Methods and Case Studies*, Fifth Edition. Upper Saddle River, NJ: Prentice Hall.

Puzone, C.A., L.E. Saltzman, M.-J. Kresnow, M.P. Thompson & J.A. Mercy (2000). "National Trends in Intimate Partner Homicide." *Violence Against Women*, 6(4):409-426.

Raymond, L. (1993). *Doing Research on Sensitive Topics*. Newbury Park, CA: Sage Publications.

Richwald, G.A., D.E. Morisky, G.R. Kyle, A.R. Kristal, M.M. Gerber & J.M. Friedland (1988). "Sexual Activities in Bathhouses in Los Angeles County: Implications for AIDS Prevention Education." *The Journal of Sex Research*, 25(2):169-180.

Riley, A.P., A.I. Hermalin & L. Rosero-Bixby (1993). "A New Look at the Determinants of Non-numeric Response to Desired Family Size: The Case of Costa Rica." *Demography*, (30)2:159-175.

Rollins, J. (1985). *Between Women: Domestics and Their Employers*. Philadelphia, PA: Temple University Press.

Rosenbaum, M. (1988). *Women on Heroin*. New Brunswick, NJ: Rutgers University Press.

Rosnow, R.L., J. Rotheram-Borus, S.J. Ceci, P.D. Blanck & G.P. Koocher (1993). "The Institutional Review Board as a Mirror of Scientific and Ethical Standards." *American Pyschologist*, 48(7):821-826.

Rossi, P.H. & H.E. Freeman (1993). *Evaluation: A Systematic Approach*, Fifth Edition. Newbury Park, CA: Sage Publications.

Rossi, P.H. (1986). "How Applied Sociology can Save Basic Sociology." *Journal of Applied Sociology*, 3(1):1-5.

Rossi, P.H., H.E. Freeman & M.W. Lipsey (1999). *Evaluation: A Systematic Approach*, Sixth Edition. Thousand Oaks, CA: Sage.

Rylko-Bauer, B., J. van Willigen & A. McElroy (1989). "Strategies for Increasing the Use of Anthropological Research in the Policy Process: A Cross-Disciplinary Analysis." In J. van Willigen, B. Rylko-Bauer & A. McElroy (eds.) *Making Our Research Useful: Case Studies in the Utilization of Anthropological Knowledge*, pp. 1-26. Boulder, CO: Westview Press.

Schiraldi, V. (1998). "Hyping School Violence." *The Washington Post*, August 25:A15.

Schutt, R.K. (2001). *Investigating the Social World: The Process and Practice of Research*, Third Edition. Thousand Oak, CA: Pine Forge Press.

Schutt, R.K. (1996). *Investigating the Social World: The Process and Practice of Research*. Thousand Oaks, CA: Pine Forge Press.

Scott, L. & K. Davies (2000). "An Examination of Women Killers in Three Georgia Counties." Currently under review.

Senese, J.D. (1997). *Applied Research Methods in Criminal Justice*. Chicago, IL: Nelson-Hall Publishers.

Shadish, W.R., T.D. Cook & D.T. Campbell (2002). *Experimental and Quasi-Experimental Designs for Generalized Causal Inference*. Boston, MA: Houghton Mifflin Company.

Shaw, C. (1930). *The Jack Roller: A Delinquent Boy's Own Story*. Chicago, IL: University of Chicago Press.

Shaw, C.R. & H.D. McKay (1942). *Juvenile Delinquency and Urban Areas*. Chicago, IL: University of Chicago Press.

Sherman, L.W. & R.A. Berk (1984). "The Specific Deterrent Effects of Arrest for Domestic Assault." *American Sociological Review*, 49(April):261-272.

Short, L., P. McMahon, D. Chervin & G. Shelley (2000). "Survivors' Identification of Protective Factors and Early Warning Signs for Intimate Partner Violence." *Violence Against Women*, 6(3):272-285.

Sil, R. (2000). "The Division of Labor in Social Science Research: Unified Methodology or 'Organic Solidarity'? *Polity*, (4):499-531.

Simon, D. (1991). *Homicide: A Year on the Killing Streets*. New York, NY: Ivy Books.

Simpson, S.S. & N.L. Piquero (2001). "The Archer Daniels Midland Antitrust Case of 1996: A Case Study." In H.N. Pontell & D. Shichor (eds.) *Contemporary Issues in Crime and Criminal Justice*, pp 175-194. Upper Saddle River, NJ: Prentice Hall.

Sinnott, J.D., C.S. Harris, M.R. Block, S. Collesano & S.G. Jacobson (1983). *Applied Research in Aging: A Guide to Methods and Resources*. Boston, MA: Little Brown and Co.

Sjoberg, G. & R. Nett (1997). *A Methodology for Social Research*. Prospect Heights, IL: Waveland Press.

Sjoberg, G., N. Williams, T.R. Vaughan & A.R. Sjoberg (1991). "The Case Study Approach in Social Research." In J. Feagin, A.M. Orum & G. Sjoberg (eds.) *A Case for the Case Study*, pp. 27-79. North Carolina: North Carolina Press.

Stainback, S. & W. Stainback (1988). *Understanding and Constructing Qualitative Research*. Dubuque, IA: Kendall/Hunt Publishing Co.

Stake, R.E. (1995). *The Art of Case Study Design*. Thousand Oaks, CA: Sage Publications.

Stark, J. E. & J.I. McEvoy (1970). "Middle Class Violence." *Psychology Today*, 4:52-65.

Sterk, C.E. (1999). *Fast Lives: Women Who Use Crack Cocaine*. Philadelphia, PA: Temple University Press.

Stewart, D. & P. Shamdasani (1990). *Focus Groups: Theory and Practice*. Newbury Park, CA: Sage.

Straus, M.A., G. Kaufman Kantor & D.W. Moore (1997). "Change in Cultural Norms Approving Marital Violence from 1968 to 1994." In G. Kaufman Kantor & J.L. Jasinski (eds.), *Out of the Darkness: Contemporary Perspectives on Family Violence*, pp. 3-16. Thousand Oaks, CA: Sage.

Strauss, A. & J. Corbin (1990). *Basics of Qualitative Research: Grounded Theory Procedures and Techniques*. Newbury Park, CA: Sage Publications.

Straus, M.A. & R.J. Gelles (1986). "Societal Changes and Change in Family Violence from 1975 to 1985 as Revealed by Two National Surveys." *Journal of Marriage and the Family*, 48:465-480.

Straus, M.A., R.J. Gelles & S.K. Steinmetz (1980). *Behind Closed Doors: Violence in the American Family*. Garden City, NY: Anchor Books.

Street, D. P. & E.A. Weinstein (1981). "Prologue: Problems and Prospects of Applied Sociology." In M.E. Olsen & M. Micklin (eds.) *Handbook of Applied Sociology: Frontiers of Contemporary Research*, pp. xiii-xxiv. New York, NY: Praeger.

Sullivan, T.J. (2001). *Methods of Social Research*. Fort Worth: Harcourt College Publishers.

Sullivan, T.J. (1992). "Applied Research Techniques." In *Applied Sociology: Research and Critical Thinking*, pp. 139-166. New York, NY: Macmillan.

Sutherland E.H. (1947). *Principles of Criminology*, Fourth Edition. Philadelphia, PA: Lippincott.

Sutherland, E. (1947). *Principles of Criminology*, Fourth Edition. New York, NY: Harper & Row.

Sutherland, E. (1945). "Is White Collar Crime Crime?" *American Sociological Review*, 10:132-139.

Sweet, N. & R.A. Tewksbury (2000). "Entry, Maintenance and Departure From a Career in the Sex Industry: Strippers' Experiences of Occupational Costs and Rewards." *Humanity and Society*, 24(2):136-161.

Sweet, J., L. Bumpass & V. Call (1988). *The Design and Content of the National Survey of Families and Households* (NSHF Working Paper #1). Madison, WI: Center for Demography and Ecology.

Tarrow, S. (1995). "Bridging the Quantitative-Qualitative Divide in Political Science." *The American Political Science Review*, 89(2):471-474.

Tewksbury, R. (2002). "Bathhouse Intercourse: Structural and Behavioral Aspects of an Erotic Oasis." *Deviant Behavior*, 23(1):75-112.

Tewksbury, R. (2001). "Acting Like an Insider: Studying Hidden Environments as a Potential Participant." In J.M. Miller & R. Tewksbury (eds.) *Extreme Methods: Innovative Approaches to Social Science Research*, pp. 72-93. Needham Heights, MA: Allyn & Bacon.

Tewksbury, R. (1993). "Men Performing as Women: Explorations in the World of Female Impersonators. *Sociological Spectrum*, 13(4):465-486.

Tewksbury, R.. (1990). "Patrons of Porn: Research Notes on the Clientele of Adult Bookstores." *Deviant Behavior*, 11(3):259-271.

Tewksbury, R. & P. Gagné (1997). "Assumed and Presumed Identities: Problems of Self-Presentation in Field Research." *Sociological Spectrum*, 17(2):127-155.

Thomas, W.I. & F. Znaniecki (1927). *The Polish Peasant in Europe and America, Vol. 2*. New York, NY: Knopf.

Thornberry, T.P. (1987). "Toward an Interactional Theory of Delinquency." *Criminology*, 25:863-91.

Thrasher, F. (1927). *The Gang: a Study of 1,313 Gangs in Chicago*. Chicago, IL: University of Chicago Press.

Tjaden, P. & N. Thoennes (2000). "Role of Stalking in Domestic Violence Crime Reports Generated by the Colorado Springs Police Department." *Violence and Victims*, 15(4):427-441.

Tjaden, P. & N. Thoennes (1998). *Violence and Threats of Violence Against Women and Men in the United States, 1994-1997*, [Computer File]. ICPSR Version. Center for Policy Research.

U.S. Department of Justice. (2000). *Crime In the United States—2000, Uniform Crime Reports*. Washington, DC: Federal Bureau of Investigation.

U.S. Department of Justice. (1999). *National Criminal Victimization Survey*. Washington, DC: Bureau of Justice Statistics.

Varano, S. P. & J.M. Cancino (2001). "An Empirical Analysis of Deviant Homicides in Chicago." *Homicide Studies*, 5(1):5-29.

Vaughan, D. (2001). "Sensational Cases, Flawed Theories." In H.N. Pontell & D. Shichor (eds.) *Contemporary Issues in Crime and Criminal Justice*, pp. 45-66. Upper Saddle River, NJ: Prentice Hall.

Vaughan, R.J. & T.F. Buss (1998). *Communicating Social Science Research to Policymakers*. Thousand Oaks, CA: Sage Publications.

Vito, G.F., T.J. Keil & J.V. Andreescu (1999). "Kentuckians' Changes in Attitudes Toward Death Penalty." *The Justice Professional*, 12:123-143.

Wallace, W. 1971. *The Logic of Science in Sociology*. New York, NY: Aldine deGruyter.

Weber, M. (1949). *The Methodology of the Social Sciences*, translated and edited by E. Shils & H. Finch. New York, NY: Free Press.

Weber, M. ([1904]1977). *The Protestant Ethic and the Spirit of Capitalism* (T. Parsons, Trans.). New York, NY: Scribner.

Weisheit, R.A. (1991). "The Intangible Rewards From Crime: The Case of Domestic Marijuana Cultivation." *Crime & Delinquency*, 27:506-527.

Whyte, W.F. (1998). "Rethinking Sociology: Applied and Basic Research." *The American Sociologist*, 29(1):16-19.

Whyte, W.F. (1982). "Interviewing in Field Research." In R.G. Burgess (ed.) *Field Research; A Sourcebook and Field Manual.* London: Allen and Unwin.

Whyte, W.F. (1955). *Street Corner Society*. Chicago, IL: University of Chicago Press.

Wilensky, H.L. (1997). "Social Science and the Public Agenda: Reflections on the Relation of Knowledge to Policy in the United States and Abroad." *Journal of Health Politics, Policy, and Law*, 22(5):1241-1265.

Williamson, J., D. Karp & J. Dalphin (1977). *The Research Craft: An Introduction to Social Science Methods*. Boston, MA: Little, Brown and Company.

Wortz, C. (1999). "Using Focus Group Research in Medical Negligence Cases." *Trial*, 35(5):38-45.

Wyson, E. & D.W. Wright (1995). "A Decade of DARE: Efficacy, Politics, and Drug Education." *Sociological Focus,* 28 (August):283-311.

Wysong, E., E. Aniskiewicz & D. Wright (1994). "Truth and DARE: Tracking Drug Education to Graduation and as Symbolic Politics." *Social Problems*, 41(3):448-472.

Yin, R.K. (1989). *Case Study Research: Design and Methods*. Newbury Park, CA: Sage.

Young, M. (1998). "Rethinking Community Resistance to Prison Siting: Results From a Community Impact Assessment." *Canadian Journal of Criminology*, 40(3):323-327.

Zagumny, M.J. & M.K. Thompson (1997). "Does D.A.R.E. Work? An Evaluation in Rural Tennessee." *Journal of Alcohol and Drug Education*, 42(2):32-41.

Zeitlin, I. M. (1990). "The Enlightenment: Philosophical Foundations." In *Ideology and the Development of Sociological Theory*, pp.1-6. Englewood Cliffs, NJ: Prentice Hall.

Contributors' Biographical Information

Lanette P. Dalley received a B.S. in Sociology from Montana State University (1984), a M.S.W. from Washington University–St. Louis, Missouri (1990), and a Ph.D. in Criminology from Indiana University of Pennsylvania (1997). She is a licensed clinical social worker and previously served as a juvenile probation officer. Currently, she is an Associate Professor at Minot State University who chairs the Institutional Review Board and also specializes in female offenders and their children.

Kim Davies is Associate Professor of Sociology and Criminal Justice at Augusta State University. She also serves as Acting Director of the Women's Studies Program at Augusta State. Dr. Davies holds a Ph.D. in sociology from The Ohio State University. Her main research interests are feminist criminology, general issues of deviance, and homicide.

Tracy L. Dietz is Associate Professor of Sociology at the University of Central Florida. She holds a Ph.D. in sociology from the University of North Texas. She is interested in the study of spouse and child abuse, ethnicity, and the process of aging.

Patricia Gagné has a Ph.D. in sociology from The Ohio State University. She is presently Associate Professor of Sociology at the University of Louisville. She has completed a number of major research projects in the areas of domestic violence, clemency for women convicted of killing abusive partners, and transexuality.

Jeffrey L. Helms is an Assistant Professor in the Department of Psychology at Kennesaw State University. He holds a Psy.D. from Spalding University and is primarily interested in forensic psychology and juvenile justice.

Jana L. Jasinksi received her Ph.D. at the University of New Hampshire where she was also a National Institute of Mental Health Post Doctoral Research Fellow at the Family Research Laboratory (1997). She is currently an Assistant Professor in the Department of Sociology and Anthropology at the University of Central Florida and the coordinator of the Graduate Certificate in Domestic Violence.

Jeanne J. Johnson is a doctoral student in Clinical Psychology at Alliant International University. Her clinical background has included work with the severely mentally ill, incarcerated women, and at-risk youth.

Kathrine Johnson is an Assistant Professor in the Department of Criminal Justice and Legal Studies at the University of West Florida where she is also the Coordinator of the Criminal Justice program at the Fort Walton Beach campus. She holds a Ph.D. in Criminology from Indiana University of Pennsylvania. Her primary areas of research interest are use/abuse of drugs and the incorporation of technology into criminal justice agencies and practices.

Julie C. Kunselman received her Ph.D. in Urban and Public Affairs from the University of Louisville. She is currently Assistant Professor in the Department of Criminal Justice and Legal Studies at the University of West Florida where she also serves as Coordinator of the Criminal Justice Program.

Alexis J. Miller is an Assistant Professor in the Department of Criminal Justice at Middle Tennessee State University. She holds a Ph.D. in Urban and Public Affairs from the University of Louisville. Her research interests center on issues of hate crimes and institutional corrections.

Elizabeth Ehrhardt Mustaine is Associate Professor of Sociology at the University of Central Florida. She has a Ph.D. in sociology from The Ohio State University. Her primary areas of research are in criminal victimization risks, domestic violence, and institutional corrections.

Richard Tewksbury is Professor of Justice Administration at the University of Louisville. He holds a Ph.D. in sociology from The Ohio State University. Presently his research focuses on issues of institutional corrections management, criminal victimization risks, men's sexuality, and undercover law enforcement practices.

Angela West is an Assistant Professor of Justice Administration at the University of Louisville. Her teaching interests include corrections, research methods, statistics, and theory. Her research involves program and policy evaluation at all levels of the justice process, race and gender-related issues, and issues pertaining to correctional release, homelessness, and recidivism.

Index

Abstract, of journal article, 35-36
Abstract macro concepts, 100
Academic audience, research evaluation and, 40
Academic research, scientific approach of, 13-14
Acceptable incompetence role, of researcher, 111
Access, to pre-existing data sets, 67-68
Ackoff, R.L., 19
Action research, 17, 20
Active consent, 55-56
Adams, J., 95
Adler, Patricia, 3, 153, 161-162
Adler, Peter, 161-162
Agency boards, researchers on, 24
Agenda setting, criminal justice policy and, 10
Age of Reason, 13
Agnew, R., 86, 87
Akers, R., 83
American Evaluation Association, 20
American Social Science Association, 20
American Sociological Association, 11
American Sociological Review, 66
American Statistical Association (ASA), locating data through, 70
Analysis
  quantitative, 46
  theory and, 87
  units of, in macro research, 93-94, 96-97
  units of, in micro research, 97-98
Analytical induction, 86
Analytic generalization, vs. statistical generalization, 156
Anderson, K., 88
Andranovich, G.D., 23
Anger, aversive environments, delinquency, and, 86
Anglin, M., 124
Anomie Theory. *See* Strain Theory
Anonymity, in research studies, 56-58

Applied research, 14
  action research, 17
  basic researchers view of, 25-26
  evaluation research, 18
  focus of, 31-32
  history of, 20
  political pressures on, 89
  purposes and goals of, 15-16
  relationship with basic research, 19-20
  social impact assessment, 17-18
  status differential with basic research, 26
  strategies to improve utilization of, 24-26
  theories and, 16
  theory utilized in, 88
  utilization of, 20-22
Archived data
  locations of, 67
  in qualitative research, 104
  Web access to, 67
Archives, locating data in, 70-71
Assessment, of criminal justice policy, 10
Audience
  for research, 14
  research evaluation and, 40-41
  rewriting technical findings for general, 23
Austin, D. Mark, 112
Author, research biases of, 33
Auxiliary theories, 86
Availability, of pre-existing data sets, 67-68
Aversive environments, juvenile delinquency and, 86

Babbie, E., 49, 55, 119, 121
Bailey, W.C., 3
Banks, C., 55
Basic research
  financial support for, 26
  as foundation for applied research, 15
  purpose and goals of, 14-15

185